Gender Relations in Sport

TEACHING GENDER

Series Editor
Patricia Leavy
USA

Scope
The *Teaching Gender* publishes monographs, anthologies and reference books that deal centrally with gender and/or sexuality. The books are intended to be used in undergraduate and graduate classes across the disciplines. The series aims to promote social justice with an emphasis on feminist, multicultural and critical perspectives.

Please email queries to the series editor at pleavy7@aol.com

International Editorial Board
Tony E. Adams, *Northeastern Illinois University, USA*
Paula Banerjee, *University of Calcutta, India*
Nitza Berkovitch, *Ben Gurion University, Israel*
Robin Boylorn, *University of Alabama, USA*
Máiréad Dunne, *University of Sussex, UK*
Mary Holmes, *Flinders University, Australia*
Laurel Richardson, *Ohio State University, Emerita, USA*
Sophie Tamas, *Queen's University, Canada*

Gender Relations in Sport

Edited by

Emily A. Roper
Department of Health and Kinesiology
Sam Houston State University
Texas, USA

SENSE PUBLISHERS
ROTTERDAM/BOSTON/TAIPEI

A C.I.P. record for this book is available from the Library of Congress.

ISBN: 978-94-6209-453-6 (paperback)
ISBN: 978-94-6209-454-3 (hardback)
ISBN: 978-94-6209-455-0 (e-book)

Published by: Sense Publishers,
P.O. Box 21858,
3001 AW Rotterdam,
The Netherlands
https://www.sensepublishers.com/

Printed on acid-free paper

Cover picture: Kolbi E. Ashorn

TABLE OF CONTENTS

Preface   vii

1. Gender and Sport Participation   1
    Karen M. Appleby & Elaine Foster

2. Theories of Gender and Sport   21
    Leslee A. Fisher, Susannah K. Knust & Alicia J. Johnson

3. Gender and Sport Media   39
    Nicole M. Lavoi

4. Sexual Identity and Sport   53
    Kerrie J. Kauer & Vikki Krane

5. Intersections of Race, Ethnicity, and Gender in Sport   73
    Akilah R. Carter-Francique & Courtney L. Flowers

6. Framing Title IX: Conceptual Metaphors at Work   95
    Theresa A. Walton

7. Studying the Athletic Body   119
    Christy Greenleaf & Trent A. Petrie

8. Sexual Harassment and Abuse in Sport   141
    Sandra Kirby & Guylaine Demers

9. Developments and Current Issues in Gender and Sport
    from a European Perspective   163
    Gertrud Pfister

Contributing Authors   181

PREFACE

Gender Relations in Sport is intended to serve as an introductory text for students, particularly those less familiar with the scholarly body of work devoted to gender and sport. The conception of this book emerged from conversations with colleagues teaching courses such as *Gender, Sport and Culture* to undergraduate and early graduate-level kinesiology students, as well as colleagues across campus in sociology, psychology, education, and history, who were also interested in integrating discussion of sport into their gender-related courses. A common theme from these conversations was the desire for an entry-level textbook that would provide a foundational understanding of the gender dynamics at play in sport.

Gender Relations in Sport is divided into nine chapters, with contributions from leading scholars in various sub-areas of "sport studies" – sport sociology, sport and exercise psychology, cultural sport studies, sport history and sport management. While each chapter focuses on a specific area of interest (e.g., race and ethnicity, Title IX, sexual harassment and abuse, sexual identity, etc.), it is important that the reader understand the overlapping and intersectional nature of the content. As one will learn, much of the content in one chapter is critical to that in another chapter. Organizing the book in this way - individual chapters - was done for educational/ teaching purposes. It is hoped that students and educators will engage in discussion of the intersecting themes and concepts.

It is important to note that the majority of the contributors are situated in U.S. academic institutions and in their chapters, share findings from studies focused primarily on North American sport participants and sport settings. While global perspectives are highlighted at various places throughout the text, Chapter Nine by Gertrud Pfister is exclusively focused on Europe. As Pfister notes in her chapter, "when writing about sport, one has to address the challenge of meanings and translations as the term sport is defined differently depending on country and culture" (p. 163). It is because of these differences that Pfister's chapter is so important – it provides the reader with exposure to cultural differences in sport and how gender is understood within different sport settings.

- In chapter one, **Gender and Sport Participation**, Karen M. Appleby and Elaine Foster provide a brief history of women's and girls' sport experiences and opportunities from the early 20th century to the present. Appleby and Foster also integrate discussion of the barriers that have kept, and continue to keep, women and men from participating in different physical activities. They conclude their chapter with examination of the recent increase in female-centered sport and exercise spaces and events.
- In chapter two, **Theories of Gender and Sport**, Leslee A. Fisher, Susannah K. Knust, and Alicia J. Johnson lay out essential definitions (e.g., gender, sex, feminism, gender identity, gender representation, etc.), as well as theories

(feminist theory, queer theory and intersectionality theory) used to examine and understand gender within the sporting context. Fisher, Knust, and Johnson close with discussion of the history and development of feminist sport studies, queer sport studies and men and masculinity studies.

- In chapter three, **Gender and Sport Media**, Nicole M. LaVoi summarizes 30 years of sport media and gender research. LaVoi begins with an overview of "first wave sport media research" which focused on the amount and quality of coverage in print and broadcast media. LaVoi then introduces "second wave sport media research" which encompasses analyses concentrated on digital media (sport blogs, Twitter, Facebook), inclusion of intersectional variables (i.e., race/ethnicity, social class, sexual identity), and understanding how various audiences (e.g., parents, athletes, fans) interpret gendered media coverage and portrayals of female athletes.

- In chapter four, **Sexual Identity and Sport**, Kerrie J. Kauer and Vikki Krane employ a queer feminist perspective and social identity foundation to examine the intersections of gender and sexuality in sport. Kauer and Krane begin by introducing the socio-historical links between sport, gender and sexuality, with specific attention devoted to the ways in which hegemonic femininity and hegemonic masculinity have created an overtly hostile and homonegative environment for lesbian, gay, bisexual and transgender (LGBT) individuals in sport. Kauer and Krane conclude their chapter with discussion of some of the positive changes in today's sport world, including the recent ally movement and other programs and initiatives aimed at creating safe and inclusive spaces in sport.

- In chapter five, **Intersections of Race, Ethnicity and Gender in Sport**, Akilah R. Carter-Francique and Courtney L. Flowers begin by explaining the role culture plays in understanding sport and its meaning for racial and ethnic groups. Using intersectionality theory, Carter-Francique and Flowers examine the ways in which the intersecting categories of race, ethnicity, and gender impact women of color in sport. Specific attention is devoted to sport participation patterns of women and girls of color at the youth/high school, college, and professional levels and their representation as sport leaders (i.e., coaches, administrators). Going beyond the statistics, Carter-Francique and Flowers review literature devoted to the *experiences* of women of color in the sporting context and the ways in which dominant ideologies influence and marginalize their experiences.

- In chapter six, **Framing Title IX: Conceptual Metaphors at Work**, Theresa A. Walton begins with a summary of Title IX policy. Using George Lakoff's concept of conceptual metaphors, Walton provides a decade-by-decade overview of the ways in which Title IX has been framed in public discourse and uses Lakoff's work on morality in political metaphors to explain how people make sense of Title IX.

- In chapter seven, **Studying the Athletic Body**, Christy Greenleaf and Trent A. Petrie summarize the extensive work devoted to the gendered nature of athletic bodies, body image(s), and eating attitudes and behaviors. Greenleaf and Petrie conclude with discussion of healthy body environments for athletes.

— In chapter eight, **Sexual Harassment and Abuse in Sport**, Sandra Kirby and Guylaine Demers begin with an overview of important definitions/language surrounding sexual abuse/exploitation. Kirby and Demers address the prevalence of the problem in sport, as well as risk factors associated with the sport culture and its participants (e.g., athletes, coaches, administrators). The cycle of abuse and grooming process and the consequences of sexual exploitation for sport, athletes, and coaches are also addressed. Kirby and Demers close with a discussion of child protection and child safeguarding, and stress the need for sport organizations to establish comprehensive prevention measures.

— In chapter nine, **Developments and Current Issues in Gender and Sport from a European Perspective**, Gertrud Pfister introduces the reader to gender and sport developments in Europe beginning in the Middle Ages to the present. Pfister documents the dramatic changes in societal attitudes, gender norms and sport opportunities for women and girls, but acknowledges that the gender gap has not yet closed. Pfister closes with discussion of the status of women and girls in today's European sport system, the gender hierarchy in key executive positions of sport organizations, and highlights new questions and issues of discussion.

I would like to close by expressing my gratitude to the many people who saw me through this book; to all those who provided support, talked things over, read, wrote, offered comments, and assisted in the editing, proofreading and design. I would specifically like to thank The Teaching Gender Series Editor, Patricia Leavy, for providing me the opportunity to publish this book. Your guidance, support and feedback throughout this process was invaluable. Thank you to the staff at Sense Publishers, specifically Production Coordinator, Jolanda Karada, for her time and prompt feedback throughout the final stages of the book. I also greatly appreciate the copy editing assistance provided by Ronda Harris at the Sam Houston State University Writing Center. I would also like to acknowledge and thank Kolbi Ashorn's parents for allowing me to use a photograph of their daughter on the book cover. When asked to select cover art, I immediately remembered seeing this photograph. I feel it is an excellent example of a young girl participating in sport that is clearly "in the game".

This book would not have been accomplished if it were not for the contributors – thank you to each of you for your exceptional contributions, timely responses, and professionalism. Most of you I know, some very well, others I have "met" throughout this project. It was a pleasure working with each of you. Above all I want to acknowledge my family – my parents, sister, and niece – who have always supported me throughout my career. And lastly, to my husband, Kevin, who continues to support my professional and personal pursuits and constantly encourages me to challenge myself and those around me.

Emily A. Roper, Ph.D.

KAREN M. APPLEBY & ELAINE FOSTER

1. GENDER AND SPORT PARTICIPATION

INTRODUCTION

Sport is both one of the most celebrated and contested institutions in our society. In ancient times, sport served various social functions, from spiritual and religious expression to applied practice for warfare. Historically, sport has been used as spectacle for the public, both for entertainment and social purposes. Sport also provides professional opportunities for athletes and coaches. Regardless of the purpose or presentation, sport is a critical element in our modern social fabric. Sport, as entertainment, is a way to have fun and enjoy positive social interaction with peers and other competitors. The context of sport, when associated with good leadership and coaching, can help athletes acquire positive personal characteristics such as moral development, leadership, and pro-social sporting behaviors (Weinberg & Gould, 2011). In recent years, sport has also served as a catalyst to social change. In sporting contexts, we have seen racial barriers broken, gender gaps decrease, and issues of inequity related to socioeconomic status challenged.

Unfortunately, the context of sport does not always lead to positive outcomes. Many sport scholars have investigated the world of sport with a critical eye which has revealed a "dark side" of sport (LaVoi & Kane, 2011, p. 376). While sport has provided opportunities, it has also reinforced damaging and dangerous social patterns such as racism, gender inequity, homophobia, and excessive violence. Sport researchers have revealed how sport both reinforces and challenges dominant ideologies that often lead to discrimination. It is through this critical lens, which challenges our common ways of thinking, that sport can start to serve as a powerful instrument for social change.

In order to begin a chapter on sport and gender, it is first important to define both of these terms. The term *gender* is a social construction used to assign a set of appropriate behaviors to the female or male sex. According to Parratt (1994), gender is a social construction that changes over time. Gender is a performed behavior that aligns to how society expects men and women to act. This performance of gender, as suggested by Parratt (1994), is fluid and can change over time, space, and discourse. A simple example of how gender is "performed" in a sporting context is looking at what sports boys and girls are encouraged to play at a young age. Our society clearly defines certain sports as appropriate for boys (i.e., football, wrestling, and boxing) and for girls (i.e., dance, gymnastics, and figure skating). There is no biological reason why a girl should not play football or why a boy should not figure skate.

E. A. Roper (Ed.), Gender Relations in Sport, 1–20.

However, due to our socially created ideas about what is suitable behavior for boys and girls, crossover performances in these sports often creates controversy.

In this chapter, we will use a critical perspective to present and discuss the intersection of sport and gender. We will begin by discussing the benefits of sport across the lifespan. Next, we will provide a brief history of sport which emphasizes women's experiences and opportunities and discuss the current status of sport involvement for girls and women, focusing on intercollegiate athletics and recreational sport activities. Finally, we will conclude this chapter with a discussion of sport as a "masculine" domain and how this prevailing ideology often provokes barriers for both female and male athletes in sport settings.

WHY WE PLAY: BENEFITS OF SPORT ACROSS THE LIFESPAN

If you were to ask a child why he or she liked to play sports, that child would likely say "Because it's fun!" In asking adults the same question, we have heard responses such as, "It's a challenge," "I like the social interaction," "For exercise," "I like competition," and/or "It's stress relief." Although the benefits of sport participation may vary between age groups, genders, and levels of competition, there is always something for everyone to gain from playing and participating in sport throughout their lives. Specifically, sport participation can elicit physical, mental, and social benefits.

Physical Benefits

Sport creates a place to be physically active, which leads to improved physical health. Concern over physical health is on center stage as obesity rates have reached an all-time high worldwide. This preventable disease is affecting people of all ages, in part because of physical inactivity. The World Health Organization (2013) reported that over 1.4 billion adults and 40 million children (under the age of five) were obese in 2008. However, youth who engage in sports reduce their chances of becoming obese and are more likely to become physically healthy adults who continue to engage in sport across the lifespan (U.S. Anti-Doping Agency, 2012). Additionally, adults who begin a regular exercise regimen can improve their health and substantially reduce the negative effects of obesity and other chronic diseases such as diabetes, high blood pressure, cardiovascular diseases, musculoskeletal disorders, osteoporosis, and certain types of cancer (U.S. Department of Health & Human Services, 2008; World Health Organization, 2013).

Mental Benefits

Not only can greater physical health be a product of sport participation, but sport can also provide a context for improved mental health. The mental benefits elicited by sport participation have been well documented (Association for Applied Sport Psychology (AASP), 2012; U.S. Anti-Doping Agency, 2012). The AASP (2012) indicates that the following are psychological benefits obtained through physical exercise (para 2): (a) improved mood, (b) reduced stress as well as an improved ability to cope with stress, (c) improved self-esteem, (d) pride in physical accomplishments, (e) increased self-satisfaction, (f) improved body image, (g) increased feelings of energy, (h) improved confidence in one's physical abilities, and (i) decreased symptoms associated with depression.

Researchers have also suggested that playing sports may reduce the chance of suicide among teens and young adults (Taliaferro, Rienzo, Miller, Pigg, & Dodd, 2008), improve academic performance in people of all grade levels (Chomitz et al., 2009; Fox, Barr-Anderson, Neumark-Sztainer, & Wall, 2010; Todd, Czyszczon, Carr, & Pratt, 2009), and promote emotional management skills in athletes (Hansen, Larson, & Dworkin, 2003). For females, sport participation may also act as a buffer against disordered eating, body dissatisfaction (Tiggemann, 2001), and teenage pregnancy (Sabo, Miller, Farrell, Barnes, & Melnick, 1998).

Social Benefits

Another reported motivator for children, adolescents, and adults to play sport is for social interaction. If you have ever witnessed a group of athletes getting together to play volleyball, you might have seen the following interaction: show up, talk for 10 minutes, warm up, talk for 5 minutes, play, laugh for 8 minutes, play again, talk for 15 minutes, leave, do it again next week! Being able to socialize because of sport is very important to many age groups, is often an indicator of ongoing participation (Dionigi, Baker, & Horton, 2011; Lim et al., 2011), and has been tied to improved health-related quality of life (Eime, Harvey, Brown, & Payne, 2010).

Not only do people have more opportunity for social interaction during sport participation, but researchers have found that playing sports can teach and reinforce positive social behaviors (U.S. Anti-Doping Agency, 2012). Mothers specifically indicate that they believe sport participation helps their children develop important social skills such as teamwork, leadership, sportsmanship, and respect (Barnett & Weber, 2008). These skills gained from sport participation can carry over into the daily interactions of life.

Overall, sport can be a catalyst for many positive feelings, emotions, outcomes, and interactions throughout one's life. Participating in sport can also help one to develop positive personal characteristics such as stress management, communication skills, and the ability to work well with others. However, in order for positive outcomes to occur, one must have an opportunity to play. Girls and women have not always had the same opportunities and access to sport as boys and men in our society. At this point, we will turn our attention to the history of women in sport in North America and provide a glimpse into current sport participation levels of women today.

3

CONTESTING AND CONTESTED: A BRIEF HISTORY OF WOMEN IN SPORT

While it is beyond the scope of this chapter to provide an in-depth analysis of the history of sport and gender, in this section we will provide a brief overview of women's participation in sport from the ancient Olympics to modern sport involvement. One of the earliest and still most popular spectacles of sport that has shaped and continues to shape our sport culture is the Olympic Games. Both the history and current status of the Olympic Games provides a glimpse into how dominant cultural ideologies of gender have been reinforced and challenged throughout history. The Greeks were the visionaries of this ancient sport exhibition. It is presumed that the Olympic Games were originally sport festivals, connected to religious rituals and sacrifices, in which wealthy, able-bodied young men played games that were fashioned to mimic the requirements of Greek warriors of the day (Coakley, 2009). The original festivities excluded women not only from participation but from spectating (Coakley, 2009). It is a widely held belief that females who were caught viewing the Olympic festivities were punished by death (Griffin, 1992).

When Baron Pierre de Coubertin resurrected the modern Olympics in 1896 not much had changed; women were still excluded from participation in accordance with the social ideologies of appropriate gender roles for men and women at the time (Borish, 1996). Baron de Coubertin was particularly staunch about his aversion to including women in the Olympic Games due to his strong ideological notions of gender. According to Leigh (1974), "Indecency, ugliness, and impropriety were strong reasons, in Coubertin's view, for excluding women from the Olympic Games. His aesthetic sense was shocked by the sight of lightly clad, sweating women engaged in strenuous activity" (p. 19). It was not until the 1900 Olympic Games that women were allowed to compete. However, even then, very few entered or were provided any type of support or media coverage (Cahn, 1994). Slowly over the years, sports for women have been added to the Olympic Games and participation for women has been encouraged and celebrated. The London 2012 Summer Olympic Games served as a gender equity milestone; it was the first Olympic Games in which all 26 sports were open for both genders and in which all countries represented included female athletes (Blyler, 2012). This Olympic Games was also the first to have more female athletes representing the United States than male athletes (Grappendorf, 2013).

As you can imagine, prevailing gender ideologies made women's participation in the Olympic Games controversial in many cases. Stereotypes about "appropriate" women's sports and the female physiology discouraged participation for women in many sports. For example, physicians in the mid-19th century believed that menstruation and reproduction were so exhausting that women could not (and should not) participate in physical exercise. According to Burton-Nelson (1994), sitting upon a bicycle saddle was "said to induce menstruation and cause contracted vaginas and collapsed uteri" (p. 16). Even more damaging to the advancement of female athletes was the notion that engaging in sports could turn a woman masculine. Boxing, for example, was discouraged for women in the late 1880s because it was thought to enhance masculine qualities such as increased shoulder size, deepened voices, and augmented musculature (Burton-Nelson, 1994).

These ideologies greatly impacted women's participation in international competition. Women's high level performances at this level often led to gender questioning and discrimination. Many successful female athletes of the time were subject to this gender speculation and many accused successful female athletes of being males disguised as females (Ljungqvist et al., 2006). As Messner (1994) suggests, "Certainly the image of a muscular – even toned – woman runs counter to traditional prescriptions for female passivity and weakness" (p. 72). Due to this rampant, and often unwarranted speculation, gender testing became standard for female athletes at major international sport competitions. Gender testing procedures, at this time, were rudimentary and required "a parade by all female competitors, in the nude, before a panel of judges" (Tucker & Collins, 2010, p. 129). Sex verification testing was protocol in the Olympic Games until just recently. In the 2000 Sydney Summer Games, this testing was provisionally discontinued and has remained discontinued through the most recent London 2012 Olympic Games (Ljungqvist et al., 2006). While gender testing is no longer a standard practice for female Olympic athletes, gender speculation still abounds in women's elite level sport. One only need look at the case of South African 800 meter world champion Caster Semenya to explore the controversial practices and unrealistic binary categories that society attributes to gender (see Cahn, 2011; Schultz, 2011; Tucker & Collins, 2010 for a more in-depth look at the controversial aspects of gender testing in modern times).

IN THE GAME: THE CURRENT STATUS OF SPORT INVOLVEMENT FOR WOMEN

While reflecting on the history of gender in the Olympic Games provides a valuable historical perspective for the exploration of women's sport participation, it only provides a glimpse into one high performance level of sport. What about the history of participation for girls and women in other, more popular settings? Next, we will discuss the history and current status of sport for girls and women in interscholastic, professional, and recreational settings.

Interscholastic Opportunities

It is in the area of interscholastic sport that girls and women in North America, in particular, have arguably made the most progress in terms of participation. This increase in participation is largely due to the passage of Title IX, a federal regulation which discouraged gender discrimination in public school settings. Prior to Title IX, the majority of interscholastic competitive sport opportunities for girls and women were intramural versus extramural (Bell, 2007). Intramural sports are those played among students at a university or college setting while extramural sports are competitions held between athletes at different institutions. Traditional intramural competitions for women in the early 20th century included contests between

5

sororities and sport clubs at the same institution. While these intramural models of sport were popular, a new model of women's sport competition was developed at this time called Play Days (Hult, 1994, p. 89). Hult (1994) describes "Play Days" as a day in which female athletes from different schools met to compete in a sport and "were divided up and played on a team of girls from all of the schools (all of the leagues or all of the clubs) at the event" (p. 89). The "Play Day" concept was quickly replaced with a more standard version of extramural competition for women and, by 1971, 278 institutions had joined the American Intercollegiate Athletics for Women (AIAW), one of the first major governing bodies for women's collegiate athletics (Hult, 1994). This governing body would be the catalyst for the current participation numbers in women's athletics at the collegiate level.

While the road to equality has been a long and formidable challenge, recent researchers suggest that girls' and women's participation in interscholastic sport is at the highest level in history (Acosta & Carpenter, 2012). Specifically, Acosta and Carpenter report that prior to 1972, the year Title IX was enacted, there was an average of only 16,000 female intercollegiate athletes. In 2012, this number had increased to a total of 200,000. This participation trend is mirrored in high school sport as well. In 1971, there were 294,015 female athletes who participated in high school sports, while in 2011/2012 a reported 3,207,533 high school girls participated (National Federation of State High School Associations, n.d.). Contrary to popular belief, the increase in girls' sport at the high school level has not led to a decrease in boy's participation in high school sports. Prior to the passage of Title IX, 3,666,917 boys played high school sports. In 2012, this number rose to 4,494,406 (Acosta & Carpenter, 2012).

There are several factors that scholars suggest may have positively impacted the participation of girls and women in interscholastic sport settings. Acosta and Carpenter (2012) report:

Perhaps it is encouraged by a long line of successful Title IX lawsuits urging non-discriminatory treatment. Perhaps it is another generation of post Title IX men and women who now know that the benefits available from sport participation enrich the lives of both females and males, their daughters and sons. Perhaps it is increased media coverage of women's sports, and perhaps it is due to the long term efforts of energetic advocacy efforts by organizations... and coalitions of a variety of organizations found under the umbrella of the National Coalition for Girls and Women in Education. Whatever the cause, female athletes are being afforded opportunities in greater numbers than ever before. (p. 2)

The passage of Title IX has not only increased the number of girls and women who participate in sports interscholastically, but it has helped ensure the equitable treatment of girls and women in sports in publicly funded institutions. It is important not just to add sports for girls and women, but to manage these sports equally to how boys and men's sports would be treated in these settings. For example, Title IX ensures the equitable treatment in relation to (but is not limited to) the following: equipment and supplies, scheduling game and practice times, travel and per diem, coaching and tutoring, facilities, medical treatment and services, housing and dining, media relations, and general support services (Moorman & Reynolds, 2011 in SPMG text). National governing bodies such as the National Collegiate Athletic Association (NCAA) have embraced the concept of gender equity in sport and continue the quest to add opportunities for women in sport who, in the past, were the underrepresented sex in the area of athletics (Miller, Heinrich, & Baker, 2000).

While the quest for gender equity at publicly funded institutions has certainly stimulated an impressive increase in participation levels for girls and women in interscholastic sport, there are still a number of gender equity issues that need to be addressed in these settings. One issue is the dearth of leadership positions held by women in collegiate sports settings (Grappendorf, 2013). According to Acosta and Carpenter (2013), prior to the implementation of Title IX in 1972, approximately 90% of coaches of women's sports were female. In 2012, the percentage of female head coaches for women's teams was 42.9% while 57.1% of women's teams were coached by men. In upper level administration at the collegiate level, only 20.3% of athletic directors are female; 79.7% males hold the position of athletic director at the collegiate level. However, this seemingly dark cloud does have a silver lining. While these raw percentages reflect a lower number of women in these positions than men, the number of women overall who hold leadership positions in sport is increasing. As Acosta and Carpenter (2012) reported, there are 501 more administrative jobs held by women at the collegiate level than there were just one decade ago.

At the professional level of sport, a similar picture emerges. In 2009, the Women's National Basketball Association (WNBA) was the only women's professional league to employ any head female coaches (LaVoi & Kane, 2011). However, over time this number has not increased. In 2012, the number of female head coaches in the WNBA decreased 8% and the number of female general managers decreased 50% (from 8 to 4) (Lapchick, Milkovich, & O'Keefe, 2012). Despite these declines in female representation in leadership positions, the WNBA has the highest representation of women in leadership of any professional women's sport organization in the United States. As LaVoi and Kane (2011) suggest, "In professional sports, females in positions of power outside of the WNBA are rare" (p. 377).

Another element related to women in professional sport is media coverage. Media and public relations are crucial elements that shape our knowledge about and understanding of sports and athletes. Those who write about sports are often those who shape our opinions about important issues in sport. They also introduce us to athletes by telling us their stories and sharing information that helps the public get to know athletes on a more personal level. Therefore, it is critical that those who write and disseminate information about sport and athletes help to highlight women in sport. Recent research, however, points to a disproportionate gender gap in the media. Lapchick et al. (2013) reported a lopsided gender breakdown of the Associated Press; a disproportionate 90.4% of sports editors are male while 90.2%

7

of sports columnists are male. This gender disparity indicates that sport media, as a profession, is male-dominated. Kian and Hardin (2009) investigated how the gender of sports writers impacts event coverage. They sought to determine how the sex of a sports writer impacted how he or she portrayed athletes in intercollegiate men's and women's basketball games. These authors found that female sports writers include female athletes more in their coverage and are less likely to reinforce traditional gender stereotypes of female athletes than male sports writers.

In regard to deterring the gender inequity among media professionals, Lapchick et al. (2013) suggested the following: recruit media personnel from diverse backgrounds and institutions, follow policies that encourage diversity in hiring practices, create an atmosphere of inclusion in the media workplace, and encourage mentoring practices that help young media professionals exercise their skills and network themselves in professional settings.

Recreational Sporting Opportunities for Women

The Olympic, collegiate, and professional levels of sport are not the only opportunities that girls and women have to be athletes and to participate in sport. Female athletes also compete at the recreational sport levels and have abundant opportunities to participate throughout the world, within a multitude of settings, and at various levels of competition. The types of sports include traditional fitness (i.e., weightlifting and aerobics), outdoor (i.e., hiking and skiing), team (i.e., lacrosse and volleyball), and even extreme activities (i.e., highline slacklining and adventure racing). The level of competition within these sports also greatly varies depending on the league (i.e., community groups, church associations, campus recreation, masters, world championships, etc.).

Specifically, women's participation in recreational sport increased dramatically in the 1970s (Granskog, 2003). This increase was due to a number of factors such as the impact of the feminist movement in the 1960s which redefined gender norms in many ways, the passage of Title IX which expanded opportunities, and the health and fitness boom which provided various outlets for competition at the recreational level (Bolin & Granskrog, 2003; Coakley, 2009). According to Lopiano (2000), "there are now more than 55 million women who participate in recreational sports and fitness activities regularly" (p. 164). Sports such as competitive cycling and triathlon have recently experienced a large increase in female participation. As reported by USA Cycling, between the years of 2005–2009, there was a 32% increase in masters (over the age of 30) women racing (T. Johnson, personal communication, November 7, 2010).

However, even before these social changes occurred, women had participated in sport at the recreational level. In the late 19th century, for example, women were widely represented in the "bicycle craze" that captivated North America. This sporting popularity "broke new ground for women's rights to public outdoor exercise" (Cahn, 1994, p. 15). As the 20th century evolved, and women's rights became a central social and political topic, women became more engaged in sporting endeavors. They actively played, participated, and competed in sports such as tennis, basketball, and track and field. These three sports, in particular, provided the widest variety of opportunity for women of color in the Post WWII era (Himes-Gissendanner, 1994).

Much like women's inclusion in the Olympics and interscholastic sport, the inclusion of women in the recreational sport scene did not come without criticism. In the late 1800s and beyond, the public still espoused widely held and unfounded beliefs about the physical dangers of women's athleticism. As Cahn (1994) suggests, social critics of female athletes of the time "claimed that excess [bicycle] riding caused women serious physiological damage," which could manifest in the forms of such ailments as "uterine displacement, spinal shock, pelvic damage, and hardened abdominal muscles" (p. 16).

Despite these cultural obstacles, women continued to play and participate even in activities that encouraged and required muscularity. In the late 1930s another fitness craze swept through the United States – the "muscle beach" fitness movement. While several men were recognized as innovators of this fitness movement, at this time the world was introduced to a female pioneer, Abby Eville (later Stockton). Eville-Stockton was one of the recognized figures in women's bodybuilding and was one of the first proponents of weight training to increase athletic ability and performance for women (McCracken, 2007). While, today it is the norm to see women and female athletes in the weight room, this concept was revolutionary at the time because it contradicted and challenged society's ideals of both femininity and the physical capabilities of women.

It was not until the 1970s that the health and fitness trend became a revolutionary movement that would propel women even deeper into athletic competition at the recreational level. Perhaps one of the most significant forces in women's recreational athletic competition at the time was distance running. It was not until 1972 that the Amateur Athletic Union (AAU) allowed women to enter sanctioned marathons. Even in the 1960s, the ancient ideologies of gender prevailed about the dangers of sport for women. As Switzer (2013) recounts, "For women…the risks of running also included getting big legs, having your uterus fall out, never having children, and turning into a burly guy" (pp. 18–19).

Despite these unfounded, but widely perpetuated "risks," women ran. Anecdotal evidence of women's previous participation in marathons was widespread. For example, Katherine Switzer entered the legendary Boston Marathon in 1967 under the alias K. V. Switzer. Race officials discovered she was female in the middle of the race and attempted to physically pull her off the course. In 1972, women were finally allowed entry into the prestigious marathon. Pioneers such as Katherine Switzer and Roberta Gibb (another Boston marathon runner who finished but never officially registered) set the stage for what would become one of the most popular community sports for women in North America – distance running. In 2012, it was estimated that over 7 million women in the United States competed in a road racing event and that women represented 41% of all marathon finishers (Fennessey, 2012; Sebor, n.d.).

9

BLOCKING THE SHOT: GENDER RELATED SPORT BARRIERS

While opportunities to play are growing, not everyone partakes in sport. Therefore, is important to reflect upon what keeps people (both men and women) from participating in certain activities. Researchers have examined many barriers that exist for both males and females when it comes to sport opportunities. These barriers include, but are not limited to: (a) living environment, (b) culture and religion, and (c) specific barriers for women.

Living Environment

Characteristics of the living environment for a person play a significant role in the sport opportunities available. Factors such as rural or urban living, the presence of sidewalks in the neighborhood, public transportation availability, and access to a recreational facility can all affect one's chances for sport participation (Davison & Lawson, 2006; U.S. Department of Health and Human Services, 2013). Children, particularly girls, who live in an urban environment often do not participate in sport because of unsafe routes or limited access to facilities and programs (Sabo & Veliz, 2008; Women's Sport Foundation, 2011). Adults and older adults also report safe routes and facility access as significant barriers to participation (Lee, Mama, McAlexander, Adamus, & Medina, 2011; Trost, Owen, Bauman, Sallis, & Brown, 2002).

Other environmental factors relating to sport opportunities are family finances and support. Older adults indicate that high costs and lack of social support often keep them from participating (Belza et al., 2004). For children, growing up in a single parent home generally means fewer available resources to accommodate the time and financial demands that sport participation requires, thus reducing the options for participation (Sabo & Veliz, 2008). For women, who often have many obligations related to their roles as wife, mother, and breadwinner, having family support plays a tremendous role in their activity levels (Appleby & Fisher, 2009; Arikawa, O'Dougherty, & Schmitz, 2011).

Culture and Religion

In the US, inequities in sport participation are also prevalent between different ethnic groups (Sabo & Veliz, 2008). Specifically, low percentages of minority boys and girls play sports. The cultural and religious expectations placed on individuals within different ethnic groups influences the opportunities to engage in certain types of sports, if participation is allowed at all. Women in particular have struggled for acceptance into the world of sports because of the expectations and ideologies found in different cultures and religions. Some cultural barriers are linked to stereotypes related to appropriate behavior for women. For example, within some Native American Indian cultures, sport may not "fit with the identity" of women and may elicit social stigmas for those who do exercise (Eyler et al., 2002, p. 248). Other cultural barriers stem from racist ideals that some societies hold. For example, many Black South African women avoid physical activity because women seen exercising are often viewed as "wasting time" or "wanting to be white" (Walter & Du Randt, 2011, p. 149). Additionally, women in this culture may be fearful of losing weight because they fear they will be accused "of being HIV positive" (p. 150). Muslim women in some countries face significant challenges when it comes to sport participation because of religious traditions and norms specifically revolving around dress code (Khan, Jamil, Khan, Kareem, & Imran, 2012). It is important to point out that many of these barriers are often cultural rather than religious in nature as Muslim women in countries such as Turkey may not have to face these same barriers (Khan et al., 2012). Recent events, however, indicate that some of these cultural barriers are easing. For example, a new initiative being introduced in the Persian Gulf, a society that has traditionally restricted girls' and women's sport participation, is opening up sport opportunities in basketball, table tennis, and athletics for girls and women (Associated Press, 2013).

Specific Barriers for Women

For young girls attempting to pursue a life filled with playing sports, significant roadblocks may limit what they are able to do. The Women's Sports Foundation (2011) indicates that girls are often faced with a lack of positive role models, fewer opportunities, and a watered down quality of sports available to them. Also, the social influences of family and friends are a huge indicator of whether a girl will be active in sports (Coleman, Cox, & Roker, 2008). Thus, if her family and friends do not participate in or value playing sports, neither will she.

If a girl can overcome these obstacles, she still faces hurdles regarding her chances of continuing to play sports. After high school, physical activity decreases by almost 50% among females (Han et al., 2008). Women often feel that even though it is acceptable for them to engage in sports, it is difficult to juggle this desire while still fulfilling their expected social roles. Specifically, as women face significant transitions such as beginning college, starting a job, getting married, or having a child, they often feel it is impossible to play sports and perform in their new responsibility (Arikawa, O'Dougherty, & Schmitz, 2011; Brown, Heesch, & Miller, 2009). Feelings of guilt and inadequacy for taking time for herself (playing sports) have also been found to reduce the likelihood of a woman engaging in sports (Appleby & Fisher, 2009).

Another common barrier women face is fear of social evaluation. Young girls, college females, and adult women (including elderly) all have indicated anxieties related to social evaluation within sport (Coleman, Cox, & Roker, 2008; Salvatore & Marecek, 2010; Trost et al. 2002). These feared assessments include the stigma of sports being masculine (Women's Sports Foundation, 2011), comparing herself to others (Huberty et al., 2008), the fear of being gazed at by a male (Calogero,

2004), and anxiety about the type of clothing that is expected to be worn (Cortis, 2009; Thøgersen-Ntoumanis, Ntoumanis, Cumming, Bartholomew, & Pearce, 2011). Additionally, many women have low self-efficacy and confidence when it comes to sport participation, worrying they will be inept in the activity and create embarrassment (Salvatore & Marecek, 2010).

GIRLS ONLY: FEMALE CENTERED ORGANIZATIONS,
EXERCISE SPACES, AND EVENTS

In an attempt to curtail the barriers that limit women's participation in sport, women's sport organizations, exercise spaces, and events have expanded in recent years. Through this women's centered movement, numerous opportunities to participate in sport have helped women feel more confident and comfortable in sport and fitness settings (Cortis, 2009).

Women-Centered Organizations

Over the years, different organizations specifically created to champion, enhance, and increase the visibility of women in sport have emerged. The National Association for Girls and Women in Sport (NAGWS), for example, was spearheaded in 1899 by Alice Foster, Sandra Berenson, Ethel Perrin, and Elizabeth Wright in an effort to create a handbook for girls' and women's basketball (NAGWS.org, n.d.). This original committee was named the Women's Basketball Rules Committee and later morphed into the currently existing NAGWS. The Women's Sports Foundation (WSF), another organization formed to advocate for women in sports, was founded in 1974 by Billie Jean King and currently provides opportunities for girls and women in sports through vehicles such as grants, scholarships, research, and awareness campaigns (WSF, n.d.).

Women-Centered Exercise Spaces

Curves for Women opened in 1992, claiming to be the first women's only fitness center (Curves, n.d.). Since then, the company can be found in over 90 countries. Thousands of gyms and fitness centers throughout the world have followed suit by creating women's exclusive facilities or times. So, why has the women's only gym become so popular worldwide? A fitness center is a unique place. Although the purpose of these venues is to provide a space to improve health and wellness, they are also often a place where the body is easily objectified (Prichard & Tiggman, 2005). Walls covered in mirrors, tight fitting apparel, and intimidating machines often deter women from fitness centers for fear of being evaluated (Salvatore & Marecek, 2010). Although all of these factors may still be found in a women's only gym, there is one thing missing – the male gaze. Some women are prohibited, due to cultural reasons, from exercising within the view of a man (Cortis, 2009), but even for those who do not have these restraints, just the thought of being under the gaze of a man can escalate body objectification (Calogero, 2004) leading to social physique anxiety (Prichard & Tiggemann, 2005).

Women's only exercise spaces have also taken root in higher education settings where women report feeling more comfortable and free in these settings allowing them to learn at their own pace without fear of criticism (Supiano, 2008). Additionally, some female college students are appreciative of women only court times as males tend to be more aggressive and physical than the women feel comfortable with. Therefore, more than just helping women to "lose weight, gain strength, and get fit" (Curves, n.d, para. 3), the creation of women's only fitness spaces has helped women break barriers that often keep them inactive.

All women's athletic leagues have also been shown to incite women's participation in a number of different ways. For example, Birrell and Richter's (1994) research on an all-women's softball league indicated that the participants valued (a) the ability to learn the techniques of the game and become highly skilled, (b) friendships, and (c) challenging competition more than just winning. These researchers also found that this all female setting discouraged the "elitism of skill" by offering "opportunities for women with little sport experience to learn the game in a supportive environment" (Birrell & Richter, 1994, p. 235). Other research indicates that all-women's training groups for sports such as triathlon offer the opportunity for participants to build valuable social connections and networks that help them navigate lifestyle difficulties such as work and child care with athletic training (Cronan & Scott, 2008). As Cronan and Scott (2008) suggest, "the all-women's atmosphere of the training program provided a space for women to talk about their lives, take time for personal development and build bonds with other women" (p. 25).

Women-Centered Events

Not only have many fitness centers and gyms facilitated women's only exercise spaces, but the women-centered movement has also found a niche in sporting events. Hundreds of bike races, triathlons, runs, obstacle races, and volleyball tournaments (to name a few) have been created just for women. Women's only events can have a positive impact on women's participation levels in sport. For example, Crofts, Schofield, and Dickson (2012) found that activity levels for almost half of the finishers of an all-women's triathlon were higher three months post-event than pre-event. Despite the positive outcomes women-centered events may have, there is evidence that the marketing of such events can often send mixed social messages. While the purpose of these events is to provide women with an opportunity to develop physical skills, health, and confidence, these outcomes can be undermined by slogans perpetuating the myth that female athletes must also be physically attractive. Slogans such as *Ride...Beautiful, Strong, and Free,* catch phrases such as *Ride... with fellow beach babes on bikes,* and references to female athletes as *Cinderella,* a *Mermaid,* or a *Goddess* can undermine the intent to empower women through sport

13

and physical activity. Therefore, it is critical that organizers of these important all-women centered events carefully consider the impact of their marketing campaigns and align them with the appropriate participation outcomes.

STILL FIGHTING: SPORT AS A MASCULINE DOMAIN

Traditionally, sports have been defined as a "masculine" domain. Masculine ideals have defined and influenced most sports creating fewer opportunities for females to participate (Hardin & Greer, 2009; Tischer, Hartmann-Tews, & Combrink, 2011). As Wachs (2003) proposes, "Like many other public environments, sports historically have been associated with masculinity" (p. 178). This ideology impacts athletes in relation to sport opportunities provided and encouraged, society's definition of appropriate sports for boys and girls/men and women, and homophobia (Wachs, 2003). All of these ideologies can negatively impact an athlete's sport options, self-confidence, and motivation to play.

Perhaps one of the most pervasive stereotypes related to sport and gender is the notion that there are "appropriate" and "inappropriate" sports for females and males. Researchers have found that sports which emphasize beauty and grace such as gymnastics, dance, and figure skating are often regarded as "feminine," while sports that include elements of violence, aggression, and physical contact such as football, boxing, and combat sports are considered "masculine" (Koivula, 2001). These notions are steeped in our social ideologies which are not created by what we *can* do but what society thinks we *should (or should not)* do. Coakley (2009) suggests these persistent ideologies limit the opportunities of sport participation for both male and female athletes:

> For both ideological and structural reasons, women have few opportunities to play professional sports. Until recently, few people would pay to watch women play anything but "ladylike" sports in which they competed alone (figure skating, golf) or competed with nets or dividers separating opponents and preventing physical contact (tennis, volleyball). Although more people today are willing to pay to watch women play various sports, the most popular spectator sports continue to be tennis, figure skating, gymnastics, and golf – all of which are consistent with traditional notions of femininity. (Coakley, 2009, p. 248)

Although sports have historically been defined as masculine or feminine, the rise of female participation in certain activities has led society to view some sports as gender neutral (Hardin & Greer, 2009). For example, in the United States, sports such as soccer, tennis, and swimming are viewed as gender neutral and "acceptable" for both males and females. This gender neutral status, however, can vary depending on the geographical location. In many countries, for example, soccer is not an acceptable activity for females to participate in (Walter & Du Randt, 2011).

These ideologies and stereotypes do not just limit choices and participation, they can also incite deep rooted forms of violence such as homophobia. Athletes, regardless of sexual orientation, who play sports deemed "inappropriate" for their gender are often subject to violence and hate that stems from cultural homophobia. In 1992, Griffin stressed that homophobia can manifest itself in the following negative ways in women's sport: (a) silence, (b) denial, (c) apology, (d) promotion of a heterosexy image, (e) attacks on lesbians, and (f) preference for male coaches (p. 253). In a presentation given 21 years later at the American Alliance for Health, Physical Education, Recreation, and Dance (AAHPERD) annual conference, Griffin (2013) noted that these homophobic attitudes and the subsequent behaviors demonstrated by female athletes are still clear and present in women's sport contexts (NAGWS Rachel Bryant Memorial Lecture, April 26th, 2013).

Researchers have also shown that these hegemonic, homophobic stereotypes are reinforced in the sports media. For example, female athletes are chronically underrepresented in the media (King, 2007). Coakley (2009) reports that coverage of female athletes and women's sports in major newspapers throughout the country is "less than 15%" (p. 420). Further, female athletes are also represented in the media as less physically capable as male athletes (Kian, Vincent, & Mondello, 2008) and are consistently portrayed in overly (hetero)sexualized manners which Knight and Guiliano (2003) term the "feminine apologetic" (p. 282). The hetero-normative representations of athletes also impacts male athletes. While female athletes must consistently display "feminine" behaviors to dissuade homophobic labeling, male athletes are always presumed to be heterosexual (Coakley, 2009; Knight & Guiliano, 2003). This labelling can be frustrating for male athletes who identify as gay because they must consistently hide their true identity from their teammates, coaches, and the public. When male athletes do reveal their sexual orientation as gay, the public are often more critical and less accepting than they are of female athletes who reveal their sexual orientation as lesbian (Knight & Giuliano, 2003).

CHAPTER SUMMARY

While the scope of this chapter certainly does not cover all issues and topics related to gender in sport, it provides a starting point for understanding why studying sport and gender is a crucial exercise. From a historical standpoint, sport has been a "contested ideological terrain" (Messner, 1994, p. 65) for women. Major international sporting events were generally unavailable to women until the early 20th century and women's sport participation in community sports was not widely accepted until the end of this same century. However, the current picture of female athletes and the inclusion of sport for women in educational settings is much brighter. Federal regulations such as Title IX have significantly increased the overall participation level and opportunities available for female athletes in interscholastic, public settings. On a recreational level, there are almost as many female athletes competing as there are male athletes.

Despite these increases in participation and opportunity, challenges still hold firm for women in sport settings. Throughout this chapter we have discussed the various barriers that are unique to women in their quest to engage in sport and fitness over the lifespan. In many cases, researchers still find that women are less likely to engage in recreation, leisure, and sporting opportunities as they age. This can be due to a number of issues including, but not limited to, parenthood, work parameters, body image, confidence, and environmental safety. Further, both male and female athletes can be discouraged from participating in certain sports based on the social ideologies that define "appropriate" sports for males and females. In certain cases, homophobic tendencies reinforced by the media can serve to deter all athletes from portraying themselves in an authentic manner.

As future professionals, it is important for you to critically consider social issues that shape our world. This includes being analytical even about institutions that may normally only be considered for entertainment such as sport. By dissecting the history, current practice, and social trends that sport follows, you can begin to appreciate both how far we have advanced in the promotion of sport for all while recognizing how far we still have to go.

REFERENCES

Acosta, R. V., & Carpenter, L. G. (2012). *Women in intercollegiate sport: A longitudinal, national study thirty-five year update: 1977–2012.* Retrieved from http://acostacarpenter.org/ AcostaCarpenter2012.pdf

Appleby, K. M., & Fisher, L. A. (2009). "Running in and out of pregnancy:" Elite distance runners' experiences of returning to competition after pregnancy. *Women in Sport and Physical Activity Journal, 18*(1), 3–17.

Arikawa, A. Y., O'Dougherty, M., & Schmitz, K. H. (2011). Adherence to a strength training intervention in adult women. *Journal of Physical Activity and Health, 8,* 111–118.

Associated Press (2013, May 9). Kuwait initiative creates first sports clubs for women in the country. *Fox News.com.* Retrieved from http://www.foxnews.com/world/2013/05/09/kuwait-initiative creates-first-sports-clubs-for-women-in-country/).

Association for Applied Sport Psychology. (2012). *Psychological Benefits of Exercise.* Retrieved from http://appliedsportpsych.org/Resource-Center/health-and-fitness/articles/psych-benefits-of-exercise

Barnett, L. A., & Weber, J. J. (2008). Perceived benefits to children from participating in different types of recreational activities. *Journal of Park and Recreation Administration, 26*(3), 1–20.

Bell, R. C. (2007). A history of women in sport prior to Title IX. *The Sport Journal, 10*(2). Retrieved from http://www.thesportjournal.org/article/history-women-sport-prior-title-ix

Belza, B., Walwick, J., Shiu-Thornton, S., Schwartz, S., Taylor, M., & LoGerfo, J. (2004). Older adult perspectives on physical activity and exercise: Voices from multiple cultures. *Preventing Chronic Disease, 1*(4), 1–12.

Birrell, S., & Richter, D. M. (1994). Is a diamond forever? Feminist transformations of sport. In S. Birrell & C. L. Cole (Eds.), *Women, Sport, and Culture* (pp. 221–244). Champaign, IL: Human Kinetics.

Blyler, L. (2012). *London Olympics offer hope for gender equity.* Retrieved from http://www.aauw.org/2012/07/09/hope-for-gender-equity/

Bolin, A., & Granskog, J. (2003). Reflexive ethnography, women, and sporting activities. In A. Bolin & J. Granskog (Eds.), *Athletic intruders: Ethnographic research on women, culture, and exercise* (pp. 7–25). Albany, NY: State University of New York Press.

Borish, L. J. (1996). Women at the Modern Olympic Games: An interdisciplinary look at American culture. *Quest, 48,* 43–56.

Brown, W. J., Heesch, K. C., & Miller, Y. D. (2009). Life events and changing physical activity patterns in women at different life stages. *The Society of Behavioral Medicine, 37,* 294–305. doi:10.1007/d12160–009-9099–2

Burton-Nelson, M. (1994). *The stronger women get, the more men love football: Sexism and the American culture of sports.* New York, NY: Harcourt Brace.

Cahn, S. (1994). *Coming on strong: Gender and sexuality in twentieth-century women's sport.* Cambridge, MA: Harvard University Press.

Cahn, S. (2011). Testing sex, attributing gender: What Caster Semenya means to women's sports. *Journal of Intercollegiate Sport, 4,* 38–48.

Calogero, R. M. (2004). A test of objectification theory: The effect of the male gaze on appearance concerns in college women. *Psychology of Women Quarterly, 28,* 16–21.

Chomitz, V. R., Slining, M. M., McGowan, R. J., Mitchell, S. E., Dawson, G. F., & Hacker, K. (2009). Is there a relationship between physical fitness and academic achievement? Positive results from public school children in the northeastern United States. *Journal of School Health, 79*(1), 30–37.

Coakley, J. (2009). *Sports in society: Issues and controversies* (Vol. 10). Boston, MA: McGraw Hill.

Coleman, L., Cox, L., & Roker, D. (2008). Girls and young women's participation in physical activity: Psychological and social influences. *Health Education Research, 23*(4), 633–647.

Cortis, N. (2009). Social inclusion and sport: Culturally diverse women's perspectives. *Australian Journal of Social Issues, 44*(1), 91–104.

Crofts, C., Schofield, G., & Dickson, G. (2012). Women-only mass participation sporting events: Does participation facilitate changes in physical activity? *Annals of Leisure Research, 15*(2), 148–160.

Cronan, M. K., & Scott, D. (2008). Triathlon and women's narratives of bodies and sport. *Leisure Sciences, 30,* 17–34.

Curves. (n.d.). *About us.* Retrieved from http://www.curves.com/about-curves/

Davison, K. K., & Lawson, C. T. (2006). Do attributes in the physical environment influence children's physical activity? A review of the literature. *International Journal of Behavioral Nutrition and Physical Activity, 3,* 19–35. doi:10.1186/1479–5868-3–19

Dionigi, R. A., Baker, J., & Horton, S. (2011). Older athletes' perceived benefits of competition. *The International Journal of Sport and Society, 2*(2), 17–28.

Eime, R. M., Harvey, J. T., Brown, W. J., & Payne, W. R. (2010). Does sports club participation contribute to health-related quality of life? *Medicine and Science in Sports and Exercise, 42*(5), 1022–1028. doi:10.1249/MSS.0b013e3181c3adaa

Eyler, A. E., Wilcox, S., Matson-Koffman, D., Evenson, K. R., Sanderson, B., Thompson, J., Wilbur, J., & Rohm-Young, D. (2002). Correlates of physical activity among women from diverse racial/ethnic groups. *Journal of Women's Health & Gender-Based Medicine, 11*(3), 239–253.

Fennessy, C. (2012). Kathrine Switzer. *Runner's World, 47*(1), 60.

Fox, C. K., Barr-Anderson, D., Neumark-Sztainer, D., & Wall, M. (2010). Physical activity and sports team participation: Associations with academic outcomes in middle school and high school students. *Journal of School Health, 80*(1), 31–37.

Granskog, J. (2003). Just "tri" and "du" it: The variable impact of female involvement in the triathlon/duathlon sport culture. In A. Bolin & J. Granskog (Eds.), *Athletic Intruders: Ethnographic research on women, culture, and exercise* (pp. 27–52). Albany, NY: State University of New York Press.

Grappendorf, H. (2013). The "year" of the women in sports: Why stop at one? *Journal of Physical Education, Recreation, and Dance, 84*(5), 7–8.

Griffin, P. (1992). Changing the game: Homophobia, sexism, and lesbians in sport. *Quest, 44,* 251–265.

Griffin, P. (2013, April). *NAGWS Rachel Bryant Memorial Lecture.* Presented at the meeting of American Alliance for Health Education, Physical Education, Recreation, and Dance, Charlotte, N.C.

Han, J. L., Dinger, M. K, Hull, H. R., Randall, N. B., Heesch, K. C., & Fields, D. A. (2008). Changes in women's physical activity during the transition to college. *American Journal of Health Education, 39*(4), 194–199.

Hansen, D. M., Larson, R. W., & Dworkin, J. B. (2003). What adolescents learn in organized youth activities: A survey of self-reported developmental experiences. *Journal of Research on Adolescence, 13*(1), 25–55. doi:10.1111/1532–7795.1301006

Hardin, M., & Greer, J. D. (2009). The influence of gender-role socialization, media use and sports participation on perceptions of gender-appropriate sports. *Journal of Sport Behavior, 32*(2), 207–226.

Himes-Gissendanner, C. (1994). African-American women and competitive sport, 1920–1960. In S. Birrell & C. L. Cole (Eds.), *Women, Sport, and Culture* (pp. 81–92). Champaign, IL: Human Kinetics.

Huberty, J. L., Ransdell, L. B., Sidman, C., Flohr, J. A., Shultz, B., Grosshans, O., & Durrant, L. (2008). Explaining long-term exercise adherence in women who complete a structured exercise program. *Research Quarterly for Exercise and Sport, 79*(3), 374–384.

Hult, J. S. (1994). The story of women's athletics: Manipulating a dream 1890–1985. In D. M. Costa & S. R. Guthrie (Eds.), *Women and Sport: Interdisciplinary Perspectives* (pp. 83–106). Champaign, IL: Human Kinetics.

Khan, M. Y., Jamil, A., Khan, U. A., Kareem, U., & Imran, G. (2012). Female students' opinion about women's participation in sports. *International Journal of Academic Research in Business and Social Sciences, 2*(9), 275–283.

Kian, E. M., & Hardin, M. (2009). Framing of sport coverage based on the sex of sports writers: Female journalists counter the traditional gendering of media coverage. *International Journal of Sport Communication, 2*, 185–204.

Kian, E. M., Vincent, J., & Mondello (2008). Masculine hegemonic hoops: An analysis of media coverage of March Madness. *Sociology of Sport Journal, 25*, 223–242.

King, C. (2007). Media portrayals of male and female athletes: A text and picture analysis of British national newspaper coverage of the Olympic Games since 1948. *International Review for the Sociology of Sport, 42*(2), 187–199.

Knight, J. L., & Giuliano, T. A. (2003). Blood, sweat, and jeers: The impact of the media's heterosexist portrayals on perceptions of male and female athletes. *Journal of Sport Behavior, 26*(3), 272–284.

Koivula, N. (2001). Perceived characteristics of sports categorized as gender-neutral, feminine, and masculine. *Journal of Sport Behavior, 24*(4), 377–393.

Lapchick, R., Milkovich, M., & O'Keefe, S. (2012). The 2012 Women's National Basketball Association Racial and Gender Report Card. Retrieved from http://web.bus.ucf.edu/documents/sport/2012-WNBA-RGRC.pdf

Lapchick, R., Burnett, C., Farris, M., Gossett, R., Orpilla, C., Phelan, J., Sherrod, T., Smith, S., Thiel, S., Walker, C., & Snively, D. (2013). The 2012 Associated Press sports editors racial and gender report card. Retrieved from http://dl. dropboxusercontent.com/u/11322904/ TIDES%20Reports/2012%20 APSE%20GRC.pdf

LaVoi, N., & Kane, M. J. (2011). Sociological aspects of sport. In P. M. Pederson, J. B. Parks, J. Quarterman, & L. Thibault (Eds.), *Contemporary Sport Management* (4th ed., pp. 374–391). Champaign, IL: Human Kinetics.

Lee, R. E., Mama, S. K., McAlexander, K. P., Adamus, H., & Medina, A. V. (2011). Neighborhood and PA: Neighborhood factors and physical activity in African American Public Housing Residents. *Journal of Physical Activity and Health, 8*(1), S83-S90.

Leigh, M. (1974). Pierre de Coubertin: A man of his time. *Quest, 22*, 19–24.

Lim, S. Y., Warner, S., Dixon, M., Berg, B., Kim, C., & Newhouse-Bailey, M. (2011). Sport participation across national contexts: A multilevel investigation of individual and systemic influences on adult sport participation. *European Sport Management Quarterly, 11*(3), 197–224.

Ljungqvist, A., Martinez-Patino, M., Martinez-Vidal, A., Zagalaz, L., Dias, P., & Mateos, C. (2006). The history and current policies on gender testing in elite athletes. *International SportMed Journal, 7*(3), 225–230.

Lopiano, D. A. (2000). Modern history of women in sports: Twenty-five years of Title IX. *The Athletic Woman, 19*(2), 163–173.

McCracken, E. (2007). The belle of the barbell. *Iron game history: The Journal of Physical Culture, 10*(1), 1.

Messner, M. (1994). Sports and male domination: The female athlete as contested ideologicalterrain. In S. Birrell & C. L. Cole (Eds.), *Women, Sport, and Culture* (pp. 65–80). Champaign, IL: Human Kinetics.

Miller, J. L., Heinrich, M. D., & Baker, R. (2000). A look at Title IX and women's participation in sport. *Physical Educator, 57*(1), 8–13.

Moorman, A. M., & Reynolds, R. C. (2011). Legal considerations in sport management. In P. M. Pederson, J. B. Parks, J. Quarterman, & L. Thibault (Eds.), *Contemporary Sport Management* (4th ed., pp. 352–371). Champaign, IL: Human Kinetics.

National Association of Girls and Women in Sport (NAGWS) (n.d.). *History.* Retrieved from http://www. aahperd.org/nagws/stories/history.cfm

National Federation of State High School Associations (n.d.). *2011–2012 high school athletics participation survey results.* Retrieved from http://www.nfhs.org/content.aspx?id=3282

Parratt, C. M. (1994). From the history of women in sport to women's sport history: A research agenda. In D. M. Costa & S. R. Guthrie (Eds.), *Women in sport: Interdisciplinary perspectives* (pp. 5–14). Champaign, IL: Human Kinetics.

Prichard, I., & Tiggemann, M. (2005). Objectification in fitness centers: Self-objectification, body dissatisfaction, and disordered eating in aerobics instructors and aerobic participants. *Sex Roles, 52,* 19–28. doi:10.1007/s11199–005-4270–0

Sabo, D., & Veliz, P. (2008). *The Women's Sports Foundation Report: Go out and play: Youth sports in America.* East Meadow, NY: Women's Sports Foundation.

Sabo, D., Miller, K., Farrell, M., Barnes, G., & Melnick, M. (1998). *The Women's Sports Foundation Report: Sport and teen pregnancy.* East Meadow, NY: Women's Sports Foundation.

Salvatore, J., & Marecek, J. (2010). Gender in the gym: Evaluation concerns as barriers to women's weight lifting. *Sex Roles, 63,* 556–567. doi:10.1007/s11199–0109800-8

Schultz, J. (2011). Caster Semenya and the "question of too:" Sex testing in elite women's sport and the issue of advantage. *Quest, 63,* 228–243.

Sebor, J. (n.d.). The history of women's running. *Women's Running.* Retrieved from http://www. active. com/women/Articles/The-History-of-Womens-Running?page=2

Supiano, B. (2008). In college gyms, a time for women only. *Chronicle of Higher Education, 54*(28), A19.

Switzer, K. (May/June, 2013). Running making the world. *Marathon & Beyond,* 16–24.

Taliaferro, L. A., Rienzo, B. A., Miller, D. M., Pigg, M. R., & Dodd, V. J. (2008). High school youth and suicide risk: Exploring protection afforded through physical activity and sport participation. *Journal of School Health, 78*(10), 545–553.

Thøgersen-Ntoumani, C., Ntoumanis, N., Cumming, J., Bartholomew, K. J., & Pearce, G. (2011). Can self-esteem protect against the deleterious consequences of self-objectification for mood and body satisfaction in physically active female university students? *Journal of Sport and Exercise Psychology, 33*(2), 289–307.

Tiggemann, M. (2001). The impact of adolescent girls' life concerns and leisure activities on body dissatisfaction, disordered eating, and self-esteem. *The Journal of Genetic Psychology, 162*(2), 133–42.

Tischer, U., Hartmann-Tews, I., & Combrink, C. (2011). Sport participation of the elderly: The role of gender, age, and social class. *European Reviews of Aging & Physical Activity, 8*(2), 83–91. doi:10.1007/s11556–011-0087–8

Todd, M., Czyszczon, G., Carr, J., & Pratt, C. (2009). Comparison of health and academic indices between campus recreation facility users and nonusers. *Recreational Sports Journal, 33*(1), 43–53.

Trost, S. G., Owen, N., Bauman, A. E., Sallis, J. F., & Brown, W. (2002). Correlates of adults' participation in physical activity: Review and update. *Medicine & Science in Sports & Exercise, 34*(12), 1996–2001. doi:10.1249/01.MSS.0000038974.76900.92

Tucker, R., & Collins, M. (2010). The science of sex verification and athletic performance. *International Journal of Sports Physiology and Performance, 5,* 127–139.

U.S. Anti-Doping Agency. (2012). *True sport: What we stand to lose in our obsession to win.* Retrieved from http://www.truesport.org/about/what-sport-means-in-america

U.S. Department of Health and Human Services. (2013). *Healthy People 2020: Physical Activity.* Retrievedfrom http://www.healthypeople.gov/2020/topicsobjectives2020/overview. aspx?topicid=33#four

U.S. Department of Health and Human Services. (2008). *2008 Physical activity guidelines for Americans: Be active, healthy and happy.* Retrieved from www.health.gov/paguidelines/ pdf/paguide.pdf

Wachs, F. L. (2003). "I was there…": Gendered limitations, expectations, and strategic assumptions in the world of co-ed softball. In A. Bolin & S. Granskog (Eds.), *Athletic intruders: Ethnographic research on women, culture, and exercise* (pp. 177–199). Albany, NY: State University of New York Press.

Walter, C. M., & Du Randt, R. (2011). Socio-cultural barriers to physical activity among black Isixhosa speaking professional women in the Nelson Mandela metropolitan municipality. *South African Journal for Research in Sport, Physical Education and Recreation, 33*(2), 143–155.

19

Weinberg, R. S., & Gould, D. (2011). *Foundations of sport and exercise psychology* (5th ed.). Champaign, IL: Human Kinetics.

Women's Sports Foundation (WSF). (2011). *Factors Influencing Girls Participation in Sports*. Retrieved from https://www.womenssportsfoundation.org/home/support-us/do-you-know-the-factors-influencing-girls-participation-in-sports.aspx

World Health Organization. (2013, March). *Obesity and overweight* (Factsheet No. 311). Retrieved from http://www.who.int/mediacentre/factsheets/fs311/en/

AFFILIATIONS

Karen M. Appleby, PhD
Department of Sport Science and Physical Education
Idaho State University

Elaine Foster, MPE-AA
Department of Sport Science and Physical Education
Idaho State University

LESLEE A. FISHER, SUSANNAH K. KNUST & ALICIA J. JOHNSON

2. THEORIES OF GENDER AND SPORT

INTRODUCTION

What is gender? Is it a *thing* people have or a process people go through (Messner & Sabo, 1990)? In this chapter, we define gender as well as a variety of theories used to examine gender including feminism and feminist theory, queer theory, and gender studies. The central categories of analysis used to explore gender such as gender identity and gendered representation are also fleshed out. Gender has been taken up and applied by researchers in multiple sport domains such as feminist sport studies, queer sport studies and men and masculinity in sport studies. A major organizing framework that we also find useful is Crenshaw and colleagues' metaphor of intersectionality (Crenshaw, Yuval-Davis, & Fine, 2009). We end with the global potential of feminist sport studies.

DEFINITIONS

What Is Gender?

Unfortunately, the terms *sex* and *gender* are often used interchangeably. However, this is not accurate. According to the American Psychological Association (APA) (2011), *sex* "refers to a person's biological status" and can be identified by "sex chromosomes, gonads, internal reproductive organs, and external genitalia" while *gender* refers to "the attitudes, feelings, and behaviors that a given culture associates with a person's biological sex" (APA, 2011).

Sport sociologist Jay Coakley (2009) suggests that *gender* is what is thought to be "masculine" or "feminine" in a society. In this gender binary system, everyone is classified into only two sex categories: male or female, with the assumption that if a baby is born male, he will be "masculine" and if a baby is born female, she will be "feminine." Sex and gender, then, are inextricably intertwined and conflated in a gender binary system. Not only are these categories set up to be "opposites," but they are interpreted as "natural" categories where "male" and "masculine" are better than "female" and "feminine." This is particularly true for cultures like the United States where males control "a disproportionate share of power and resources" (p. 258). As Coakley (2009) wrote:

> All people in the male category are believed to be naturally different from all people in the female category, and they are held to different normative

E. A. Roper (Ed.), Gender Relations in Sport, 21–38.
© *2013 Sense Publishers. All rights reserved.*

expectations when it comes to feelings, thoughts, and actions…The two-category gender classification model is so central to the way people see the world that they resist thinking about gender critically and are likely to feel uncomfortable when people don't fit neatly into one sex category or the other. (p. 258)

Butler (1990) extended critical thinking about gender as she defined gender as a "performance." Butler stated that gender is actually only brought into being when a person "performs" his/her gender identity. This involves how s/he dresses, speaks, plays, talks, etc. "Performing" gender is not voluntary in most cultures, including the United States; gender norms prescribe what gender performances are probable and in what ways they are to be performed. Butler (1990) believed that people who identify with a particular version of gender that is *outside* of cultural norms are rejected by most members of that society.

Like Butler, Layton (2004) speculated that hegemonic masculinity and femininity (e.g., the dominant and "taken-for-granted" notions about "normal" masculinity and femininity) are likely to be the most powerful gender internalizations. Each is associated with its own modes of action and response in relationship. For example, the "traditional" modes of action for males in North American society are assertion, agency, and aggression; the "traditional" modes of action for females are restraint, constraint, and passivity. The "traditional" mode of response in relationship for males is non-responsiveness while the "traditional" mode of response for females is responsiveness.

Layton (2004) furthered that these "traditional," dominant and hegemonic modes of action and relationship are not the only ones that people experience. Both males and females maintain not just one but multiple gender identities, each associated with its own unique modes of action and response in relationship. For example, the same girl could grow up to be "athletic in relation to an active mother or father, passive and small in relation to a caretaking mother or father, flirty in relation to a seductive or distracted mother or father" (p. 54), depending upon her social environment. Further, an upper-class Caucasian girl, for example, will receive very different messages about how she can act and what she can do in the world as compared to a lower-class Caucasian girl, a girl of color, a middle-class Hispanic boy, etc. Lastly, Layton (2004) asserted that gendered experience is not fixed in stone at a particular age or stage of development; rather, gendered experience evolves with our evolving sets of developing relationships. In other words, gender is developed in relationship.

What Is Feminism and Feminist Theory?

bell hooks (2000), professor, author, and social activist, defined *feminism* as "a movement to end sexism, sexist exploitation, and oppression" (p. 1). The basic goals of feminism are to promote women's rights, transform society, privilege women's ways of knowing, and include their voices in research (e.g., Andermahr, Lovell,

& Wolkowitz, 1997; Harnois, 2013; Villanueva Gardner, 2006). *Feminist theory* is an umbrella term for a variety of theories used to examine the social injustices, including sexism, sexist exploitation, and oppression, that many women suffer because of their gender.

Feminist theories have developed and evolved after women's experiences and perceptions were finally included in academic research after many years of being ignored. According to Harnois (2013):

> early approaches to feminist research in the social sciences aimed to transform traditional academic disciplines. Feminist scholars sought to centralize women's issues within the humanities, social sciences, and biological sciences. They introduced new questions and considered new sources of information. They challenged gender bias and sexism in the research process and worked to give intellectual legitimacy to a variety of issues related to women and gender more broadly. (p. 19)

Each theory of feminism includes different analyses of the causes of and remedies for gendered oppression. For example, there is liberal feminism, Marxist feminism, radical feminism, socialist feminism, ecofeminism, cultural feminism, anarchist feminism, Asian American feminism, Black feminism, existential feminism, feminist communication theory, feminist family theory, feminist legal theory, feminist political theory, feminist social work theory, feminist rhetorical theory, feminist-vegetarian critical theory, French feminism, global feminism, Italian feminism, Latina feminism, lesbian feminism, multicultural feminism, Native American feminism, postmodern feminism, and psychoanalytic feminism. The sheer numbers of feminist theories amaze a lot of people who think that feminism is one thing and that feminists are "one kind" of people.

Feminism and feminist theories are also linked to different time periods or waves. In the United States from the mid-1800s to 1920, the first wave of feminism began as women fought for the equal right to vote and to own property. During this wave, liberal feminists believed that sexist oppression would decrease when women had the same rights as men did in these arenas. There was a lull in feminist activity during the first and second world wars (Villanueva Gardner, 2006). Then, in the 1960s and 1970s, those in the second wave of feminism focused on seeking justice and equality for women through individual freedom and equal opportunity in the public realm. Liberal feminists did this by trying to reform North American patriarchal legal and social systems. Most reforms focused on creating equal rights in marital law, women's reproductive health, and education.

During this time, liberal feminists highlighted the similarities between men and women rather than the differences (Brake, 2010). Out of this focus came the push for Title IX, a federal law passed in 1972 that prohibited sex discrimination in education programs which receive federal funding (Brake, 2010). Contrary to public perception, Title IX focused on all educational activities and is not limited to equality for men and women only in interscholastic sport. However, Title IX has had

23

a huge impact on women's involvement in sport. In 1971, less than 300,000 young women competed in high school athletics (Brake, 2010). In contrast, during 2010–2011, more than 3 million young women competed at that same level (National Federation of State High School Associations, 2011). In order to be in compliance with Title IX and continue to receive federal funding, institutions must meet at least one of a three-pronged test: (a) provide proportionate participation opportunities based on enrolment and sex; (b) continue to expand programs for women in response to their interests and abilities; and (c) demonstrate that women have been fully accommodated by the program (ED.gov, 2013).

Also during the second wave of feminism, some feminists in the United States split from liberal feminism. This was because even though women's' legal and civil rights had improved, they still endured sexist oppression. These radical feminists began to fight for equal rights related to the private sphere, using the slogan "the personal is political." They sought equality related to sexuality, their bodies, reproductive rights, and violence against women (Villanueva Gardner, 2006). Radical feminists believe that the primary source for all oppression is patriarchy. They have encouraged women to participate in female-only sports where the emphasis is on cooperation rather than competition (Theberge, 1987). They have also raised criticism about how most sports have been designed to emphasize the need for upper body strength (a "traditionally" masculine trait) rather than agility (a "traditionally" feminine trait) (Costa & Guthrie, 1994).

Further, cultural feminism developed out of radical feminism. Unlike liberal feminists who focus on the similarities between men and women, cultural feminists focus on the differences in experience, thinking, virtue, and ethics between men and women. They encourage social reform based on these distinctions. For example, feminine ethics includes women's moral reasoning and a focus on care, pacifism, and cooperation. Other foci of cultural feminists include mothering, spirituality, lesbianism, and women-centeredness (Villanueva Gardner, 2006). If cultural feminism were the foundation of athletic teams, Jay (1997) suggested three ways feminine ethics could be implemented in sport: (a) having nurturing (i.e., supportive) teams; (b) having interconnected (i.e., relational) teams; and (c) having non-competitive teams. Jay believes that the "male" model of sport is aggressive, physical, and competitive; however, if we were to use a "female" model of sport, athletes would be caring and cooperative toward each other, but they still may be competitive. Thus, females might choose to participate in male-created sports that have a high interconnection such as basketball, soccer, and lacrosse or in non-traditional sports that could have both males and females participating such as rock-climbing and sailing. Sports such as rock-climbing and also martial arts are examples of activities where instructors may "…emphasize self-confidence, cooperation, and reliance upon others for success, as opposed to competitiveness" (Jay, 1997, p. 34).

The third wave of feminism began in the mid-1980s as a reaction to the second wave. Women in the third wave movement included Third world feminists and feminists of color who pointed out that women face multiple systems of oppression because of their race, class, and nationality (Humm, 1995; Villanueva Gardner, 2006). Third wave feminists sought to end all oppression. Like Butler (1990), they believed that gender and other identities were "performed" (Heywood, 2008). Heywood (2008) wrote that women who were born after 1980 did not experience gender the same way that older women had. Rather than feeling pressure to perform only "traditional" feminine gender roles (e.g., wife, mother), they had the opportunity to have a career as well as compete as athletes. As Heywood (2008) stated, these women had been able to "experience all possibilities in the modality of both/and rather than either/or" (p. 72). An example of a competitive athlete who represents this possibility is Lisa Andersen, a four-time world surfing champion, who was recognized for her blend of masculine and feminine approaches as she both attacked the waves and "went with the flow" (Andersen, 2005). She is an example of third wave feminism because she was able to balance "traditional" male/masculine characteristics (e.g., achievement) with "traditional" female/feminine characteristics (e.g., female "beauty culture") (Heywood, 2008). Queer theory was also being developed during this time.

What Is Queer Theory?

Scholarship on gender and feminist theory contributed to the development of queer theory. In fact, both feminist and queer theory have benefitted from the development of one another (Weed, 1996). Weed (1996) suggested that these two theoretical orientations are "…two branches of the same family tree of knowledge and politics, just as in most bookstores they are most easily found on shelves located side by side or back to back" (p. vii). What makes queer theory both interesting and challenging is that it is difficult to define and always in flux (Jagose, 1996). However, as Butler (1990) suggested, to "normalize" anything "queer" would probably be the end of it.

Both feminist theorists and queer theorists resist and oppose binary definitions of gender and sexual orientation. However, the central focus of queer theory is on exploring "the processes through which sexual identity is, and has been, constituted in contemporary and past societies" (Edgar & Sedgwick, 2002, p. 321). In other words, queer theorists investigate how sexual identity is created by societal norms during different historical time periods.

Similar to gender, sexual identity and orientation are often seen as operating from a binary system made up of the two categories of either "heterosexual" or "homosexual." However, the APA (2011) defines sexual identity as occurring along a continuum or spectrum from "exclusive homosexuality" to "exclusive heterosexuality." This continuum is often referred to as the Lesbian, Gay, Bisexual, Transgender (LGBT) spectrum. In other words, sexual identity and orientation are thought to be more fluid than most people think. In addition, some people might find it difficult to identify with just one category. So, queer theorists suggest that the use of the term "queer" may allow a person to define his/her identity as a process that is in constant flux and perhaps even gender-neutral (Gamson, 2000).

25

There is some research in sport studies that utilizes a queer theory framework. Most of the scholars who use this framework study sexual identity. For example, Sykes (1998) used a feminist-queer theory framework to gather life histories of six female physical education teachers, three of whom identified as homosexual and three who identified as heterosexual. Sykes examined how these participants accepted or resisted the lesbian closet (e.g., not being "out" in the open about their sexual identity). Sykes also utilized queer theory in order to highlight the heteronormative status of physical education; she found that the field of physical education encourages individuals who identify as LGBT to stay in the closet so as to not disrupt the heteronormative environment. By employing queer theory during the analysis, Sykes was able to identify the silence that participants described while being inside the lesbian closet as well as the pressure of heteronormative talk when outside of it.

Sykes (1998) also discussed three different types of heterosexual closets including: (a) the closet of (an)other where a homosexual person discloses his/her sexual orientation to a heterosexual ally who now has to maintain the secret; (b) the closet of association where a heterosexual person is very close with a homosexual person, and suspicion of homosexuality arises if the heterosexual person does not explicitly discuss his/her heterosexuality in public, and (c) the paranoid closet where heterosexual persons may become suspicious of their own heterosexuality when a homosexual person comes out of the closet. Sykes' results challenge the hetero/homosexual binary, which is one of the purposes of queer theory.

What Is Gender Studies?

In *gender studies*, gender is used to investigate a broad range of disciplines. As Leslie Heywood and Shari Dworkin (1997) write:

> Within the third wave of feminism…as well as in queer studies and post-structuralism, there is little agreement that women are or should be "feminine" or "masculine." In fact, to some, these terms have little currency and are seen as limiting stereotypes. Consequently, a revaluation of the masculine within feminism is currently taking place within a younger generation that is sometimes dubbed postfeminist, though more accurate names for it are 'gender studies,' 'queer theory,' or 'third wave feminism'.…some of us highly value the masculine as well as feminine parts of ourselves (especially when we are not stigmatized for doing so). (p. 65)

Heywood and Dworkin suggest further that in sport, gender studies can be said to follow what Kane (1995) describes as the gender continuum model. In this gender continuum model of sport, Kane suggests that since athletes are encouraged to partake in "gender appropriate" sports (e.g., cheerleading for females and football for males) and that the media does not report when male and female athletes partake in what society views as gender inappropriate sports (e.g., powerlifting for females and dance for males), sport subdues any indication of a gender continuum (e.g., where women demonstrate "traditional" masculine characteristics and where men demonstrate "traditional" feminine characteristics). As a result, people come to believe that rather than being located on different points along the sport continuum, female athletes who participate in "traditional" male sports are "acting like men" and male athletes who participate in "traditional" female sports are "acting like women" (see also Heyword and Dworkin's (1997) discussion of Kane's model). Heywood and Dworkin go on to suggest that it is critically important for males and females to engage in what has been seen as "gender inappropriate" sports; this is because it is precisely by destabilizing traditional gender categories that we can open up possibilities for a more inclusive sport participation for all. Gender studies can also be defined as those studies which focus upon two central categories of analysis: *gender identity* and *gendered representation* (Whitman College, 2013).

CENTRAL CATEGORIES OF ANALYSIS

What Is Gender Identity?

Identity is an important topic in sport research. Researchers recognize that peoples' identities are fragmented and intersectional (e.g., Cole, 1993; Crenshaw, 1991; Krane & Barber, 2005; Ryba & Wright, 2005). According to the American Psychological Association (APA) (2011), *gender identity* is defined as "the psychological sense of being male or female" (APA Answers, 2011). This psychological sense of being "male" or "female" also develops within the context of relationships and cultural spaces.

In fact, Bornstein (2012, September 15) suggested that gender is one of 15 cultural spaces where identity develops. These other cultural spaces include: class, race, age, ability status, mental health, religion, family/children, politics, appearance, language, habitat/ecology, citizenship, sexuality, and humanity. Further, Bornstein stated that in these spheres, identity is not just developing; she suggested that cultural regulation related to binaries is also occurring, making people feel as though they must fit into either the "male/masculine" or the "female/feminine" category (Bornstein, 2012).

What Is Gender Representation?

Cultural regulation of gender identity can frequently be seen in the media. According to Firoz (2009), *media representation* is:

> The process of presenting information about the world to the world....The key issue here is to explore, who is being represented and why, and by whom and how? Fairness of representation has always been a critical area of enquiry in Media Studies. According to Patricia J. Williams, "The media do not merely represent; they also recreate the world as desirable, and saleable. What they reproduce is chosen, not random, not neutral, and not without consequence."

27

Further, The Media Literacy Clearinghouse (2013) suggested that "Texts are only representations but people process images as reality." As an example, MissRepresentation.org (2013) recently released statistics related to the differences in gender representation in film and television. A summary of selected findings suggests that teens are exposed to 14,000 sexual references and innuendos per year on TV. In addition, between the years 1999 and 2009, the amount of degrading sexualization found in song lyrics tripled. And, when men are shown in the background of a video, they are most often fully clothed; however, when women are in the background, approximately half the time they are dressed in ways that expose or focus on their breasts and rear ends. The key questions to ask yourself as a consumer are: Who produces these images? Who are the images targeted at? What is missing? Why? And, how does this relate to sport?

What is important for those of us in sport studies to remember about gender representation – especially in the media – is that:

> ...market conditions can be oppressive to some, empowering to others, and offer the potential to do progressive and regressive cultural work, sometimes simultaneously.... Market conditions...could begin to sell a strong female athlete icon to a more financially powerful female demographic. (Heywood & Dworkin, 2003, p. 11)

DOMAINS, METHODS AND CONTENT

In the next section, we tackle the question of which academic domains and research methods have been used to explore gender, gender identity, feminist theory and queer theory, relative to sport. A large mixture of theoretical approaches has been used to study gender in sport. We have chosen to review feminist sport studies, queer sport studies, and men and masculinity studies.

What Is Feminist Sport Studies?

According to Markula (2005), feminist sport studies reaches across many subdisciplinary areas related to the study of sport. In North America, sport studies originally arose out of physical education during the 1960s and 1970s. However, not all subdisciplinary areas within physical education – now often called kinesiology – have well-developed feminist sport studies scholarship (Markula, 2005).

During the 1980s and 1990s, feminist research related to women's sport had moved away from the study of psychological sex differences and sex roles to a focus on patriarchy, gender relations, and the sex/gender system (Markula, 2005). According to Markula (2005), this is when feminist sport studies became theoretically grounded and focused mainly on relational research (Birrell, 1988). Feminist sport studies researchers aimed for their work to be liberating for women, as they also tried to connect their research with activism. As Theberge (1987) wrote, "The liberatory possibility of sport lies in the opportunity for women to experience the creativity and energy of their bodily power and to develop this power in the community of women" (p. 393).

Feminist sport studies researchers during this time period intended to raise the consciousness of others about women's issues (e.g., Grewal & Kaplan, 1994; Humm, 1995; Theberge, 1987), how sport could be empowering for women (e.g., Birrell & Richter, 1987; Theberge, 1985/1994; Young & White, 1995), how it could also be disempowering (e.g., Inglis, Danylchuck, & Pastore, 2000; Krane & Barber, 2005) and how it could promote personal, group, and institutional political change for women (e.g., Hargreaves, 1990; Hartsock, 1985; Kane, 1995). Researchers also expanded the analysis to include media representations of sporting women.

More recently, feminist sport studies research has been called postmodern or poststructural (Markula, 2005) with an emphasis on considerations of power, representation, identity, gender and social differences within sport (e.g., Cole, 1993; Krane, Choi, Baird, Aimar, & Kauer, 2004; Ryba & Wright, 2005). Both sport and women's bodies are situated within political, cultural, historical, and economic sport structures and cannot be separated from them (e.g., Chow, 1999; Cole, 1993; Fisher, Butryn, & Roper, 2003; Hartsock, 1985; Ryba & Wright, 2005). As previously mentioned, sport can be both liberating and confining. On the one hand, it allows women the freedom to move their bodies powerfully and gracefully; on the other, women still experience the expectation to "perform femininity" (Butler, 1990) because of societal structures.

Since gender and gender identity develop *relationally* in a cultural space like sport, feminist sport researchers believe that it is important to examine power within that cultural space (Van Ingen, 2003). Through targeted messages from significant others who have power in sport like coaches, administrators, and parents, athletes learn how to be a "real man" or a "real woman." As previously mentioned, sports that require power and strength (i.e., ice hockey, football) are considered "masculine" sports that create "real men" while sports that require grace and beauty (i.e., figure skating, synchronized swimming) are considered "feminine" sports that create "real women" (Hargreaves, 1993).

Different values are also given to different bodies. For example, the "ideal" woman's body is seen as stereotypically "feminine," heterosexual, and Caucasian. This leaves the bodies of women of color, lesbians, and women with disabilities (to name only a few) marginalized (Holliday & Hassard, 2001). The media presents images similar to this ideal rather than highlighting the differences inherent in women's bodies (Bordo, 1993). This production of a certain image is then strengthened and reproduced by many parents, coaches, administrators, the media, and fans.

The image that has been projected in the media is what researchers call "hegemonic femininity." This is the expectation that women look and act like heterosexual "traditionally attractive" Caucasian women (e.g., Bordo, 1993; Hall, 1996; Krane, 2001; Krane et al., 2004; Wright & Clarke, 1999). Many female athletes struggle to balance striving for excellence in their sport (especially those requiring muscularity) with the social value of appearing hegemonically feminine (e.g., Cole, 1993; Krane, 2001; Krane et al., 2004). To produce a hegemonically feminine body, women may feel pressure to diet, work out, purchase certain athletic clothing, and join a gym (Cole, 1993). In addition, athletes who are "appropriately" feminine are privileged over those that are not (e.g., Choi, 2000; Krane, 2001; Lenskyj, 1994); privileges include media attention, endorsements, fan support, and reduced discrimination (Krane, 2001). "Inappropriately" feminine athletes – or those who are "queering" sport – can experience oppression such as verbal harassment in athletic, academic, and social settings (e.g., about how they should dress); they have also been cut from their teams (Krane, 1997, 2001).

What Is Queer Sport Studies?

Like feminist sport studies, *queer studies* can also be found in many different domains or disciplines. In fact, during the 1990s there was a rapid increase and development of lesbian and gay studies in university programs. However, as Kauer (2009) described, it has been only since the late 1990s/early 2000s that queer studies became present within research on women's sport (Caudwell, 1999; Griffin, 1998; Krane & Barber, 2005; Sykes, 1998, 2001).

There is largely a qualitative research focus within queer studies. One possible reason that qualitative methods (interviews, participant-observations, etc.) are more prevalent than quantitative methods (scales, surveys, etc.) could be because there is a history of research studies conducted to identify the "cause" of and the "cure" for homosexuality using quantitative methodology. In addition, qualitative researchers focus on meaning creation, understanding the experiences of everyday life, and bringing forward previously silent voices (Gamson, 2000).

One challenge relative to queer qualitative research is that because not all persons who identify as LGBT are "out" or allow the public to know they identify as LGBT, it can be difficult to find participants. However, researchers may choose to incorporate snowball sampling into their methods in order to obtain participants that self-identify as LGBT. Snowball sampling is similar to a referral network where once the researcher has an "in" with one participant (often a personal or professional contact), that participant is asked to refer the researcher to anybody else that fits the criteria for the study (Taylor & Bogdan, 1998). This method of research participant selection allows the voices of persons who identify as LGBT to be included in the research while still maintaining confidentiality in terms of their identity.

What Is Men and Masculinity Studies?

While the above disciplinary research reviewed had a focus on women, beginning in the 1980s, a new field of *men and masculinity studies* also emerged. According to Kimmel (1987), men and masculinity studies focus on reforming men's roles, male/

female relationships, men in domestic settings, sexual orientation, and gender and race, to name a few. Scholars in men's studies have explored such topics as men's life histories, how men handle the end of their careers (including in sport), the role of homonegativism in the construction of masculinity (particularly for American heterosexual males), and examples of group sexual harassment (Kimmel, 1987). These scholars study specific groups of men to unearth their values, how they see their roles changing, and how their self-images may also be changing as a result.

Pivotal work on the connections between men, masculinity and sport has been undertaken by scholars like Michael A. Messner, Don Sabo and R.W. Connell. For example, in their book, *Sport, Men, and the Gender Order: Critical Feminist Perspectives*, Michael Messner and Don Sabo (1990) argue that gender is not a "thing" that people have; rather, it is a process that people go through. R.W. Connell has also tried to reconcile a variety of approaches to gender in his books *Which Way is Up? Essays on Sex, Class, and Culture* (Connell, 1983), *Gender and Power: Society, the Person, and Sexual Politics* (Connell, 1987), and *Gender* (Connell, 2002). In the latter, Connell tackles revisions to his earlier work in light of recent scholarship focusing on (a) poststructuralist and postmodernist ideas about gender, bodies and sexuality; (b) the rise of meta-analysis in the psychology of difference; (c) the rapid growth of research on men and masculinity; (d) new sophisticated research on gender in organizations; and (e) the growing debate about gender in relation to imperialism, neo-colonialism, and contemporary globalization (Connell, 2002). A major strength of Connell's work is his stance that gender theory needs to be continually revisited – like feminist theory – in light of global and diverse cultures as well as an inherent research bias toward Western models of gender. In addition, his examination of the diversity of men's gender outlooks suggests an unlimited range of gender possibilities related to men's lived experiences, possible alliances, and progressive politics (Connell, 2002).

APPLICATION: INTERSECTIONALITY IN SPORT

In the last part of this chapter, we apply the concept of intersectionality in sport. We do this by describing how knowledge and appreciation about human diversity in sport is important for future sport professionals. We also discuss understanding the role of intersectionality in the gendered realities of athletes as well as the importance of future researchers looking globally. We end with some brief concluding remarks.

Knowledge and Appreciation of Human Diversity in Sport

It is valuable to recognize that sport encompasses a much broader community of people than is often represented. As we have suggested, sport participants come from a variety of backgrounds and have different motivations and identities related to their lived sport experience. Learning about the privilege and oppression that people experience – often simultaneously – is important because these experiences

31

shape who they are and how they react in various situations. "Privilege" in sport is often represented by Caucasian, American, heterosexual, able-bodied men who play football, baseball, basketball, or ice hockey. These are the athletes highlighted on ESPN's SportsCenter and other mainstream media outlets. However, it is important to be aware of and respect *all* athletes, especially those who have one or more oppressed identities (e.g., female athletes, athletes of color, athletes born in a variety of countries, LGBT athletes, athletes with disabilities, competitors in "minor" sports). This is because their experiences, abilities, and accomplishments are most often not shared via the media. Sport should be representative of everyone, and, as future professionals, it is important to remember this.

A good practice for future professionals to engage in is to identify their positionality or current biases and assumptions related to gender and their future practice. Pat Griffin, a leading scholar in LGBT studies in sport, is a good example of a professional engaged in this type of practice. Griffin (1993) claims the following assumptions in her research and writing related to homophobia in sport:

- We all have some degree of discomfort with the topic of homosexuality because we live in a culture that teaches us to fear or condemn lesbians and gay men and makes it difficult for us to gather accurate information about homosexuality.
- This discomfort with homosexuality has negative effects on all of our lives, regardless of our sexual orientation. It affects friendships, family relationships, and personal choices as we try to avoid association with homosexuality.
- No sexual orientation (heterosexual, homosexual, or bisexual) is inherently any more natural, normal, or acceptable than any other.
- Not all readers will agree with the first three assumptions. (p. 194)

Here Griffin not only outlines her assumptions, but she also recognizes that not everyone is going to agree with these assumptions.

The Role of Intersectionality in the Gendered Realities of Athletes

Crenshaw (1991) described *intersectionality* as the idea "that the intersection of racism and sexism factors into Black women's lives in ways that cannot be captured wholly by looking at the race or gender dimensions of those experiences separately" (p. 1244). She uses the concept of an intersection – with four different points where cars meet at the traffic light – to explore this idea. Athletes have multiple, fragmented, and conflicting identities (e.g., Krane & Barber, 2003, 2005; Krane et al., 2004; Ryba & Wright, 2005). Not only do athletes navigate personal identities, but they also navigate social/cultural identities. These identities include but are not limited to: race, class, gender, sexual orientation, religion, country of origin, and ability status (see Fisher, Roper, & Butryn, 2009; Gill & Kamphoff, 2009; Hill, 1993; Kontos & Breland-Noble, 2002; Martens, Mobley, & Zizzi, 2000; Schinke, Hanrahan, & Catina, 2009). As these identities intersect, they allow some to experience privilege while others experience oppression (McIntosh, 1988). For example, a woman who is

Caucasian, middle-class, heterosexual, Christian, American, and able-bodied would most likely have a much different experience in sport than a woman who has even one more intersecting identity (Holliday & Hassard, 2001). Beal (1970) wrote that African-American women experience "double jeopardy," meaning that their two minority identities cause much more oppression than what occurs with just one minority identity. Imagine, therefore, the added difficulties that an African-American lesbian female athlete or a Chinese-American female athlete with a disability might experience.

The reality is that: (a) female athletes who have multiple minority identities have been marginalized; and (b) their gender difference is magnified by their other minority identity. As women, they also already have less power than men in a patriarchal society. In addition, these women are not represented very often in the media.

The Importance of Looking Globally

Imagine that you are a young girl living in Saudi Arabia and that you have a deep passion for sport. However, it is not possible for you to enter the world of sport because there are very limited opportunities for women and girls to participate in sport or physical activity in Saudi Arabia. In fact, in 2012, the Saudi Arabian Sports Minister and Prince Nawwaf al-Faisal stated, "Female sports activity has not existed [in the kingdom] and there is no move thereto in this regard" (Human Rights Watch, 2012). Soon after that statement was released, the Saudi Arabian Olympic Committee was pressured to send female athletes to the 2012 London Summer Olympic Games. And, in March of 2013 it was announced that Saudi Arabia would license women's sports clubs for the first time in the country's history (McDowall & Roche, 2013).

This example is just one of many related to the denial of women and girls' right to participate in sport and physical activity and demonstrates the need for scholars to take a critical feminist sport studies approach to such situations. Currently, much of the research completed in the area of critical feminist sport studies, including the research that has been discussed in this chapter, is set within a North American college context. However, the applicability of and need for critical feminist sport studies extends far beyond this context and has led to a call for more critical feminist sport studies research that focuses on issues of women and girls' sport and physical activity participation around the world (Giles & Lynch, 2012).

Farooq (2010) is one example of a scholar who has used a post-colonial feminist theoretical framework to study a global issue related to women and girls' sport participation. Farooq examined the sport experiences of 20 British born Muslim women of Bangladeshi and Pakistani heritage. They included students and working professionals who lived in the UK and played basketball in their local community. Farooq used the method of ethnography to challenge uncritical and simplistic knowledge about this group and to gain a better understanding of global issues related to women and girls' sport and physical activity participation. Her findings suggested that these women struggled against the imposition of a particular kind of "Muslim woman" identity that enforced a particular way of life upon them that restricted their sport access. However, Farooq found that these women did have power to define their selfhoods in unique ways.

In a time where women account for nearly half of the world's population (e.g., 49.7% of the 2013 projected population) (U.S. Census Bureau International Database, 2013), issues of gender inequality continue to prevail around the world. On a positive note, women were specifically included in three of the eight United Nation's (UN) recent 2000 Millennial Development Goals (MDG) (United Nations, 2005) and sport has been listed as one of the ways in which these goals can be met (United Nations, 2000). Since 2000, the UN has been a leader in the growth of using sport as a means of achieving development and peace around the world. In fact, the UN declared 2005 as the Year of Development and Peace through Sport (United Nations, 2005).

CHAPTER SUMMARY

Through an academic analysis using the lenses of gender, feminism, feminist theory, queer theory, men and masculinity studies, and feminist sport studies, sport has been identified as a site for both the empowerment of and oppression of men and women, boys and girls. However, it also has the potential to enhance health and well-being, foster self-esteem and empowerment, facilitate social inclusion and integration, challenge gender norms, and provide opportunities for leadership and achievement (Larkin, 2007). While there appears to be a recent movement at the governmental level related to empowering women through sport, a lack of academic research using a critical feminist sport studies lens still remains. This has led to a call for more research using an intersectional, global feminist sport studies lens focusing on the lived experiences of athletes – particularly those that are marginalized – in both North America and around the world (Giles & Lynch, 2012).

REFERENCES

American Psychological Association (APA). (2011). Definition of terms: Sex, gender, gender identity, sexual orientation. *The Guideline for Psychological Practice with Lesbian, Gay, and Bisexual Clients*. Retrieved June 7, 2013 from http://www.apa.org/pi/lgbt/ resources/sexuality-definitions.pdf.

Andermahr, S., Lovell, T., & Wolkowitz, C. (1997). *A glossary of feminist theory*. New York: St. Martin's Press, Inc.

Andersen, L. (Actor). Roe, J. (Director). (2005). *Firsthand* [Television broadcast]. Los Angeles, CA: Fuel TV.

Beal, F. (1970). Double jeopardy: To be black and female. In T. Cade (Bambara) (Ed.), *The Black woman: An Anthology*. New York: New American Library.

Birrell, S. (1988). Discourses on the gender/sport relationship: From women in sport to gender relations. *Exercise and Sport Sciences Review*, 16, 459–502.

Birrell, S., & Richter, D. M. (1987). Is a diamond forever: Feminist transformation of sport. *Women's Studies International Forum, 10*(4), 395–409.

Bordo, S. (1993). *Unbearable weight: Feminism, Western culture, and the body*. Berkeley: University of California Press.

Bornstein, K. (2012, September 15). 15 spaces of cultural regulations and the binaries they pretend to be. Retrieved on June 7, 2013 from http://katebornstein.typepad.com/date_bornsteins_blog /2012/09/15-spaces-of-cultural-regulations-and-the-binaries-they-pretend-to-be.html.

Brake, D. L. (2010). *Getting in the game: Title IX and the women's sports revolution.* New York: UP.

Butler, J. (1990). *Gender trouble: Feminism and the subversion of identity.* New York, NY: Routledge.

Caudwell, J. (1999). Women's football in the United Kingdom: Theorizing gender and unpacking the butch lesbian image. *Journal of Sport and Social Issues, 23,* 390–402.

Choi, P. Y. L. (2000). *Femininity and the physically active woman.* London: Routledge.

Chow, R. (1999). When Whiteness feminizes…Some consequences of a supplementary logic. *Differences, 11*(3), 137–168.

Coakley, J. (2009). *Sports in society: Issues and controversies.* New York, NY: McGraw-Hill.

Cole, C. L. (1993). Resisting the canon: Feminist cultural studies, sport, and technologies of the body. *Journal of Sport and Social Issues, 17*(2), 77–97.

Connell, R. W. (1983). *Which way is up? Essays on sex, class, and culture.* Sydney, Australia: Allen & Unwin.

Connell, R. W. (1987). *Gender and power: Society, the person, and sexual politics.* Cambridge UK: Polity.

Connell, R. W. (2002). *Gender.* Oxford UK: Blackwell Publishers Ltd.

Costa, D. M., & Guthrie, S. (1994). Feminist perspectives: Intersections with women and sport. *Women and sport: Interdisciplinary perspectives (pp. 235–252).* Champaign, IL: Human Kinetics.

Crenshaw, K. (1991). Mapping the margins: Intersectionality, identity politics, and violence against women of color. *Stanford Law Review,* 43: 1241–99.

Crenshaw, K., Yuval-Davis, N., & Fine, M. (2009). A conversation with founding scholars of intersectionality. In M. T. Berger & K. Guidroz (Eds.), *The intersectional approach: Transforming the academy through race, class, and gender.* Chapel Hill, NC: The University of North Carolina Press.

ED.gov (2013, May 14). *Clarification of Intercollegiate Athletics policy guidance: The three-part test.* Office for Civil Rights, U.S. Department of Education [Policy Interpretation, 44, Fed Reg, 71,418]. Retrieved from http://www2.ed.gov/about/offices/list/ocr/docs/clarific.html.

Edgar, A., & Sedgwick, P. (2002). *Cultural theory: The key concepts.* London: Routledge.

Farooq (S.). 2010. "Muslim women"' Islam, and sport: "Race," culture and identity in post-colonial Britain (Unpublished doctoral dissertation). University of Warwick, UK.

Firoz (2009). *Four key concepts in media studies.* Retrieved June 7, 2013 from http://learning-media. blogspot.com/2009/09/four-key-concepts-in-media-studies.html.

Fisher, L. A., Butryn, T. M., & Roper, E. A. (2003). Diversifying sport psychology through cultural studies: A promising perspective. *The Sport Psychologist, 17,* 391–405.

Fisher, L. A., Roper, E. A., & Butryn, T. M. (2009). Engaging cultural studies and traditional sport psychology. In R. J. Schinke & S. J. Hanrahan (Eds.), *Cultural sport psychology* (pp. 23–31). Champaign, IL: Human Kinetics.

Gamson, J. (2000). Sexualities, queer theory, and qualitative research. In N. K. Denzin & Y. S. Lincoln (Eds.), *Handbook of qualitative research* (2nd ed.) (pp. 347–365). Thousand Oaks, CA: Sage Publications.

Giles, A. R., & Lynch, M. (2012). Postcolonial and feminist critiques of sport for development. In R. J. Schinke & S. J. Hanrahan (Eds.), *Sport for development, peace, and social justice* (pp. 89–104). Morgantown, WV: Fitness Information Technology.

Gill, D. L., & Kamphoff, C. S. (2009). Cultural diversity in applied sport psychology. In R. J. Schinke & S. J. Hanrahan (Eds.), *Cultural sport psychology* (pp. 45–56). Champaign, IL: Human Kinetics.

Grewal, I & Kaplan, C. (1994). *Scattered hegemonies: Postmodernity and transnational feminist practices.* Minneapolis, MN: University of Minnesota Press.

Griffin, P. (1993). Homophobia in women's sports: The fear that divides us. In G. L. Cohen, *Women in sport: Issues and Controversies,* (pp. 193–203). Newbury Park, CA: Sage.

Griffin, P. (1998). *Strong women, deep closets: Lesbians and homophobia in sport.* Champaign, IL: Human Kinetics.

Hargreaves, J. A. (1990). Gender on the sports agenda. *International Review for the Sociology of Sport, 25*(4), 287–307.

Hargreaves, J. A. (1993). *Sporting females: Critical issues in the history and sociology of women's sports*. New York: Routledge.

Harnois, C. E. (2013). *Feminist measures in survey research*. Los Angeles, CA: Sage.

Hartsock, M. (1985). *Money, sex and power*. Boston: Northeastern University Press.

Heywood, L. (2008). Third-wave feminism, the global economy, and women's surfing: Sport as a stealth feminism in girls' surf culture. In A. Harris (Ed.), *Next wave cultures: Feminism, subcultures, activism*, (pp. 63–82). New York, NY: Routledge.

Heywood, L., & Dworkin, S. (1997). *Third wave agenda: Being feminist, doing feminism*. Minneapolis, MN: University of Minnesota Press.

Heywood, L., & Dworkin, S. (2003). *Built to win: The female athlete as cultural icon*. Minneapolis, MN: University of Minnesota Press.

Hill, T. L. (1993). Sport psychology and the collegiate athlete: One size does not fit all. *Counseling Psychologist, 21*, 436–440.

Holliday, R., & Hassard, J. (2001). Contested bodies: An introduction. In R. Holliday & J. Hassard (Eds.), *Contested Bodies* (pp. 1–17). New York: Routledge.

hooks, b. (2000). *Feminism is for everybody: Passionate politics*. Cambridge, MA: South End Press.

Human Rights Watch. (2013, June 7). Saudi Arabia: Sports minister confirms women's exclusion. Retrieved from http://www.hrw.org/news/2012/04/05/saudi-arabia-sports-minister-confirms-women-s-exclusion.

Humm, M. (1995). *The dictionary of feminist theory*. Columbus, OH: Ohio State University Press.

Inglis, S. Danylchuk, K., & Pastore, D. L. (2000). Understanding retention factors in coaching and athletic management positions. *Journal of Sport Management, 10*, 237–249.

Jagose, A. (1996). *Queer theory: An introduction*. New York: New York University Press.

Jay, J. E. (1997). Women's participation in sport: Four feminist perspectives. *Texas Journal of Women and the Law, 7*, 1–36.

Kane, M. J. (1995). Resistance/Transformation of the oppositional binary: Exposing sport as a continuum. *Journal of Sport and Social Issues, 19*(1), 191–218.

Kimmel, M. S. (1987). *Changing men: New directions in research on men and masculinity*. Newbury Park, CA: Sage Publications.

Kontos, A. P., & Breland-Noble, A. M. (2002). Racial/ethnic diversity in applied sport psychology: A multicultural introduction to working with athletes of color. *The Sport Psychologist, 16*, 296–315.

Krane, V. (1997). Homonegativism experienced by lesbian collegiate athletes. *Women in Sport and Physical Activity Journal, 6*, 141–163.

Krane, V. (2001). We can be athletic and feminine, but do we want to? Challenging hegemonic femininity in women's sport. *Quest, 53*, 115–133.

Krane, V., & Barber, H. (2003). Lesbian experiences in sport: A social identity perspective. *Quest, 55*, 328–346.

Krane, V., & Barber, H. (2005). Identity tensions in lesbian intercollegiate coaches. *Research Quarterly for Exercise and Sport, 76*(1), 67–81.

Krane, V., Choi, P. Y. L., Baird, S. M., Aimar, C. M., & Kauer, K. J. (2004). Living the paradox: Female athletes negotiate femininity and muscularity. *Sex Roles, 50*(5/6), 315–329.

Kauer, K. (2009). Queering lesbian sexualities in collegiate sporting spaces. *Journal of Lesbian Studies, 13*, 306–318. doi: 10.1080/10894160902876804.

Larkin, J. (2007). Gender, sport, and development (pp. 89–123). Retrieved on June 7, 2013 from http://righttoplay.com/International/news-andmedia/Documents/Policy%20Reports%20docs/Literature%20Reviews%20SDP.pdf#page=89.

Layton, L. (2004). *Who's that girl? Who's that boy? Clinical practice meets postmodern gender theory*. Hillsdale, NJ: Analytic Press.

Lenskyj, H. J. (1994). Sexuality and femininity in sport context: Issues and alternatives. *Journal of Sport and Social Issues, 18*, 356–376.

Markula, P. (2005). *Feminist sport studies: Sharing experiences of joy and pain*. New York: SUNY Press.

Martens, M. P., Mobley, M., & Zizzi, S. J. (2000). Multicultural training in applied sport psychology. *The Sport Psychologist, 14*, 81–97.

McDowall, A., & Roche, A. (2013). Saudi Arabia to allow women's sports clubs: Paper. Retrieved from http://www.reuters.com/article/2013/03/30/us-saudi-women-sports-idUSBRE92T05620 130330.

McIntosh, P. (1988). *White privilege and male privilege: A personal account of coming to see correspondences through work in women's studies.* Paper presented at the meeting of the American Educational Research Association, Boston.

Media Literacy Clearinghouse (2013, June 7). Texts. Retrieved from http://www.frankwbaker.com/genrep.htm.

Messner, M., & Sabo, D. (1990). *Sport, men, and the gender order: Critical feminist perspectives.* Champaign, IL: Human Kinetics Press.

Missrepresentation.org (2013, April 12). Statistics on women in the media. Retrieved from http://www.missrepresentation.org/about-us/resources/gender-resources/.

National Federation of State High School Associations (NFSHSA) (2011). High school sports participation continues upward climb. Retrieved May 14, 2013, from http://www.nfhs.org/content.aspx?id=5752.

Ryba, T. V., & Wright, H. K. (2005). From mental game to cultural praxis: A cultural studies model's implications for the future of sport psychology. *Quest, 57,* 192–212.

Schinke, R. J., Hanrahan, S. J., & Catina, P. (2009). Introduction to cultural sport psychology. In R. J. Schinke & S. J. Hanrahan (Eds.), *Cultural sport psychology* (pp. 3–12). Champaign, IL: Human Kinetics.

Sykes, H. (1998). Turning the closets inside/out: Towards a queer-feminist theory in women's physical education. *Sociology of Sport Journal, 15,* 154–173.

Sykes, H. (2001). Understanding and overstanding: Feminist-postructural life histories of physical education teachers. *Qualitative Studies in Education, 14,* 13–31.

Taylor, S. T., & Bogdan, R. (1998). *Introduction to qualitative research methods: A guidebook and resource* (3rd ed.). New York: John Wiley & Sons.

Theberge, N. (1985/1994). Toward a feminist alternative to sport as a male preserve. In S. Birrell & C. L. Cole (Eds.), *Women, sport, and culture* (pp. 181–192). Champaign, IL: Human Kinetics. (Reprinted from *Quest, 37,* 193–202).

Theberge, N. (1987). Sport and women's empowerment. *Women's Studies International Forum, 10*(4), 387–393. United Nations. (2000a). *United Nations Millenium Declaration.* Resolution adopted by the General Assembly. New York: United Nations.

The Media Clearinghouse. (2013). Retrieved from www.frankwbaker.com/genrep.htm.

United Nations (2000). Contribution of sport to the Millennium Development Goals. Retrieved on June 7, 2013 from http://www.un.org/wcm/content/site/sport/home/sport/sportandmdgs.

United Nations (2005). *International year of sport and physical education.* New York: United Nations.

U.S. Census Bureau, Population Division. (2013, June 7). World population by age and sex. *International Data Base.* Retrieved from http://www.census.gov/cgi-bin/broker.

Van Ingen, C. (2003). Geographies of gender, sexuality and race: Reframing the focus on space in sport sociology. *International Review for the Sociology of Sport, 38*(2), 201–216.

Villanueva Gardner, C. (2006). *The A to Z feminist philosophy.* Lanham, MD: The Scarecrow Press, Inc.

Weed, E. (1996). Introduction. In E. Weed & N. Schor (Eds.), *Feminism meets queer theory* (pp. vii–xiii). Bloomington: Indiana University Press.

Whitman College (2013, April 12). Definitions of gender studies. Retrieved from http://www.whitman.edu/academics/courses-of-study/gender-studies.

Wright, J., & Clarke, G. (1999). Sport, the media and the construction of compulsory heterosexuality, *International Review for the Sociology of Sport, 34,* 227–234.

Young, K., & White, P. (1995). Sport, physical danger, and injury: The experiences of elite women athletes. *Journal of Sport and Social Issues, 19,* 45–61.

AFFILIATIONS

Leslee A. Fisher, PhD
Department of Kinesiology, Recreation, and Sport Studies
University of Tennessee

Susannah K. Knust, PhD
Comprehensive Soldier and Family Fitness
Fort Campbell, KY

Alicia J. Johnson, M.S.
Department of Kinesiology, Recreation, and Sport Studies
University of Tennessee

NICOLE M. LAVOI

3. GENDER AND SPORT MEDIA

INTRODUCTION

Thirty years of sport media and gender research will be summarized in this chapter. In what some scholars call *mediasport,* a site where sport is not experienced in the space where it happens but represented through media, differences such as gender, class, race, sexuality, identity, disability and nationalism are naturalized and reproduced (Bruce, 2013, p. 126). In the sport-media complex (Jhally, 1989) where sport and media are inextricably linked, what and how athletes and sport are portrayed indicate and communicate to individuals in a particular society what is important, valued, relevant and known, and what is and who are not. These representations and intertwined relationships among sport, gender, and media are inherently power relations, which are not easily shifted or changed. To begin, a summary of first wave sport media research and prevalent theoretical frameworks will be provided, followed by emerging data for what is now referred to as *second wave* sport media research (Kane, LaVoi, & Fink, 2013).

First Wave Sport Media Research

The first wave of sport media research comprises studies utilizing a range of theoretical and methodological approaches across many disciplines over the last thirty years, a majority of which has been dedicated to the amount and quality of content analyses and readings of media texts with a focus on how media reproduce, legitimize, and occasionally challenge ideologies of gender (Billings, 2011; Bruce, 2013; Kane et al., 2013). Given this emphasis and a large body of empirical evidence, a comprehensive treatment of gender and sport media within the space limitations of this chapter is impossible. The goal herein is to provide a representative illustration of sport media literature in summary, with a focus on gender pertaining first to female athletes, and then male athletes.

Female athletes and women's sport. Despite historic participation statistics for female athletes at all levels of competition in the United States due to the passage of Title IX in 1972 and the fact that approximately 40% of all high school and college sport participants are female, a similar rise in the *amount* and *quality* of sport media coverage of female athletes and women's sport has not occurred. In fact, according to the most recent data outlined, the amount of coverage for women's sport in the United States over the last 30 years has *declined.* And in the infrequent

E. A. Roper (Ed.), Gender Relations in Sport, 39–52.

instance where female athletes are covered, the quality of coverage is startling—athletic accomplishments and athleticism are minimized and a focus on femininity, hypersexuality, and heterosexuality is commonplace. As sports journalist for the *New York Times* Karen Crouse (2013) puts it, "To be a female athlete is to feel as if she is the sum total of her physical assets—or invisible" (p. 3). The two trends of underrepresentation and sexualization have been stable and persistent in both traditional print and broadcast journalism.

Scholars estimate that less than 5% of all broadcast sport media pertains to female athletes (Bruce, 2013). Longitudinal research by Messner and colleagues illustrates televised coverage of women's sport has *declined* over the last 20 years, and data from the latest report in 2009 indicate an all-time low for network news (1.6%) and ESPN SportsCenter (1.3%) coverage of sportswomen (Cooky, Messner, & Hextrum, 2013). In another set of studies, Tuggle and his colleagues (Adams & Tuggle, 2004; Tuggle, 1997) examined the coverage of a sample of sportscasts on ESPN SportsCenter and similarly found coverage of women's sport had declined from 1995 to 2002.

Researchers examining the amount of print media coverage of sportswomen longitudinally and cross-sectionally—mainly magazines and newspapers—have found similar trends to those found in broadcast media. In general, Bruce (2013) reports less than 10% of print media coverage is devoted to sportswomen. In the most comprehensive survey to date which included 80 newspapers in 22 countries, researchers found that sportswomen were the main focus of only 9% of articles (Toft, 2011). Kaiser and Skoglund (2006) analysed the column inches and feature photos "above the fold" on the front page of the sports section in two U.S. newspapers from 1940 to 2005 and found coverage of sportswomen never surpassed 10% and had declined over time. As a result, Kaiser and Skoglund argued that Title IX did not appear to be a great change agent in creating equal recognition in sport media.

In periodical print media, female athletes are rarely (less than 5%) seen on the covers of the most important U.S. sport periodicals such *Sports Illustrated* (*SI*) and *ESPN The Magazine*—a number that has remained remarkably stable. In the most recent analysis of *SI* covers from 2000 to 2011, Weber and Carini (2013) found females athletes appeared on 4.9% of covers (not including the popular Swimsuit Issue). This percentage is similar to analyses in the 1980s and 1990s and lower than a similar analysis completed in 1954–1965 where 12.6% of covers contained female athletes. In the rare instances where females did appear on the cover of *SI* they were often marginalized through sexual objectification, appearing with male athletes or the women highlighted were not related to sports participation (Weber & Carini, 2013). The trends for feature stories about and content including female athletes inside the magazine are only marginally better. In a study that examined *SI* feature articles from 1990 to 1999, Lumpkin (2009) found that only 9.7% of feature articles pertained to female athletes or women's sports. Clearly, sportswomen are underrepresented in sport media across all traditional mediums, and when they are included the quality of representation is limited.

In sum, across both print and broadcast sport media, respectful quality coverage of female athletes is rare. The ways in which female athletes' talent and power is contained and undermined are many. They are often portrayed in stereotypical ways that highlight traditional femininity and sex-appeal that do little to increase respect for and sustain real interest in women's sport (Kane et al., 2013; Meân & Kassing, 2008). Female athletes are typically constructed as "less than" and different in (selective) ability and talent compared to male counterparts (Kane, 1995). On TV, negative (e.g., fights, assaults, scandals) aspects are highlighted, and sexualized gag stories often stand alone as the only women's sports story in a particular broadcast (Cooky, Messner, et al., 2013). Recognition and coverage of athleticism in sports where the masculine-typed traits such as strength, speed, power and aggression are required (e.g., ice hockey, rugby) is much less than coverage of female athletes in traditionally feminine-typed sports (e.g., gymnastics, figure skating, tennis) (Kane, 1995).

Ambivalence is another well-documented sport media pattern which marginalizes and trivializes sportswomen. Ambivalent coverage is defined by two contradictory or mixed-message statements and/or images in a single presentation—one statement/ image that is positive and focused on talent, coupled with another focused on faults or aspects unrelated to sport that are meant to undermine athleticism (e.g., excessive dependence on others, identity conflicts, emotional issues) (Duncan & Hasbrook, 1988). A classic example of both marginalization and ambivalence involved WNBA standout Candace Parker, who appeared pregnant on the March 23, 2009 cover of *ESPN The Magazine*. The first paragraph of the accompanying feature article denoted a mixed-message about Parker's athleticism and femininity:

Candace Parker is beautiful. Breathtaking, really, with flawless skin, endless legs and a C cup she is proud of but never flaunts. She is also the best at what she does, a record-setter, a rule-breaker, a redefiner. She is a woman who plays like a man, one of the boys, if the boys had C cups and flawless skin. She's nice, too. Sweet, even. Kind to animals and children, she is the sort of woman who worries about others more than about herself, a saint in high-tops. (Glock, 2009)

In comparison, ambivalent and incongruent media messages about male athletes are far less common.

Kane (1995) describes another way media marginalize sportswomen by constructing highly talented female athletes who deviate from norms of traditional femininity as "deviant-mutants"—whereby their biological sex is questioned and/ or even subjected to sex verification testing. College standout and current WNBA basketball player Brittney Griner is a recent example of a media-constructed "deviant mutant" because of her exceptional, game-changing talent on the court, coupled with above average height (6'8") and deep ("masculine") voice. South African runner Caster Semenya, because of her "suspicious" speed and masculine, muscular appearance, was similarly cast as an outlier and endured years of public scrutiny and demands for sex verification testing (Cooky, Dycus, et al., 2013). Griner and Semenya, female athletes who do not conform to dominant notions of femininity, were subjects of ridicule and targets of racist and sexist backlash and commentary (Cooky, Wachs, Messner, & Dworkin, 2010).

Labeling female athletes who are non-conformant to femininity norms, possess or exhibit masculine qualities, or play masculine sport types as lesbian is another way sportswomen are contained and marginalized in sport media (Kane, 1995). While sociocultural norms and beliefs about non-heterosexual individuals in general have shifted since Kane made her contention in 1995, nearly 20 years later, labeling competent sportswomen as lesbians is still a powerful mechanism of containment because some still view gay men and lesbians negatively. Sport sociologist Helen Lenskyj (2013) comments regarding the heteronormativity, homophobia, and heterosexism which permeates sport media: "After more than five decades of liberal sport feminist activism, starting with the Western women's movements of the 1960s, the mainstream media's obsession with female athletes' heterosexual appeal (or perceived lack thereof) has continued virtually uninterrupted" (p. 141). In sport media, lesbian athletes and coaches are nearly invisible while coverage of motherhood and social roles such as heterosexual wife, fiancé, or girlfriend abound. This pattern persists despite Lenskyj's (2013) contention that mainstream sport media assume that all female athletes are gay, especially when participating in masculine-typed sports. When gays and lesbians are recognized by the media it is usually based on reports of discrimination, harassment, job loss, or loss of endorsements (Hardin & LaVoi, 2013; Lenskyj, 2013). Take for example the media attention given to Louisiana State University head women's basketball coach Pokey Chatman who in 2007 "left" LSU before the NCAA Tournament under allegations of improper conduct with a former player. In 2011, former University of Minnesota associate women's golf coach Katie Brenny was in the news when she filed a discrimination lawsuit based on allegations she was demoted when the Director of Golf found out she was a lesbian. On a positive note, and perhaps a sign of cultural change, in early 2013 the media gave considerable coverage to the public coming-out stories of both Griner and NBA player Jason Collins, the anti-bullying *It Gets Better Project*, and pro-gay marriage statements by high-profile male athletes and professional teams. Such attention by mainstream media may help create a less homophobic environment for all athletes.

It is clear that for-profit, commercial sport media entities routinely marginalize sportswomen, but evidence suggests that some non-profit media (e.g., intercollegiate) may project slightly more equitable and realistic—though not yet fully equal—portrayals. Huffman, Tuggle and Rosengard (2004) found male athletes were the primary focus of print (72.7%) and broadcast (81.5%) stories in campus newspapers and television stations. Similarly, examination of images of athletes in the *NCAA News* indicated female athletes were still underrepresented (32%) but featured at a greater rate than in commercial media (Cooper & Cooper, 2009). In longitudinal examination of feature photos on the covers of intercollegiate sport media guides—a powerful and public tool used to market and promote teams—Buysse and colleagues used three categories to determine if gender ideologies were challenged or reproduced: in vs. out of uniform, on vs. off the court, and active vs. passive poses (Buysse, 1992; Buysse & Embser-Herbert, 2004; Buysse & Wolter, 2013; Kane & Buysse, 2005). Despite improvements in serious and competent portrayals of female college athletes in 2004, the most recent data from 2009 indicate a backward slide in all three categories and as Buysse and Wolter (2013) conclude, it seems the battle for equality was only temporarily won.

Theoretical frameworks. To better understand these perplexing trends, scholars have employed a variety of theoretical frameworks to analyze visual and written sport media texts. A few of the more prevalent theories will be briefly summarized. Tuchman's (1978, 2012) theory has been used to argue female athletes have been, and continue to be, *symbolically annihilated* by mass media through omission, trivialization, and condemnation of their accomplishments. Through the lens of *critical feminist theory*, scholars have consistently demonstrated that sportswomen are underrepresented, marginalized, and feminized in sport media coverage due to the existing power and privilege held by men (e.g., Cooky, Messner, Hextrum, 2013; Fink & Kensicki, 2002; Jones, 2006; Kane et al., 2013; Kane & Buysse, 2005). Some scholars have used Gramci's (1971) *hegemony theory* to describe the ways in which a dominant social class (i.e., males) get the marginalized class to uncritically adopt a common sense "that's just the way it is" ideology in which dominance is created and maintained (Kian, Vincent, & Mondello, 2008). Connell's (1987, 2005) blending of hegemony with gender and power produced the concept of *hegemonic masculinity* which has been widely used to analyze male-dominated social structures, gender hierarchies, male dominance, and female subordination. Other scholars have used *framing theory* to analyze phrases, words, pictures and repetition of themes that persist over time which help "frame" both the issue as well as what is silenced or omitted. Framing theory in sport media can forward understanding of how cultural norms, values and ideologies are formed and reproduced and sometimes challenged within power hierarchies (e.g., Calhoun, LaVoi, & Johnson, 2011; Cooky, Dykus, & Dworkin, 2013; Hardin & Whiteside, 2009; Kian & Hardin, 2009). Many scholars combine multiple theories to provide a more complete understanding of the sport-media-commercial complex and its effects.

Whatever the theoretical perspective employed, scholars agree that limited coverage and sexualized portrayals not only trivialize female athletes, but severely limit their ability to challenge or change men's ideological and institutional control of sport (Bruce, 2013; Kane et al., 2013; Messner, 1988). When sport is by, for and about men, the transformative potential of sport for females is at best limited, and at worst, lost. Cooky, Messner and Hextrum (2013) and Kane et al. (2013) contend that the amount of coverage and the quality of sport media coverage constructs a reality that builds and sustains audience interest and thus the "demand" for men's sports, while constraining audience interest for women's sports. When audience interest is constrained, decision makers commonly cite "lack of interest" to justify their deficiency in coverage of female athletes. Kane and colleagues (2013) argue, however, that in reality a "lack of interest in women's sport" narrative is a way to suppress knowledge and deny the reality of expanding interest and participation in sport and the increasing athleticism of female athletes. According to Kane et al. (2013):

> The key point here is that the "nobody's interested" narrative that media— in the form of producers, editors, and journalists—use to justify their own continued and systematic lack of interest ignores the fact that when women's sports are covered the audience frequently responds in record-setting numbers. By ignoring this reality, they conveniently avoid another one: their own role and responsibility in building (read, hyping) an audience for men's sports while simultaneously suppressing interest in women's. (p. 3)

Bruce (2013) states the remaining question is "whether and how the articulation of sport and masculinity can be disrupted on an everyday, long-term basis" (p. 132). Hardin (2013) suggests that one way to challenge hegemonic ideologies and the culture of sport is to increase the number of women who write about and cover sports. Hardin's research asserts that women think, value, and write about sports differently and that women believe female athletes deserve better coverage than they are currently afforded in comparison to their male counterparts. Yet given the scarcity of female sport journalists in every position (<10%), the current impact of women is limited. Sports journalist Karen Crouse (2013) suggests advocates and fans of women's sport, such as parents of girls and the next generation of female athletes, need to demand parity in sports coverage, otherwise the status quo will remain. Until change occurs, sport media will remain an especially effective tool for preserving male power and privilege (Kane, 2011). Considerably fewer researchers have focused attention on analyses of gender, male athletes, and sport media which will be summarized next.

Male athletes and men's sport. From the literature summarized thus far, ample evidence exists to make the claim that sport media is a male domain "that produces coverage by men, for men, and about men" (Bruce, 2013, p. 128). There is an unending tide of respectful pictures and celebratory stories of males as competent athletes, and proportionally far fewer that are negative, derogatory, or sexual in nature that trivialize male athletes in comparison to female counterparts (Cooky, Messner, et al., 2013). However, some argue that the fact that sport is constructed as a "male preserve," in part by the media, is not unproblematic. Scholars point out that males who are unable or unwilling to participate in sport or consume sport are often marginalized because they do not conform to societal standards of hegemonic masculinity (Curry, Arrigada, Cornwell, 2002). Messner (2013) argues all males are targets as:

the sports–media–commercial complex consistently sells boys and men a glorified package of what masculinity is and should be, regularly nudges us with reminders that we do not measure up to this standard, and then offers compensatory products—beer, underwear, cars, shaving products and, yes, erectile dysfunction medications—that promise transcendence from the shameful knowledge that, even if our team is in first place, we individual men are in fact losers…who might hope to consume their way out of their insecurities. (p. 118)

Indeed, hegemonic masculinity is heavily policed in sport and reproduced and maintained in sport media. For male athletes, depictions that deviate from masculine athlete to alternative roles of father, husband, boyfriend, or a caring, loving partner are scarce and serve to narrowly construct what it looks like to be a "real man." These constraints construct a false reality of manhood for men, and when combined with the pervasive "Televised Sports Manhood Formula" (TSMF) (Messner, Dunbar, & Hunt, 2000) the effects are potentially far reaching. Messner and colleagues examined televised sport media outlets and summarized the tenets of the TSMF as follows: men are the center and voice of authority in broadcast content and commercials; women are constructed as sexual objects present for men's reward and consumption; aggressive play is lauded; violence and violent plays are normalized; and sacrificing the body for the team is expected, among others. When the sport-media-commercial complex is consumed uncritically, males learn to view females as not fully human which decreases the likelihood of successful intimate and professional relationships with women, and an adoption of the belief that to be successful in sport, health and well-being are secondary (Messner et al., 2000).

Gaps in first wave research.   First wave sport media research has been defined by content analysis of traditional (i.e., print and broadcast) media. While this large and important body of work has produced awareness of gender inequality and problematic portrayal patterns, some gaps in the literature remain. Three of the most notable gaps include intersectionality, digital media, and audience reception. Contributing scholars filling existing gaps are included in "second wave" research and their work is summarized next.

Second Wave Sport Media Research

A majority of first wave research included analysis of one demographic variable (predominately gender) as a way to analyze media content and quality. As theoretical frameworks from other disciplines, namely cultural studies, began to inform sport media research, scholars have called for a more nuanced approach in order to address other social variables—that is, an intersectional analysis that explores how power, gender, social class, race/ethnicity, sexuality, and other identities intersect within sporting contexts and in the broader society (Lenskyj, 2013; Lisec & McDonald,

2012; McDonald & Birrell, 1999). Intersectional analysis allows a more complete understanding of how multidimensional identities are constructed and influenced within sport by the media, as well as the consequences of racism, sexism and inequality (Lisec & McDonald, 2012). One example of intersectional sport media research was conducted by Cooky and colleagues where they examined mainstream print news media's response to radio talk show host Don Imus's comment about the Rutgers' women's basketball team as "nappy-headed ho's" (Cooky, Wachs, Messner, & Dworkin, 2010). They argued that the Imus controversy provided an opportunity for intersectional understanding of how gender, race, class, and sexuality operate in contemporary sporting contexts. An increasing number of scholars are attempting to draw intersectional analysis into their research, while others are taking a different methodological approach.

A small and expanding body of audience reception research is emerging in which researchers examine how consumers (i.e., audiences) interpret media texts. Stuart Hall's (1974) classic work on encoding/decoding cultural texts is one theory informing this line of inquiry. Hall argued that although producers of media texts encode their messages with preferred meanings which reinforce dominant ideologies, it does not automatically guarantee that the audience member will decode/receive the message the producer intended. This is particularly true given the lived experiences and multiple identities individuals use to understand texts. A small group of researchers across different academic disciplines have used audience reception to begin to understand how a variety of audiences interpret gendered media coverage and portrayals of female athletes (Antil, Burton, & Robinson, 2012; Daniels, 2012; Daniels & Wartena, 2011; Kane et al., 2013; Kane & Maxwell, 2011; Krane et al., 2010). The consistent take home message from this growing body of research is that sexualized portrayals of female athletes are not an effective way to market and promote women's sport. The data also challenge the assumption and practice that "sex sells" women's sport. This approach is not only ineffective but counterproductive: Female fans, female athletes, dads with daughters, families with girls, and girls themselves—the core demographic for women's sports—react negatively to hypersexualized images of sportswomen. As Kane (2011) emphatically states in a piece she wrote for *The Nation*, "sex sells sex, not women's sport" (p. 28). Researchers exploring digital media are trying to discern if the "sex sells" narrative is firmly embedded, or being challenged.

Sport media 2.0 research: Digital platforms. Another line of inquiry which characterizes second wave sport media research pertains to digital media (therefore 2.0)—forms of electronic interactive media that integrate data, text, pictures, and sounds, are stored in a digital format (not analog), and are distributed through networks. Sport media 2.0 research has lagged behind the growth and popularity of digital media in society, and despite a recent increase in digital sport media studies in the last five years, only a handful of studies include a critical feminist or intersectional theoretical framework (LaVoi & Calhoun, 2013). At the time of press, research about blogs, Facebook, Twitter and Web sites exist, but research on other popular digital sources is non-existent.

Without reliance on traditional sports editors and journalists—most of whom are White men (Lapchick, 2013)—to cover female athletes and women's sport events, some argue digital media is the way to respectfully market and promote sportswomen. However, based on a small amount of data, sport blogs are not challenging but instead are reproducing dominant gender ideologies. Sport blogs are problematic for several reasons: (a) most of the (male) bloggers are untrained in journalism or ethics and lack progressive orientations toward women's sport (Hardin, Zhong, & Corrigan, 2012); (b) female bloggers who try to give women's sport visibility occupy marginal positions within the sport blogsphere (Antunovic & Hardin, 2012); and (c) blog discussion boards serve as an unedited, unfiltered, unmediated source of homophobic, misogynistic, and sexist responses to women in sport, which, compared to traditional media, occur in more blatant, profane, and stronger forms of language (Lisec & McDonald, 2012).

To extend amount and quality analyses commonly used in traditional media, Clavio and Eagleman (2011) examined portrayals of female athletes in the 10 most popular sport blogs and found similar trends—female athletes, women's teams, or leagues were rarely featured and when a photograph of a female was present it was overwhelmingly a non-athlete, cheerleader, dancer or model portrayed in a sexualized way. One research team indicated female "fan bloggers" of *Women Talk Sports*—a blog network of the best blogs relating to women's sports—frequently advocated for women's sport but rarely challenged dominant ideologies and gender hierarchies that supress and limit sportswomen, and failed to engage with other bloggers around these issues (Antunovic & Hardin, 2012). In conclusion, the lack of diversity in the sport blogosphere and the marginal or niche positions of female bloggers or those that blog about women's sport, ensures nearly homogenous content (i.e., by, for, and about men) and guarantees the reproduction of gender stereotypes and ideologies found in traditional media (Hardin et al., 2012).

Research pertaining to popular digital media tools, such as Twitter and Facebook, in which researchers employed a critical gender analysis, is extremely limited to date (LaVoi & Calhoun, 2013). Smith (2011) used hegemonic masculinity in framing an examination of Twitter feeds of Division IA sport conferences while Wallace, Wilson and Miloch (2011) conducted a content analysis of NCAA and Big 12 athletic department Facebook pages and, while they did not go into the study with a gendered lens, gender differences emerged. Based on the results in both studies, it is evident that tweets, retweets, posts, and "likes" pertaining to men's sports far surpassed those for women's sports which unfortunately reinforces the assumption that interest in women's sports is minimal. What goes unreported and unchallenged is the responsibility of media producers—in this case sports information staff at universities that are required by law to be committed to gender equity—to create content in equal amount and quality for men's and women's team, that would in turn generate interest.

47

Nearly all intercollegiate athletic departments produce digital media and convey a large amount of information about their teams and athletes to the public through multiple and integrated platforms. Some scholars have examined institutionally endorsed athletic Web sites at the Division I intercollegiate level and found women's teams are marginalized through receiving less coverage (Sagas, Cunningham, Wigley, & Asley 2000), advertisements, photographs, and multimedia (Cooper & Cooper, 2009) than men's teams. In a follow-up study, only schools in NCAA Division III provided equitable coverage to male and female athletes on athletic department webpages (Cooper & Pierce, 2011).

Institutional athletic Web sites marginalize in other ways as well, including near erasure of non-heterosexual identities. Using framing theory, Calhoun et al. (2011) analyzed text for the presence or absence of family narratives— specific mention of a wife, spouse, same sex partner, children, and grandchildren—in a national sample of online college coach biographies. Based on the data, a near absence of explicit LGBT coaches and their families and an overwhelming presence of heteronormative frames were present—only 2 of 1855 (.01%) coaches in their sample identified as openly gay. Calhoun et al. (2011) asserted that digital content of intercollegiate athletic department Web sites reproduce dominant gender ideologies and are plagued with the same overt and subtle homophobia and gender ideologies found in the locker room and on the playing field, and suggested athletic departments develop and adopt a digital media plan that is inclusive of all family narratives. Data for commercial digital sport media platforms reveals similar trends.

Researchers studying commercial digital media, such as ESPN.com or CBSSports. com, have found these sites also reinforce traditional gender ideologies and marginalize sportswomen. Marginalization of sportswomen occurs via minimal or lack of content, "othering" them in comparison to male counterparts, out-dated or repeated stories and photographs, content unrelated to athletic prowess, and photographs or stories about a losing effort (e.g., Kachgal, 2001; Kian, Mondello & Vincent, 2009). These collective patterns communicate a lack of value, importance, interest in and respect for women's sport in comparison to men's sport (LaVoi & Calhoun, 2013). So while some argue that digital sport media sources have the potential to be a transformational, empowering, and positive space where sportswomen are valued, where women's sport is advanced, where masculine hegemony can be contested, and where ideological and institutional control is shifted away from men, based on current data this vision is currently tenuous and unrealized (Hardin et al., 2012; LaVoi & Calhoun, 2013).

CHAPTER SUMMARY

Existing data encompassing 30 years of sport media research across first and second wave eras were summarized in this chapter. A diverse range of approaches, theoretical frameworks, and methodologies to study sport media exist across a variety of academic disciplines. First wave sport media research was characterized by a focus on the amount and quality of media content in print and broadcast media. Second wave researchers are focused on continued content documentation initiated in the first wave, and are adding analyses concentrated on digital media, inclusion of intersectional variables, and gleaning information on audience reception.

Despite overwhelming evidence which demonstrates girls and women are highly skilled athletes who participate in sports in record numbers, coverage and portrayals of sportswomen in both traditional and digital media depict a much different picture. The dominant narrative created by the sport-media-commercial complex does not create a reality-based picture of sportswomen that highlights athletic competence and in turn engenders feelings of respect and admiration (Kane et al., 2013). Given this contradiction, it is clear that sport in general and sport media specifically is still fully "entrenched in safeguarding traditional definitions of sport and gender norms" (Hardin, 2013) that sustain the marginalization of sportswomen. What is also clear is that females' entrance into sport in the post-Title IX era created what Mike Messner in 1988 called "contested terrain," and that if sportswomen were to achieve full participation and respectful coverage with a primary focus on athleticism it would undercut detrimental and out-dated stereotypes, and therefore male power (Curry et al., 2002). As Kane and colleagues assert, "As long as sportswomen are portrayed in ways that sexually objectify them, they will not gain the respect they deserve. Nor, we suggest, will they gain an equal foothold [in the institution of sport]" (2013, p. 25). Respectful coverage of sportswomen would also send a message to young girls and boys that physical attractiveness is less important than athletic prowess, which may help change gender socialization and lead to healthier self-perceptions for girls, as well as high quality professional and personal relationships (Daniels & LaVoi, 2013). For male athletes, a move away from "The Televised Sports Manhood Formula" in which media construct and portrays normative masculinity as violent, aggressive, and powerful and with a disregard for health and well-being (Messner et al., 2000) toward broader and realistic portrayals of masculinity would serve sportsmen well.

In conclusion, individuals must be aware of how "mediasport" constructs unhealthy, narrow, limited, and unrealistic portrayals of both male and female athletes that do little to advance gender equality or social change efforts. Sport matters because it is one of the largest, most popular, and most central social institutions and it both reflects and influences what is societally valued, reveals aspects of collective identity, and connects to politics, economics, culture and power in ways that shape daily existence (Boyle, 2013).

REFERENCES

Adams, T., & Tuggle, C. A. (2004). ESPN SportsCenter and coverage of women's athletics: "It's a Boys' Club." *Mass Communication and Society, 7,* 237–248.

Antil, J. H., Burton, E., & Robinson, M. (2012). Exploring the challenges facing female athletes as endorsers. *Journal of Brand Strategy, 1*(3), 292–307.

Antunovic, D., & Hardin, M. (2012). Activism in women's sports blogs: Fandom and feminist potential. *International Journal of Sport Communication, 5,* 305–322.

49

Billings, A. (2011). *Sports media: Transformation, integration, consumption.* New York, NY: Routledge.

Boyle, R. (2013). Reflections of communication and sport: On journalism and digital culture. *Communication and Sport, 1*(1/2), 88–99.

Bruce, T. (2013). Reflections on communication and sport: On women and femininities. *Communication and Sport.* doi: 10.1177/2167479512472883

Buysse, J. M. (1992). *Media constructions of gender difference and hierarchy in sport: An analysis of intercollegiate media guide cover photographs.* (Unpublished doctoral dissertation). University of Minnesota, Minneapolis.

Buysse, J., & Embser-Herbert, M. S. (2004). Constructions of gender in sport: An analysis of intercollegiate media guide cover photographs. *Gender and Society, 18*(1), 66–81.

Buysse, J., & Wolter, S. (2013). Gender representation in 2010 NCAA Division I media guides: The battle for equity was only temporarily won. *Journal of Issues in Intercollegiate Athletics, 6*, 1–21.

Calhoun, A. S., LaVoi, N. M., & Johnson, A. (2011). Framing with family: Examining online coaching biographies for heteronormative and heterosexist narratives. *International Journal of Sport Communication, 4*(3), 300–316.

Clavio, G., & Eagleman, A. N. (2011).Gender and sexually suggestive images in sports blogs. Journal of *Sport Management, 7*, 295–304.

Connell, R. W. (1987). *Gender and power.* Stanford, CA: Stanford University Press.

Connell, R. W. (2005). *Masculinities* (2nd ed.). Berkeley, CA: University of California.

Cooky, C., Dycus, R., & Dworkin, S. L. (2013). "What makes a woman a woman?" vs. "Our first lady of sport:" A comparative analysis of United States and South African media coverage of Caster Semenya. *Journal of Sport and Social Issues, 37*, 31–56.

Cooky, C., Messner, M., & Hextrum, R. (2013). Women play sport, but not on TV: A longitudinal study of televised news media. *Communication and Sport.* doi:10.1177/2167479513476947

Cooky, C., Wachs, F., Messner, M., & Dworkin, S. (2010). It's not about the game: Don Imus, race, class, gender and sexuality in contemporary media. *Sociology of Sport Journal, 27*, 139–159.

Cooper, C. G., & Cooper, B. D. (2009). NCAA website coverage: Do athletic departments provide equitable gender coverage on their athletic home web pages? *The Sport Journal, 12*(2). Retrieved from http://www.thesportjournal.org/article/ncaa-website-coverage-do-athletic-departments-provide-equitable-gender-coverage-their-athlet

Cooper, C. G., & Pierce, D. (2011). The role of divisional affiliation in athletic department web site coverage. *International Journal of Sport Communication, 4*, 70–82.

Crouse, K. (2013). Why female athletes remain on sport's periphery. *Communication & Sport.* doi: 10.1177/2167479513487722

Curry, T. J., Arriagada, P. A., & Cornwell, B. (2002). Images of sport in popular nonsport magazines: Power and performance versus pleasure and participation. *Sociological Perspectives, 45(4).* 397–413.

Daniels, E. A. (2012). Sexy versus strong: What girls and women think of female athletes. *Journal of Applied Developmental Psychology, 33*, 79–90.

Daniels, E., & LaVoi, N. M. (2013). Athletics as solution and problem: Sports participation for girls and the sexualization of female athletes. In E. L. Zubriggen & T. A. Roberts (Eds.), *The sexualization of girls and girlhood: Causes, consequences and resistance* (pp. 63–83). New York, NY: Oxford University Press.

Daniels, E., & Wartena, H. (2011). Athlete or sex symbol: What boys think of media representations of female athletes. *Sex Roles, 65*, 566–579.

Duncan, M. C., & Hasbrook, C. A. (1988). Denial of power in televised women's sports. *Sociology of Sport Journal, 5*, 1–21.

Fink, J. S., & Kensicki, L. J. (2002). An imperceptible difference: Visual and textual constructions of femininity in *Sports Illustrated* and *Sports Illustrated for Women. Mass Communication and Society, 5(3),* 317–339.

Glock, A. (2009). The selling of Candace Parker. Retrieved from http://sports.espn.go.com/espnmag/story?id=3967891

Gramsci, A. (1971). *Selections from the prison notebooks.* New York, NY: International Publishers.

Hall, S. (1974). *Encoding and decoding in the television discourse* (Centre for Contemporary Cultural Studies, paper No. 7). Birmingham, England: University of Birmingham.

Hardin, M. (2013). Want changes in content? Change the decision makers. *Communication and Sport.* doi: 10.1177/2167479513486985

Hardin, M., & LaVoi, N. M. (2013). Inappropriate behavior and lesbianism: The contrasting falls of two women's college basketball coaches. In L. Wenner (Ed.) *Fallen sports Heroes, media, and celebrity culture* (p. 267–283). New York, NY Peter Lang Publishing.

Hardin, M., & Whiteside, E. (2009). The Rene Portland case: New homophobia and heterosexism in women's sports coverage. In H. L. Hundley & A. C. Billings (Eds.), *Examining identity in sports media* (pp. 17–36). Thousand Oaks, CA: Sage Publications.

Hardin, M., Zhong, B., & Corrigan, T. F. (2012). The funhouse mirror: The blogosphere's reflection. In T. Dumova & R. Fiordo (Eds.), *Blogging in the global society: Cultural, political and geographical aspects* (pp. 55–71). Hershey, PA: IGI Global.

Huffman, S., Tuggle, C. A., Rosengard, D. S. (2004). How campus media cover sports: The gender-equity issue, one generation later. *Mass Communication and Society, 4,* 475–489.

Jhally, S. (1989). Media sports, culture and power: Critical issues in the communication of sport. In L. A. Wenner (Ed.), *Media, sports, and society: Research on the communication of sport* (pp. 70–93). Thousand Oaks, CA: Sage Publications.

Jones, D. (2006). The representation of female athletes in online images of successive Olympic Games. *Pacific Journalism Review, 12*(1), 108–129.

Kachgal, T. M. (2001). Home court disadvantage? Examining the coverage of female athletes on leading sports websites: A pilot study. *National Convention of the Association for Education in Journalism and Mass Communication*, Washington, DC. Retrieved from http://list.msu.edu/cgi-bin/wa?A3=ind0 109a&L=AEJMC&E=8bit&P=4297846&B=--%3D%3D%3D%3D%3D%3D%3D%3D%3D%3D%3D% 3D%3D%3D%3D%3D%3D%3D%3D%3D%3D%3D_85286876%3D%3D_&T=text%2Fplain;%20 charset=iso-8859-1

Kaiser, K., & Skoglund, E. (2006), *Prominence of men and women in newspaper sports coverage as an indicator of gender equality pre- and post-Title IX.* Paper presented at the annual meeting of the Association for Education in Journalism and Mass Communication Convention, San Francisco, CA.

Kane, M. J. (2011). Sex sells sex, not women's sports. *The Nation.* Retrieved from: http://www.thenation. com/article/162390/sex-sells-sex-not-womens-sports#axzz2Wbuy16qm

Kane, M. J. (1995). Resistance/Transformation of the oppositional binary: Exposing sport as a continuum. *Journal of Sport and Social Issues, 19*(1), 191–218.

Kane, M. J., & Buysse, J. (2005). Intercollegiate media guides as contested terrain: A longitudinal analysis. *Sociology of Sport Journal, 22,* 214–238.

Kane, M. J., LaVoi, N. M., Fink, J. S. (2013). Exploring elite female athletes' interpretations of sport media images: A window into the construction of social identity and "selling sex" in women's sports. *Communication and Sport,* 1–31. doi: 0.1177/2167479512473585

Kane, M. J., & Maxwell, H. D. (2011). Expanding the boundaries of sport media research: Using critical theory to explore consumer responses to representations of women's sports. *Journal of Sport Management, 25,* 202–216.

Kian, E. M., & Hardin, M. (2009). Framing of sport coverage based on the sex of sport writers: Female journalists counter traditional gendering of media coverage. *International Journal of Sport Communication, 2,* 185–204.

Kian, E. M., Mondello, M., & Vincent, J. (2009). ESPN—The women's sports network? A content analysis of internet coverage of March Madness. *Journal of Broadcasting and Electronic Media, 53*(3), 477–495.

Kian, E. M., Vincent, J., & Mondello, M. (2008). Masculine hegemonic hoops: An analysis of media coverage of March Madness. *Sociology of Sport Journal, 25,* 223–242.

Krane, V., Ross, S. R., Miller, M., Rowse, J. L., Ganoie, K., Andrzejczyk, J. A., & Lucas, C. B. (2010). Power and focus: Self-representation of female college athletes. *Qualitative Research in Sport and Exercise, 2,* 175–195.

Lapchick, R. (2013, February 25). Diversity progress, diversity hiring in sports media still poor. *Sports Business Daily Global Journal.* Retrieved from http://www.sportsbusinessdaily. com/Journal/ Issues/2013/02/25/Opinion/Richard-Lapchick.aspx

LaVoi, N. M., & Calhoun, A. S. (In Press, Jan, 2014). Digital media and female athletes. In A. Billings & M. Hardin (Eds.), *Handbook of Sport and New Media*. New York, NY: Routledge.

Lenkyj, H. J. (2013). Reflections on communication and sport: On heteronormativity and gender identities. *Communication and Sport, 1*(1/2), 138–150.

Lisec, J., & McDonald M. (2012). Gender inequality in the new millennium: An analysis of WNBA representations in sport blogs. *Journal of Sports Media, 7*(2), 153–178.

Lumpkin, A. (2009). Female representation in feather articles published by *Sports Illustrated* in the 1990s. *Women in Sport and Physical Activity Journal, 18(2),* 38–51.

McDonald, M., & Birrell, S. (1999). Reading sport critically: A methodology for interrogating power. *Sociology of Sport Journal, 16(4),* 283–300.

Meân, L. J., & Kassing, J. W. (2008). "I would just like to be known as an athlete": Managing hegemony, femininity, and heterosexuality in female sport. *Western Journal of Communication, 72,* 126–144.

Messner, M. A. (1988). Sports and male domination: The female athlete as contested ideological terrain. *Sociology of Sport Journal, 5,* 197–211.

Messner, M. A. (2013). Reflections on communication and sport: On men and masculinities. *Communication and Sport, 1*(1/2), 113–124. doi: 10.1177/2167479512467977

Messner, M. A., Dunbar, M., & Hunt, D. (2000) The televised sports manhood formula. *Journal of Sport and Social Issues, 24,* 380–394.

Sagas, M., Cunningham, G. B., Wigley, B. J., & Asley, F. B. (2000). Internet coverage of university softball and baseball web sites: The inequity continues. *Sociology of Sport Journal, 17,* 198–205.

Smith, L. (2011). The less you say: An initial study of gender coverage in sports on Twitter. In A. C. Billings (Ed.), *Sports media: Transformation, integration, consumption* (pp. 146–161). Hoboken, NJ: Taylor & Francis.

Toft, D. (2011, October 3). New sports press survey: Newspapers focus narrowly on sports results. *Play the game.* Retrieved from http://www.playthegame.org/knowledge-bank/articles/new-sports-press-survey-newspapers-focus-narrowly-on-sports-results-5248.html

Tuchman, G. (2012). *Edging women out: Victorian novelists, publishers and social change.* New York, NY: Routledge.

Tuchman, G. (1978). Introduction: The symbolic annihilation of women by the mass media. In G. Tuchman, A. Daniels, & J. Benét (Eds.), *Hearth and home: Images of women in the mass media* (pp. 3–38). New York, NY: Oxford University Press.

Tuggle, C. A. (1997). Differences in television sports reporting of men's and women's athletics: ESPN SportsCenter and CNN Sports Tonight. Journal of Broadcasting & Electronic Media, 41, 4–34.

Wallace, L., Wilson, J., & Miloch, K. (2011). Sporting Facebook: A content analysis of NCAA organizational sport pages and Big 12 conference athletic department pages. *International Journal of Sport Communication, 4,* 422–444.

Weber, J. D., & Carini, R. M. (2013). Where are the female athletes in *Sports Illustrated*? A content analysis of covers (2000–2011). *International Review for the Sociology of Sport, 48*(2), 196–203.

AFFILIATION

Nicole M. LaVoi, PhD
School of Kinesiology
Tucker Center for Research on Girls and Women in Sport
University of Minnesota

KERRIE J. KAUER & VIKKI KRANE

4. SEXUAL IDENTITY AND SPORT

INTRODUCTION

Within two weeks of each other in the spring of 2013, two professional athletes publicly came out as lesbian and gay. Brittney Griner, U.S. university player of the year 2012 and 2013, and first round Women's National Basketball Association (WNBA) draft pick to the Phoenix Mercury, announced that she was a lesbian. Griners' "announcement" was subtle, and did not gain a lot of press. But, her coming out was significant given the few professional lesbian athletes who are open about their sexuality. The fact that a major news media outlet, *The New York Times*, picked up the story is indicative of the anomaly of college and professional athletes publicly discussing their sexual orientation. Two weeks after Griner's story, Jason Collins, a National Basketball Association (NBA) free agent became the first male athlete in one of the "big four" professional sport leagues (NBA, Major League Baseball, National Football League, or National Hockey League) to come out publicly as gay while still actively competing. Collins' announcement created a media storm, including a feature story for the May 2013 issue of *Sports Illustrated* which contained the personal story that Collins wrote. Collins soon received tweets from NBA stars such as Kobe Bryant and a telephone call from United States President Barack Obama in support of his declaration of being a gay athlete. The perception of these two professional athletes, Griner and Collins, differed in many regards. Most striking was the lack of media coverage in response to Griner's announcement in comparison to the media storm surrounding Collins' proclamation. While Collins' announcement was littered through sport and news media, Griner's subtle affirmation was largely ignored. Additionally, while Griner's coming out is evidence of the progress towards greater inclusiveness in women's sport, stories also emerged of Baylor University's homonegative culture and the insistence from her coach, Kim Mulkey, that lesbian athletes should not disclose their sexuality for fear of negative repercussions around recruiting (Fagan, 2013).

As we will discuss in this chapter, the ways in which gender and sexuality in sport are experienced by its participants varies widely depending on social and cultural norms that are prevalent in men's and women's sports. These two contemporary incidents provide an introduction for questioning the relationship between sexuality and sport: Why is it newsworthy when lesbian or gay male athletes announce their sexuality? What is the culture like regarding lesbian, gay male, bisexual, and

E. A. Roper (Ed.), Gender Relations in Sport, 53–71.
© *2013 Sense Publishers. All rights reserved.*

transgender (LGBT) athletes in sport? What is the history of LGBT inclusion in sport and how does this history help us conceptualize or make sense of sexuality in sport today? We aim to address these questions and more in this chapter. In this chapter, we will examine the historical roots of gendered scripts in sport, their impact on perspectives related to sexual identity in sport, and challenges to expectations surrounding gender and sexuality and discrimination based on sexual identity in contemporary sport.

DEFINING SEXUALITY IN SPORT

When examining sport in Western society, it is hard to avoid noticing the strong gender scripts and codes that are promoted. Boys and girls learn the expected and acceptable ways to act consistent with their gender; boys learn the importance of being skilled, competitive, and assertive while girls learn that they can play hard, but not to be too skilled, competitive, or assertive. In other words, boys learn to be masculine while girls learn that even in the physical arena of sport, there are rewards for being feminine and punishments for pushing the boundaries of femininity. When an athlete does not neatly fit into normative gender categories, her or his sexuality, or sexual orientation, often is questioned. For example, boys who show an interest in figure skating or gymnastics often are called "sissy" or "faggot" because they are not ascribing to masculine gender ideology. Girls and women who develop attributes for success in sport, such as muscularity, assertiveness, and competitiveness often are labeled "butch," "dyke," or "lesbian."

This type of prejudice is targeted at gender non-conformity (Espelage, Aragon, Birkett, & Koenig, 2008; Krane, 2008) and these stances conflate sex, gender, and sexual orientation. Briefly, *sex* refers to the biological body whereas *gender* is socially and culturally constructed and refers to attitudes and behaviors that have been associated with masculinity and femininity (Krane & Symons, in press). *Sexual orientation* is one's emotional and sexual attraction to another person (Cho, Laub, Wall, Daley, & Joslin, 2004) and the term *sexual identity* is used to convey one's sense of self (i.e., identity) consistent with emotional and sexual attractions as well as membership in a community with other people who share this orientation (APA, 2008). *Gender identity* refers to one's internal sense of being female or male; this identity may or may not align with one's physical body (i.e., sex) (Enke, 2012). People who have a gender identity that is not consistent with their physical sex assigned at birth and a gender expression that differs from conventional expectations associated with the assigned sex may identify as *transgender* (Krane, in press). *Intersex* people are born with internal or external genitalia, hormonal and chromosomal make-up, and/or internal reproductive organs that are inconsistent with one sex. That is, they may have a combination of male and female physical characteristics or ambiguous sex characteristics (Krane, in press).

Very often, in sport, masculine acting males and feminine acting females are privileged over other sportspeople. This expectation, that girls be feminine and boys be masculine, is the foundation for much discrimination against LGBT people. Often, when boys act in ways consistent with femininity or girls act in masculine ways, their sexual orientation is called into question. *Homonegative* sport climates are openly prejudiced and people who are LGBT face negative stereotypes, bigotry, and discrimination (Krane, 1997). This hostility can range from denigrating comments or jokes to physical assaults. Although common in the popular press and everyday language, we purposely do not use the term homophobia (Krane, 1997; Herek, 2000). A *phobia* is an irrational reaction or fear, such as a fear of spiders or heights. Contrary, discrimination against LGBT people often is rooted in deliberate attitudes reflecting social, religious, political, or other ideological beliefs. When prejudice is aimed at someone due to her/his gender expression or gender identity, it is considered *trans prejudice* or *transnegativism* (Krane & Symons, in press).

THEORETICAL FRAMEWORK

Our understanding and discussion of sexual identity in sport is guided by a queer feminist foundation and social identity perspective. In general, a feminist framework puts gender at the core of analysis. Feminists recognize the social hierarchies that tend to privilege males and masculinity over females and femininity. Queer theory extends feminist analysis with an emphasis on confronting heteronormativity, or the privileging and normalizing of heterosexuality in our society. To confront heteronormativity includes resisting the privileging of heterosexuality as well as being open and inclusive of all expressions of gender and sexuality (e.g., lesbian, transgender, bisexual). Altogether, our queer feminist foundation (Krane, Waldron, Kauer, & Smerjian, 2010) provides the framework for challenging dominant notions of sex, gender, and sexuality in sport. In particular, we contest on how sex, gender, and sexuality are socially constructed and reinforced in sport. This framework also posits a strong social justice theme.

The institution of sport has been one of the social and cultural spaces that has constructed and maintained binary categories of sex, gender, and sexual orientation. This means that these constructs are defined as opposites; to be male is the opposite of being female. Additionally, what it means to be male includes not being female. This framework also fits gender (i.e., to be masculine means not being feminine) and sexual orientation (heterosexual is the opposite of homosexual). This binary conceptualization is problematic because it negates the possibility that there is a middle ground. For example, the existence of bisexual people is erased or made invisible. Additionally, dichotomous categories of gender and sexuality set up hierarchies where one gender or orientation has power over the other. In Western culture, men are given more power than women, and heterosexuals have more power than LGBT people. Such binary categorization also creates stereotypes intermingling sex, gender, and sexual orientation. Stereotypically speaking, to be perceived as a heterosexual male, one must have a male appearing body as well as masculine mannerisms and personality.

While queer feminism provides a framework for understanding the social milieu surrounding athletes as they learn to negotiate expectations surrounding sex, gender, and sexuality, social identity perspective helps us understand group behaviors in sport. Previous research has applied this framework to understand prejudice against sexual minorities and how individuals with marginalized sexual identities navigate sport (e.g., Kauer & Krane, 2006; Krane & Barber, 2005). Identity, in this perspective, is conceived to emerge from social group membership and the emotional attachments people have to these social groups (Tajfel & Turner, 1979). Individuals recognize various social groups and categorize or define themselves as a member of particular groups (Hogg & Abrams, 1990). For example, an individual will recognize him or herself as a member of a religious or ethnic group. If membership within this category is considered important, that individual will embrace this social identity, be emotionally attached to it, and she or he will behave consistent with the values and social expectations of this group. Individuals have multiple social identities, for example based on gender, sexual orientation, race, social class, school, or athletic team. And, as Wright points out, it is important to recognize the "fluid and dynamic nature of collective identities" (2009, p. 864). That is, at different times and in different contexts different social identities become more salient. For example, as a Muslim, gay male athlete, in some circumstances his religious identity may be important whereas in others his athlete identity will be most relevant. Further, in some settings he may conceal his sexual identity and in others he may conceal his religious identity. There is a constant shifting in how some individuals may present themselves; when one's social identities conflict or are associated with different social status, there also is a constant negotiation regarding how people act when with different social groups.

When individuals join a new group, such as an athletic team, they will learn and adopt the *social norms* (i.e., expected behaviors, attitudes, and values) of that group through the process of *depersonalization* (Turner, Hogg, Oakes, Reichter, & Wetherell, 1987). Wanting to be accepted and recognized as a group member, people will downplay their individuality and act in manners consistent with the group (e.g., talk or dress similarly). Through depersonalization, new members redefine themselves as group members, engage in normative behavior, and adopt group values and attitudes (Turner et al., 1987). *Collective esteem*, or feelings of self-worth gained from group membership (Crocker & Luhtanen, 1990), emerge from acceptance as a group member. In other words, individuals feel good about themselves when they are recognized as a member of a group that is important to them.

Social identity perspective explains that not only do groups differ in social status, but that members of high status groups may work to maintain their social standing while members of low status groups may act to improve their standing. For example, in sport there has been a long-standing stereotype that gay men are effeminate and therefore cannot be good athletes. Thus, the social norms within high status men's sport teams have reinforced the importance of highly masculine appearance and behavior. This has led to discrimination against boys and men who are not heterosexual or who do not appear heterosexual. Members of low status social groups will engage in social change actions when they perceive that the treatment of their group is unjust and they can envision that social change will be successful (Wright, 2009). Members of high status groups also will fight for social justice and support low status groups when they perceive the treatment of the low status group is unfair and the inequity is pervasive (Ellemers & Barroto, 2009; Iyer & Ryan, 2009).

SOCIO-HISTORICAL LINKS BETWEEN SPORT, GENDER, AND SEXUALITY

The social identity perspective helps us understand the development of stereotypes and historic negative treatment of LGBTs in sport. In the past, high status athletes were those who possessed characteristics associated with hegemonic masculinity and femininity. While hegemonic forms of masculinity and femininity are not always the most common, they are the most revered (Connell, 2005; Krane, 2001). Further, hegemonic beliefs often are so commonly accepted that they are considered "natural" and are not questioned. Adherence with hegemonic masculinity and femininity also create hierarchies. People who adhere to these ideals are admired, gain respect from their peers, and have access to greater privilege and resources than other athletes. For example, hegemonically feminine female athletes gain greater media attention and fan support. Their peers who admire them, support this hierarchy as they emulate hegemonic ideals and strive to gain the associated privileges. This has created a system in which privileged sportspeople (i.e., feminine females and masculine males) strive to maintain their power and social status.

Hegemonic masculinity, in particular, has guided the historic development of gender norms in sport. The goal of early sport in the US was to prepare boys and men for war. Particularly around the time of the industrial revolution, in the absence of physical labor for men, there became a fear that men would become feminized (Rader, 2008). Sport became a cultural site where socially constructed masculine traits, such as aggression and competition, would be instilled in young boys and men; this was an attempt to encourage masculinity and discourage femininity in them (Messner, 1990). Hughes and Coakley (1991) referred to this behavior as the sport ethic, composed of four primary characteristics: sacrificing oneself for "the game," relentless pursuit of perfection, playing through pain, and accepting no limits. This ethic has become melded with hegemonic masculinity. Ideal athletes will have ideal masculinity by sacrificing their bodies, being aggressive towards opponents, and doing whatever it takes to win. Athletes who cannot live up to these standards were considered not masculine enough -- they were labeled feminine or gay. Historically, hegemonic masculinity became the foundation for being an accepted teammate and successful athlete.

Consistent with the social identity perspective, males learn the social norms of masculinity and strive to engage in masculine behaviors (i.e., they depersonalize). For male athletes, hegemonic masculinity was an ideal to live up to; when athletes failed to do so, they were called gay. For females, acting in ways too closely associated with hegemonic masculinity led to being labeled masculine, which was equated with being lesbian (Cahn, 1993). Ironically, simply participating in sport and being athletic often led to girls and women being stereotyped as masculine (i.e., lesbian). However, males who participated in most sports (not including feminine-typed sports such as gymnastics or figure skating) were automatically marked as masculine. Accordingly, stereotypes emerged suggesting that gay men did not exist in sport whereas most female athletes were perceived as lesbians. While differently constructed, these two cultural archetypes, hegemonic masculinity and hegemonic femininity, created an overtly hostile, or homonegative, environment for LGBT people in sport as they both emphasize distancing from, or even hostility towards, homosexuality.

Hegemonic Masculinity

Masculinity is a recurring theme in the reading of sport as a cultural construct and has greatly influenced the treatment and acceptance of gay men in sport. Historically, important components of being appropriately masculine included displaying overtly heterosexual behavior, commodification of women as sexualized objects, use of homonegative discourse (bragging about heterosexual conquests by heterosexual males in exclusively heterosexual spaces such as athletic locker rooms), and avoidance and intolerance of effeminate behavior which is associated with homosexuality (Anderson, 2005). Anderson (2005) referred to this type of behavior as orthodox masculinity. The more closely male athletes adhered to the sport ethic combined with homonegative and sexist conduct created masculine capital. This masculine capital refers to his worth, based on skills and adherence to these highly gendered attributes (Anderson, 2005).

Athletes with high masculine capital were the most privileged and revered. They also tended to be the most successful and often were team leaders. Since the social assumption was that such masculine men could not be gay, this morphed into the strongly held belief that gay men did not exist within the masculine culture of sport for boys and men. This was particularly true for men of color, specifically Black men, who had been oppressed and excluded from much of sport's history. Once feared, the Black male body became the epitome of masculinity in sport and of (hetero)sexual prowess (Kian & Anderson, 2009).

As gay men were perceived to not be present, heterosexism, homonegativism, and sexism became part of the dominant discourse. It was commonly accepted that less skilled players were called derogatory terms referring to femininity and homosexuality. For Black athletes, an already marginalized and oppressed group, conforming to hegemonic forms of masculinity became a way to raise their masculine capital (Kian & Anderson, 2009). It also is important to point out the strict limits of the boundaries of hegemonic or orthodox masculinity. These terms refer to highly selective behavior and are aimed at describing the most privileged athletes. As such, the dominant form of masculinity is associated with White, able-bodied, heterosexual, athletically skilled men (Anderson, 2005).

Hegemonic Femininity

Historically in women's sport, being feminine was held up as the standard. Early participation in sport for girls and women was guided by the misperceptions that female bodies were not strong enough for sport and that being too competitive or athletic would interfere with potential fertility (Cahn, 1993). Additionally, US sporting cultures for girls and women were guided by physical educators who emphasized Victorian ideals of femininity in which females were perceived as weak, docile, dependent, maternal, and as not having stamina needed for physical activity. Thus, efforts to avoid fertility problems associated with too much physical activity were coupled with a strong emphasis on being feminine.

Particularly around the time of the Second World War, there was a surge in female sport and physical activity (Cahn, 1993). At this time, physical activity and sport for girls and young women were integrated into the education system. To gain and maintain respect and support of male physical educators and coaches, female physical educators placed great import on femininity. Teaching proper posture, wearing make-up, and feminine attire were integral parts of physical education for women, with the goal to dissolve impressions of physically active women as masculine or to deter attributes associated with men and masculinity (Cahn, 1993). Similar to hegemonic masculinity, a hegemonic form of femininity also emerged, one that was consistent with White, upper class values. Sportswomen were to be graceful, composed, humble, and restrained. Too much exertion, sweating, competitiveness, and aggression were to be avoided. Under these conditions, and overtime, a social and moral shift took place in social views of women's participation in physical activity (Wushanely, 2004). Women who competed in sport and physical activity slowly were legitimized as long as they were perceived as feminine (Rader, 2008).

While White girls and women were encouraged to be feminine in sport, Black girls and women in the United States were not receiving equal opportunities in education which housed many sport opportunities for females (Cahn, 1994). And, Black sportswomen simply could not meet expectations associated with White, upper class femininity. As such, their sporting history differs from the educationally-based sport for White girls and women. Athletic programs open to Black females were developed through church leagues, community organizations such as the YWCA, and historically black colleges and universities. Similarly, working class women also could not meet the expectations of hegemonic femininity and they created sporting opportunities through industrial leagues. Both Black and working class female athletes pursued highly competitive and assertive sport which differed greatly from the socially sanctioned sport in which White middle- and upper-class sportswomen participated. While many White women in sport and physical education emphasized individual health, Black women leaders promoted community health and spirit as well as highly competitive athletic endeavors (Cahn, 1994). While they were supported and encouraged within their communities, broader society denigrated Black sportswomen as too masculine.

After World War II, as Cahn (1993) explained, the stereotype of the "mannish lesbian" emerged as an attempt to revert women back to domesticity, a code word for heterosexuality. While during the war, women were needed to fill in for the males who were overseas fighting. However, after the war, social expectations were that women would no longer engage in these male pursuits (e.g., being in the workforce, participating in sport). Masculine characteristics associated with sport, such as muscularity and assertiveness, were either perceived to imply lesbianism or thought capable of turning all female athletes into lesbians (Cahn, 1994). The long history of avoiding masculinity in girls and women's sport combined with the strong associations between masculinity and lesbians created a climate strongly prejudiced against women who did not meet the demands of hegemonic femininity.

While hegemonic masculinity provided an ideal for male athletes, an ideal form of femininity also has emerged for female athletes. Coined hegemonic femininity (Choi, 2000; Krane, 2001), it also sets up a hierarchy of more and less privileged sportswomen. In other words, women who display characteristics such as gracefulness, compassion, gentleness, emotionalism, and weakness (Krane & Symons, in press) have what might be considered feminine capital and are privileged in sport. However, females who participate in sport often develop characteristics perceived to be in opposition to hegemonic femininity. Their bodies and personalities that help them achieve their sport goals contrasts social standards of femininity (Krane, 2001). Therefore, female athletes are stereotyped as masculine and many sporting women become targets of prejudice and discrimination. For example, in the 1980s, Martina Navratilova rose to prominence on the international tennis circuit. She was scrutinized for her muscular physique and dominance as a tennis player because of the societal belief that a "real woman" could never accomplish such strength and athletic prowess (Cahn, 1993). "Americans simply could not separate the concept of athletic superiority from its cultural affiliation with masculine sport and the male body" (Cahn, 1993, p. 2). Instead of praising Navratilova's success, work ethic, and talent, she was criticized for being too muscular and powerful.

Female athletes who excel in sports where strength and muscularity are essential for success, challenge socially constructed ideals of what it means to be feminine (Krane, 2001). Consistent with social identity perspective, discrimination occurs because they conflict with socially sanctioned norms of femininity. In particular, they are stereotyped as lesbian. This lesbian stereotype has become a way to stigmatize women who participate in sport and discourages young girls and women from entering the historically masculine terrain (Cahn, 1993; Griffin, 1998). The use of the lesbian label impacts all women in sport as it oppresses and denigrates all females' accomplishments. Some sport scholars argue that social construction of gender and hegemonic femininity are central to the attempts to ostracize, denigrate, and exclude women from sport (Kane, 1995; Wright & Clarke, 1999; Young, 1997). In other words, the dominant groups in society form opinions regarding how females should look and behave. Female athletes who do not conform to hegemonic femininity are perceived to threaten dominant gender-role ideologies (Veri, 1999).

Homonegative and Heteronormative Sport Cultures

Expectations surrounding hegemonic masculinity and femininity have created highly negative environments for athletes who do not have high masculine or feminine capital, and especially for LGBT people. By constantly marginalizing males with low masculine capital and associating gay men with femininity, sport has maintained the notion that homosexuality and athleticism are incompatible (Butterworth, 2006; Sierra, 2013). Similarly, in women's sport, the association between a lack of femininity, masculinity and being considered a lesbian has served to marginalize women's sport as a whole and denigrate individuals perceived to lack feminine appeal.

As explained by social identity perspective, sportspeople with high masculine or feminine capital will attempt to maintain their privileged status by reiterating and reinforcing hegemonic ideals. Since athletes who achieve these ideals are most likely to rise into leadership positions (Krane, 2008; Messner, 2002; Waldron & Krane, 2005), they will continue to reward others who follow in their footsteps. Athletes perceived as LGBT are marginalized or rejected by teammates, creating a homonegative climate in which LGBT athletes quit or hide their sexual identity.

Some sport settings are overtly homo- or transnegative and LGBT athletes or those perceived as LGBT are bullied by coaches and teammates. In these settings, athletes may be called names, lose playing time, be cut from teams, or be socially ostracized because of their sexual or gender identities. Even if not aimed at a specific player, the common use of homonegative epithets against all athletes reinforces the lack of acceptance of LGBT players. As Fletcher, Smith, and Dyson (2010) explained, homo- and transnegative language is a form of control over gender expression. Abusive terms such as "dyke" or "fag" serve to assert the importance of being perceived as acceptably masculine or feminine. According to Fletcher et al. (2010), "such terms are applied as a way of punishing perceived gender transgressions, regardless of someone's known (or assumed) sexuality" (p. 7).

Other sport settings may be described as *heteronormative*. That means that heterosexuality is considered the norm and there is a hierarchical privileging of heterosexuality. Because of the assumption that all sportspeople are heterosexual, the culture of sport often neglects people who are LGBT. This bias often is subtle, yet pervasive. For example, when reading coach profiles, heterosexual coaches often include information about their families (e.g., mention their wives or husbands and children; Buyssee & Wolter, 2013; Kane, LaVoi, & Fink, 2013). Lesbian or gay male coaches will not include this personal information. While seemingly innocuous, the repeated omission of same sex partners reinforces their invisibility (or the perception that they do not exist). Their omission also sets a standard in that new LGBT coaches also do not disclose this information, furthering the perception that all coaches are heterosexual.

Heteronormative environments often are described using the analogy of the former US military policy of "don't ask, don't tell." LGBT athletes and coaches are accepted in these sport settings as long as they don't talk about their sexual identity or openly reveal it. The foundation for heteronormativity is *heterosexism*, which is an ideology that stigmatizes, denies, and denigrates identities, behaviors, and relationships that are not heterosexual (Herek, 2000). As Krane and Symons (in press) explained,

heterosexism specifically refers to discriminatory attitudes that disregard people who are not heterosexual, whereas heteronormativity reflects an ever-present cultural bias in favour of heterosexuality and the omission of other forms of sexuality.

Both heterosexism and heteronormativity often operate at the institutional level and are reflected in policies and attitudes that do not include LGBT people. The lack of inclusion of LGBT people creates that illusion that we do not exist and, therefore, we do not need to be supported. Heteronormative and heterosexist sport settings also may be prejudiced overtly against LGBTs. While heterosexism often is grounded in the lack of attention or assumed absence of LGBT athletes, some sport climates are outright hostile towards LGBT people.

Negative recruiting is an example of homonegative discrimination faced by female coaches and women's sport teams in US universities. The Women's Sport Foundation (2011a) defines negative recruiting as,

an unethical recruitment strategy within women's collegiate sports, essentially attempting to give their own programs an un-fair advantage based on perpetuating stereotypes, myths, and misconceptions. By implying to a recruit, that a rival college or university's coach is gay, or that an opposing team is "full of lesbians," school recruiters use this tactic to prey on unsubstantiated fears, one of which is that a gay coach or gay players might negatively influence the sexual orientation of potential recruits. (p. 1)

An example of negative recruiting is when a coach discourages recruits from attending a rival school by labeling the team or the coaches' as lesbian. In other words, when two coaches from rival schools compete for the same athlete, some coaches will use the lesbian scare tactic (e.g., "You don't want to play for a coach with that lifestyle") to discourage an athlete from attending the competing university. Although unethical and contrary to the National Collegiate Athletics Association (NCAA) policy, this practice has been reported frequently among the college coaching ranks (Ionnatta & Kane, 2006; Kauer, 2009; Krane & Barber, 2005) and is used to intimidate and discriminate against collegiate coaches in the recruiting process of athletes. Athlete recruitment is not an issue that should be taken lightly. At many elite level Division I institutions, getting the most talented athletes is a high stakes battle. The fear of negative recruiting has kept many coaches afraid to come out, and also has led to some coaches keeping their current players closeted, such as the case of Brittney Griner and her coach's insistence that her sexuality be kept private for fear of losing recruits (Fagan, 2013).

Heterosexism, heteronormativity, homonegativism and transnegativism have pervasive social and personal consequences. Socially, explicit or implicit acceptance of homonegativism and transnegativism creates social norms that maintain the social hierarchical privileging of heterosexual and gender-conforming athletes. In other words, discrimination becomes the accepted action. On an individual level, when LGBT athletes perceive sport climates as intolerant, they are likely to attempt to conceal their sexual identity. Doing so can become highly stressful and interfere with sport performance (e.g., Anderson, 2005; Griffin, 1998; Krane, 1997). For example, Griner stated that early years at Baylor presented many personal challenges, at one point she was forced to delete a "Tweet" to an ex-girlfriend and that Mulkey never truly supported "all of her," quashing an important part of her identity as a lesbian (Fagan, 2013). Contrary, when Megan Rapinoe, US Olympic soccer player, publically announced that she is a lesbian, she stated, "I guess it seems like a weight off my shoulders, because I've been playing a lot better than I've ever played before" (Buzinski, 2012).

When athletes are subject to harassment and bullying, they become likely to experience a decline in overall psychological well-being; this may include decreased self-confidence and self-esteem, and increased stress, depression, and suicidal thoughts or attempts (Krane, Surface, & Alexander, 2005; Russell, Ryan, Toomey, Diaz, & Sanchez, 2011). These effects can be even more pronounced in youth who are questioning their sexuality and who are being teased or bullied as if they are LGBT (Espelage et al., 2008). Once individuals have come out, they are able to seek out supportive friends, family, and sport personnel. However, questioning youth still are working through their identity development and have not yet created these support networks.

CONTEMPORARY SPORT CLIMATES

We are experiencing a sea of change in today's sport world. On one hand, we find LGBT athletes who are comfortable coming out to teammates (Sierra, 2013; Stoelting, 2011). In high school and college sports, there are openly LGBT coaches, administrators, and athletic trainers. Some professional athletes also are revealing LGBT identities publicly: Jason Collins (NBA), Brittney Griner (WNBA), Robbie Rogers (LA Galaxy/Soccer), and Fallon Fox (transgender MMA fighter) (see http://www.outsports.com/out-gay-athletes). These athletes are the new trendsetters and role models; no longer considered a shocking anomaly, they are being supported by teammates, coaches, and staff. At the same time, we also are seeing examples of highly homonegative sport settings. For instance, recent news stories have highlighted a video of Rutgers University men's basketball coach Mike Rice hurling homonegative slurs at his players (Gregory, 2013). The reality of sport today is that there is a wide range in the level of acceptance of LGBT athletes. While publicly we are seeing greater support, there still are many places where education and change is needed.

A recent report by the Gay, Lesbian, and Straight Education Network (GLSEN) (2013) revealed that many LGBT student-athletes, in US middle and high schools, still are experiencing bullying and harassment in school sports and that some settings remain openly hostile for athletes who are not heterosexual. Young athletes have described that bullying is common in locker rooms (Birkett, Espelage, & Koenig, 2009) and LGBT students reported feeling unsafe in locker rooms and gyms (GLSEN, 2011). Similarly, Australian same-sex attracted young people expressed feeling "least safe at sporting events" (Hillier, Turner, & Mitchell, 2005). In their examination of heterosexual athletes' attitudes towards gay men and lesbians, Roper and Halloran (2007) found that negative mindsets still exist. More specifically, male student-athletes held more negative attitudes toward gay men and lesbians than did female athletes. And, the male athletes held more negative attitudes toward gay men than they did lesbians. While negative attitudes are still evident, studies have shown that overall attitudes towards LGBTs in sport and physical activity are generally positive and that students, athletes, and athletic trainers who knew and had contact with lesbians or gay men had more positive attitudes than their peers (Ensign, Yiamouyiannis, White, & Ridpath, 2011; Gill, Morrow, Collins, Lucey, & Schultz, 2006; Roper & Halloran, 2007; Southall, Anderson, Nagel, Polite, & Southall, 2011).

Positive Changes in Sport

As Hargreaves (2000) asserted, sport provides a public and popular channel for social change to occur regarding LGBT athletes. Sport, as a social institution, provides a platform for athletes and sport organizations to create powerful structures and movements that help change the landscape of our culture. Climate changes towards greater inclusiveness regarding sexuality is occurring in men's and women's sport. As athletes are coming out to teammates, their teammates are responding positively (e.g., Adams & Anderson, 2012; Fink, Burton, Farrell, & Parker, 2012; Kauer & Krane, 2006; Sierra, 2013; Stoelting, 2011). Altogether they are creating supportive, inclusive teams and changing the previously heteronormative culture of sport. Anderson (2011a) describes a shift in the conditions of men's sport environments; while previously he expressed that orthodox masculinity created a homonegative sport culture for men, today he is finding a more inclusive form of masculinity which embraces diverse masculinities and sexualities. In his research, he is finding that gay male athletes in high school and universities are less fearful in disclosing their sexual orientation to their teams than in previous generations and that teammates are supportive of their gay teammates (Anderson, 2011b). Popular press and research literature are supporting similar trends in women's sport (Fagan, 2013; Fink et al., 2012; Stoelting, 2011).

Kauer and Krane (2006) found that in teams where diverse sexual identities were accepted, heterosexual athletes as well as lesbian and bisexual athletes worked to create more open and accepting environments. Their research revealed that female athletes who had high collective esteem about their athletic identity spoke out against heterosexist language or stood up for lesbian/bisexual teammates in the face of discrimination. Having openly LGBT teammates, supportive coaches, or having at least one ally in athletics departments is an important component towards creating safe sport settings (Fink et al., 2012; Sierra, 2013; Stoelting, 2011). And, when athletes construed their sport climates as safe, they were more likely to disclose their sexual orientation. As Anderson (2011b) stated regarding gay male athletes, "there is a complex web of variables that most athletes use to make such decisions: team climate, social networks, the attitudes of their coach, and a host of other identifiable and unidentifiable factors" (p. 265). Seemingly, in today's sporting cultures, more and more LGBT athletes are perceiving the climate as safe and are feeling supported and accepted.

In contrast to the goals of negative recruiting, which we previously discussed, interviewed lesbian athletes were drawn to particular teams and universities because they were known for having accepting social climates (Stoelting, 2011). Kauer (2009) also found that lesbian and bisexual coaches who are publically out are creating positive change in athletic department policy, normalizing partnerships and children in same-sex relationships, and breaking down barriers around negative recruiting. When referring to normalizing lesbian identities and relationships, coaches and athletes aimed to make being lesbian or having a same sex partner just as "normal" as heterosexual identities and partnerships. That is, all people are treated the same regardless of sexual identity. Coaches who normalized their same sex relationships (e.g., had pictures of partners in the office; their partners attended athletic events) often were met with acceptance from athletes as well as administrators (Ionnatta & Kane, 2006; Kauer, 2009).

Positive changes with regard to transgender athletes also are occurring. Transgender athletes are becoming more visible; Keelin Godsey competed in the US Olympic trials for the hammer throw and Kye Allums competed on the Georgetown University women's basketball team (Torre & Epstein, 2012). Taylor Edelmann, a university volleyball player, began his college athletic career on the women's team and then moved to the men's team after beginning hormone therapy and publicly identifying as a transgender male (DeFrancesco, 2013). As a true sign of his acceptance by his male teammates, he was voted team captain for his senior year. There also is growing support for transgender youth. For example, when 9 year old Jazz, a transgender girl, wanted to play on a Florida girls' soccer team, she was prohibited from doing so by the Florida Youth Soccer Association (Woog, 2013). However, when her parents appealed the decision to the U.S. Soccer Federation, the board of directors almost unanimously overturned the previous decision. They also appointed a special committee that developed a policy of transgender inclusion and that applies to all soccer programs under the US Soccer federation.

The Ally Movement

In addition to the research documenting attempts to reduce homophobia in women's sport, several activist organizations have spearheaded campaigns to create change and social justice for LGBTs in sport. One of the most influential programs in this regard was the Women's Sports Foundation's, *It Takes a Team.* As described by the WSF,

65

It Takes A Team! Education Campaign for Lesbian, Gay, Bisexual and Transgender (LGBT) Issues in Sport is an education project focused on eliminating homophobia as a barrier to all women and men participating in sport. Our primary goals are to develop and disseminate practical educational information and resources to athletic administrators, coaches, parents and athletes at the high school and college levels to make sport safe and welcoming for all. (WSF, 2011b)

The director, Pat Griffin, provided educational workshops on issues related to heterosexism and homongativism in sport to hundreds of high school and college athletes, coaches, and administrators. *It Takes a Team* has an educational kit including instructional and curriculum resources; action guides to help coaches, parents, athletes, and administrators address practical issues; administrative resources for addressing the athletic department climate; and legal resources. While this program no longer is active, it was one of the first of its kind to provide readily available, practical tools for people working in sport and athletics.

Another organization working to diminish heterosexism and homophobia is the National Center for Lesbian Rights (NCLR, http://www.nclrights.org/). Since 2001, the NCLR has taken on the legal cases of lesbian athletes and coaches who have been fired or dismissed from their positions due to their sexual orientation. Several high profile cases, such as that of basketball player Jennifer Harris against Rene Portland and Pennsylvania State University, have been handled by the NCLR's Sports Project. Coach Rene Portland had a longstanding and well known "no lesbians" policy on her teams; however, due to the courage of athletes and the litigation provided by the NCLR, Portland no longer is coaching at Penn State (for a complete discussion of this case, see Newhall & Buzuvis, 2008). Through advocacy, litigation, and outreach, the NCLR's Sports Project is creating practical social change for all women in sport who are affected by homonegativism and heterosexism. The *GLSEN Sports Project* (sports.glsen.org) is another example of an organization working toward equality and acceptance. The Sports Project is an education and advocacy program that strives to create positive experiences in sport and physical education in kindergarten through high school settings for all students regardless of sexual identity or gender expression. Spearheaded by Pat Griffin, the program aims to "change the game" and eliminate homonegativism in sports.

The Nike Corporation also has taken a leadership role in addressing heterosexism, homonegativsm, and transnegativism in sport. Nike held its first ever LGBT Sport Summit in the Spring of 2012 at their World Headquarters. Nike teamed up with many of the aforementioned organizations and brought together 30 sport leaders to speak at the conference, and promote strategies for making sport more accepting and safe for LGBT athletes. Following its own lead, Nike has promised endorsement deals to openly LGBT professional athletes; Brittney Griner of the Phoenix Mercury will be one of those athletes.

Recently, a number of ally programs have emerged. These programs were created by heterosexual allies compelled to work towards supporting LGBTs and creating inclusive sport settings. *Athlete Ally* (http://www.athleteally.com/) is one such organization working toward creating positive climates in sport for all members. On the website, athletes, coaches, fans, and parents can sign a pledge to welcome all athletes and make all players feel respected, regardless of perceived or actual sexual orientation, gender identity or gender expression. Thousands of people associated with all levels of sport have signed the pledge. As professional tennis player James Blake expressed, he is an ally and views inclusion less about political acts, and more about basic human rights for all athletes (Hernandez, 2013).

Founded by three professional ice hockey players, Patrick Burke, Brian Kitts, and Glenn Witman, and partnered with the NHL, the *You Can Play Project* (http://youcanplayproject.org) promotes locker rooms and sport venues that are "free from homophobia." The site provides video messages and other resources to help create positive experiences for all athletes without regard for sexual orientation. Athletes can take the Captain's Challenge and pledge to be respectful and to educate teammates when confronted with homonegativism. Other sport ally programs also exist; some of them include:

- It Gets Better campaign (http://www.itgetsbetter.org/)
- br{ache the silence (http://www.freedomsounds.org/index.html)
- Step Up! Speak Out!(http://www.caaws.ca/stepupspeakout/e/index.cfm).

Additionally, it is becoming more common for professional athletes to take public stances in support of LGBT teammates and other sportspeople as well as take public stands supporting social justice for LGBT causes. In particular, NFL players Chris Kluwe and Brendon Ayanbadejo wrote and filed an amicus brief in the state of California in support of same-sex marriage (McManus, 2013). They have been outspoken advocates of accepting gay teammates (although no current athlete in the NFL is publically "out") and have been at the forefront of creating a dialogue about LGBT rights in American football.

BECOMING AN ALLY AND CREATING SAFE SPACES IN SPORT

In spite of all the positive changes, there still is an important need to continue dialogue and education in sport and athletics. One important yet relatively simple way to work toward change and acceptance for LGBT athletes is to use and encourage appropriate language. For example, using the phrase, "that's so gay" reinforces negative stereotypes about LGBT people, even though those who use this phrase are rarely referring to LGBT people. Coaches, athletes, administrators, and parents can interject when they hear someone using any kind of gay slurs. Additionally, people in sport can use language that does not reproduce heteronormative assumptions about someone's gender identity or presumed sexual orientation. For example, coaches talking to a team of female athletes can use language such as "partner" or "significant other" instead of "boyfriend," which assumes all team members are heterosexual. In the same vein, administrators can be sure to use inclusive language in policy, memos, and athletic department documents, as well openly encouraging LGBT coaches who want to include partners or families in athletic media guides in similar ways that heterosexual coaches are granted. Roper and Halloran (2007) argued that universities can incorporate diversity coursework and workshops which can result in enhancing heterosexual athletes' and coaches' attitudes towards LGBTs. Additionally, many high schools and universities have Lesbian, Gay, Bisexual, Transgender, and Straight Ally groups on campus where students can come together in an organized club to work toward social justice and social change for athletes. Education and proactively addressing trans- or homonegative actions are important steps towards creating safe and inclusive sport climates.

CHAPTER SUMMARY

Sport, as a major social institution, is an important part of many people's lives—as participants or fans. Sport also can be a powerful space for social change and social justice to occur. All people who participate in sport should be able to do so in an environment that is safe, inclusive, and accepting. As we have highlighted in this chapter, the history of sport has not always been inclusive and safe for LGBT athletes, and while significant positive change is happening, there also is much work to be done to continue this trend. As we explore the intersections of gender and sexuality in sport, dialogue will continue and these important aspects of people will gain acceptance. We look forward to when coming out as an athlete or coach is no longer newsworthy and when athletes such as Brittney Griner and Jason Collins simply can be themselves throughout their sport careers.

REFERENCES

Adams, A., & Anderson, E. (2012). Exploring the relationship between homosexuality and sport among the teammates of a small, Midwestern Catholic college soccer team. *Sport, Education and Society, 17*(3), 347–363.

Anderson, E. (2005). *In the game: Gay athletes and the cult of masculinity.* New York: SUNY Press.

Anderson, E. (2011a). Updating the outcome. *Gender and Society, 25*(2), 250–268.

Anderson, E. (2011b). Masculinities and sexualities in sport and physical cultures: Three decades of evolving research. *Journal of Homosexuality, 58*(5), 565–578.

American Psychological Association (2008). *Answers to your questions: For better understanding of sexual orientation and homosexuality.* Retrieved from www.apa.org/topics/sorientation.pdf

Birkett, M., Espelage, D. L., & Koenig, B. (2009). LGB and questioning students in schools: The moderating effects of homophobic bullying and school climate on negative outcomes. *Journal of Youth and Adolescence, 38*(7), 989–1000.

Butterworth, M. L. (2006). Pitchers and catchers: Mike Piazza and the discourse of gay identity in the national pastime. *Journal of Sport and Social Issues, 30,* 138–157.

Buysse, J. A., & Wolter, S. (2013). Gender Representation in 2010 NCAA Division I Media Guides: The Battle for Equity was only Temporarily Won. *Journal of Issues in Intercollegiate Athletics, 6,* 1–21.

Buzinski, J. (2012, Aug. 8). U.S. soccer's Megan Rapinoe says coming out before Olympics 'weight off my shoulders.' Retrieved from http://www.sbnation.com/london-olympics-2012/2012/8/8/3228890/u-s-womens-soccer-megan-rapinoe-lesbian-london-olympics-gay

Cahn, S. K. (1993). From the" muscle moll" to the" butch" ballplayer: Mannishness, lesbianism, and homophobia in US women's sport. *Feminist Studies, 19*(2), 343–368

Cahn, S. K. (1994). *Coming on strong: Gender and sexuality in twentieth-century women's sport.* Boston, MA: Harvard.

Cho, S., Laub, C., Wall, S., Daley, C., & Joslin, C. (2004). Beyond the binary: A tool kit for gender identity activism in schools. *Retrieved on September, 15, 2008.*

Crocker, J., & Luhtanen, R. (1990). Collective self-esteem and ingroup bias. *Journal of Personality and Social Psychology, 58,* 60–67.

Choi, P. Y .L. (2000). *Femininity and the physically active woman.* New York: Routledge.

Connell, R. W. (2005). *Masculinities* (2nd ed.). Berkeley: University of California Press.

DeFrancesco, D. (2013, May 7). Student athlete finds support in gender change. The (Westchester County, N.Y.) Journal News, Retrieved from http://www.usatoday.com/story/news/nation /2013/05/07/ student-athlete-gender-change/2143267/

Ellemers, N., & Barreto, M. (2009). Collective action in modern times: How modern expressions of prejudice prevent collective action. *Journal of Social Issues, 65*(4), 749–768.

Enke, A. F. (2012). Note on terms and concepts. In A. Enke (Ed.), *Transfeminist perspectives: In and beyond transgender and gender studies* (pp. 16–20). Philadelphia: Temple University Press.

Ensign, K. A., Yiamouyiannis, A., White, K. M., & Ridpath, B. (2011). Athletic trainers' attitudes toward lesbian, gay, and bisexual national collegiate athletic association student-athletes. *Journal of Athletic Training, 46*(1), 69–75.

Espelage, D. L., Aragon, S. R., Birkett, M., & Koenig, B. W. (2008). Homophobic teasing, psychological outcomes, and sexual orientation among high school students: What influence do parents and schools have? *School Psychology Review, 37,* 202–216.

Fagan, K. (2013). Owning the middle. Retrieved from http://espn.go.com/espn/story/_/id /9316697/ owning-middle

Fink, J. S., Burton, L. J., Farrell, A. O., Parker, H. M. (2012). Playing it out: Female intercollegiate athletes' experiences in revealing their sexual identities. *Journal for the Study of Sports and Athletes in Education, 6,* 83–106.

Fletcher, G., Smith, L., & Dyson, S. (2010). *Fair Go, Sport! Promoting sexual and gender diversity in hockey: A literature review.* Victoria, Australia: Victorian Equal Opportunity and Human Rights Commission.

Gill, D. L., Morrow, R. G.,Collins, K. E., Lucey, A. B., & Schultz, A. M. (2006). Attitudes and sexual prejudice in sport and physical activity. *Journal of Sport Management, 20,* 554–564.

Gay, Lesbian, and Straight Education Network (GLSEN). (2013). *The Experiences of LGBT Students in School Athletics (Research Brief).* New York: GLSEN. Retrieved from http://www.glsen.org/binary-data/GLSEN_ ATTACHMENTS/ file/000/002/2140–1.pdf

Gay, Lesbian, and Straight Education Network (GLSEN). (2011). The 2011 national school climate survey: The experiences of lesbian, gay, bisexual and transgender youth in our nation's schools. New York: GLSEN. Retrieved from http://www.glsen.org/binary-data/GLSEN _ATTACHMENTS/ file/000/002/2105–1.pdf

Gregory, S. (2013, April 03). Rutgers coach fired after hurling homophobic slurs, basketballs at players. *Time.* Retrieved from http://keepingscore.blogs.time.com/2013/04/03/watch-college-hoops-coach-hurls-homophobic-slurs-basketballs-at-players/

Griffin, P. (1998). *Strong women, deep closets: Lesbians and homophobia in sport.* Campaign, IL: Human Kinetics Publishers.

Hargreaves, J. (2000). *Heroines of sport: The politics of difference and identity.* New York: Routledge.

Herek, G. M. (2000). The psychology of sexual prejudice. *Current Directions in Psychological Science, 9*(1), 19–22.

Hernandez, G. (2013). American tennis star James Blake speaks out against homophobia in sport. Retrieved from http://www.gaystarnews.com/article/american-tennis-star-james-blake-speaks-out-against-homophobia-sport280513

Hillier, L., Turner, A., & Mitchell, A. (2005). *Writing themselves in again: 6 Years on [the 2nd national report on the sexuality, health and well-being of same-sex attracted young people].* Australian Research Centre in Sex, Health and Society.

Hogg, J., & Abrams, D. (1990). *Social identifications: A social psychology of intergroup relations and group processes.* New York: Routledge.

69

Hughes, R., & Coakley, J. (1991). Positive deviance among athletes: The implications of overconformity to the sport ethic. *Sociology of Sport Journal, 8*, 361–74.

Ionnatta, J. C., & Kane, M. J. (2002). Sexual stories as resistance narratives in women's sports: reconceptualizing identity performance. *Sociology of Sport Journal, 19*, 347–369.

Iyer, A., & Ryan, M. K. (2009). Why do men and women challenge gender discrimination in the workplace? The role of group status and in-group identification in predicting pathways to collective action. *Journal of Social Issues, 65*(4), 791–814.

Kane, M. J. (1995). Resistance/transformation of the oppositional binary: Exposing sport as a continuum. *Journal of Sport and Social Issues, 19*, 191–218.

Kane, M. J., LaVoi, N. M., & Fink, J. S. (2013). Exploring elite female athletes' interpretations of sport media images: A window into the construction of social identity and ''selling sex''' in women's sports. *Communication and Sport.* doi:10.1177/2167479512473585

Kauer, K. J. (2009). Queering lesbian sexualities in collegiate sporting spaces. *Journal of Lesbian Studies, 13*, 306–318.

Kauer, K. J., & Krane, V. (2006). "Scary dykes" and "feminine queens:" Stereotypes and female collegiate athletes. *Women in Sport and Physical Activity Journal, 15*(1), 42–52.

Kian, E. T. M., & Anderson, E. (2009). John Amaechi: Changing the way sport reporters examine gay athletes. *Journal of Homosexuality, 56*(7), 799–818. doi:10.1080/00918360903187788

Krane, V. (1997). Homonegativism experienced by lesbian collegiate athletes. *Women in Sport and Physical Activity Journal, 6*(2), 141–163.

Krane, V. (2001). We can be athletic and feminine, but do we want to? Challenging hegemonic femininity in women's sport. *Quest, 53*(1), 115–133.

Krane, V. (2008). Gendered social dynamics in sport. In M. Beauchamp & M. Eys (Eds.), *Group dynamics advances in sport and exercise psychology: Contemporary themes* (pp. 159–176). New York: Routledge.

Krane, V. (in press). Gender nonconformity, sex variation, and sport. In R. Schinke & K. McGannon (Eds.), *The psychology of sub-culture in sport and physical activity: A critical approach.* New York: Psychology Press.

Krane, V., & Barber, H. (2005). Identity tensions in lesbian intercollegiate coaches. *Research Quarterly for Exercise and Sport, 76*(1), 67–81.

Krane, V., Surface, H., & Alexander, L. (2005). Health implications of heterosexism and homonegativism for girls and women in sport. In L. Ransdall & L. Petlichkoff (Eds.), *Ensuring the health of active and athletic girls and women* (pp. 327–346). Reston, VA: National Association for Girls and Women in Sport.

Krane, V., & Symons, C. (in press). Gender and sexual orientation. In A. Papaioannou & D. Hackfort (Eds.), *Fundamental concepts in sport and exercise psychology* (chapter 8). Taylor & Francis.

Krane, V., Waldron, J. J., Kauer, K. J., & Semerjian, T. (2010). Queering sport psychology. In T. Ryba, R. Schinke, & G. Tennenbaum (Eds.), *The cultural turn in sport and exercise psychology* (pp.153–180). Morgantown, West Virginia: Fitness Information Technology.

McManus, J. (2013, February 28). NFLers show support of gay marriage. ESPNNewYork.com. Retrieved from http://espn.go.com/nfl/story/_/id/9000545/chris-kluwe-brendon-ayanbadejo-file-amicus-brief-california-favoring-same-sex-marriage

Messner, M. (1990). Boyhood, organized sports, and the construction of masculinities. *Journal of Contemporary Ethnography, 18*(4), 416–444.

Messner, M. A. (2002). *Taking the field: Women, men, and sports.* Minneapolis: University of Minnesota Press.

Newhall, K. E., & Buzuvis, E. E. (2008). (e)Racing Jennifer Harris: Sexuality and race, law and discourse in Harris v. Portland. *Journal of Sport and Social Issues, 32*, 345–368.

Rader, B. (2008). *American sports: From the age of folk games to the age of televised sports* (6th ed). Upper Saddle River, NJ: Pearson.

Roper, E. A., & Halloran, E. (2007). Attitudes toward gay men and lesbians among heterosexual male and female student-athletes. *Sex Roles, 57*(11–12), 919–928.

Russell, S. T., Ryan, C., Toomey, R. B., Diaz, R. M., & Sanchez, J. (2011). Lesbian, gay, bisexual, and transgender adolescent school victimization: Implications for young adult health and adjustment. Journal of School Health, 81(5), 223–230.

Sierra, D. (2013). Singled out: A narrative exploration into sexuality, sport, and masculinity. Master's thesis, Bowling Green State University.

Southall, R. M., Anderson, E. D., Nagel, M. S., Polite, F. G., & Southall, C. (2011). An investigation of ethnicity as a variable related to US male college athletes' sexual-orientation behaviours and attitudes. Ethnic and Racial Studies, 34(2), 293–313.

Stoelting, S. (2011). Disclosure as an Interaction: Why Lesbian Athletes Disclose Their Sexual Identities in Intercollegiate Sport. Journal of Homosexuality, 58(9), 1187–1210.

Tajfel, H., & Turner, J. C. (1979). An integrative theory of intergroup conflict. The Social Psychology of Intergroup Relations, 33, 47.

Torre, P. S., & Epstein, D. (2012). The transgender athlete. Sports Illustrated, 116(22), 66–73.

Turner, J. C., Hogg, M. A., Oakes, P. J., Reichter, S. D., & Wetherell, M. S. (1987). Rediscovering the social group: A self-categorization theory. Oxford, UK: Basil Blackwell.

Veri, M. J. (1999). Homophobic discourse surrounding the female athlete. Quest, 51, 355–368.

Waldron, J. J., & Krane, V. (2005). Whatever it takes: Health compromising behaviors in female athletes. Quest, 57, 315–329.

Women's Sport Foundation (WSF). (2011a). Recruiting – Negative recruiting/slander based on sexuality: The Foundation position. Retrieved from http://www.womenssportsfoundation.org / home/ advocate/ foundation-positions/lgbt-issues/negative_recruiting

Women's Sport Foundation (WSF). (2011b). About It Takes A Team! Retrieved from http://www. womenssportsfoundation.org/en/home/athletes/for-athletes/know-your-rights/coach-and-athletic-director-resources/about-itat

Woog, D. (2013, March 06). The OutField: U.S. Soccer, and All that Trans Jazz. The Rainbow Times. Retrieved from http://www.therainbowtimesmass.com/2013/03/06/the-outfield-u-s-soccer-and-all-that-trans-jazz/

Wright, S. C. (2009). The next generation of collective action research. Journal of Social Issues, 65(4), 859–879.

Wright, J., & Clarke, G. (1999). Sport, the media and the construction of compulsory heterosexuality. International Review for the Sociology of Sport, 34, 227–243.

Wushanely, Y. (2004). Playing nice and losing: The struggle for control of women's intercollegiate athletics, 1960–2000. New York: Syracuse University Press.

Young, K. (1997). Women, sport, and physicality. International Review for the Sociology of Sport, 32, 297–305.

AFFILIATIONS

Kerrie J. Kauer, PhD
Department of Kinesiology
California State University, Long Beach

Vikki Krane, PhD
Department of Human Movement, Sport, and Leisure Studies
Bowling Green State University

AKILAH R. CARTER-FRANCIQUE & COURTNEY L. FLOWERS

5. INTERSECTIONS OF RACE, ETHNICITY, AND GENDER IN SPORT

INTRODUCTION

The purpose of this chapter is to describe the relationship between gender, race, and ethnicity in sport. Gender has been a topic of conversation in sport for many decades, with Title IX of the Education Amendments of 1972 (Title IX) anchoring many of those conversations (Acosta & Carpenter, 2012). Title IX celebrated its fortieth anniversary in the spring of 2012. In honor of this historic celebration, Arne Duncan, United States Director of Education, explained Title IX's significance to college sport specifically stating, "Student-athletes learn lessons on the court and the playing field that are hard to learn anywhere else—lessons about teamwork, commitment, adaptation, and discipline" (U.S. Department of Education, 2012). In addition, Duncan stated:

> When Title IX was enacted in 1972, less than 30,000 female students participated in sports and recreational programs at NCAA [National Collegiate Athletic Association] member institutions nationwide. Today, that number has increased nearly six-fold. And at the high school level, the number of girls participating in athletics has increased ten-fold since 1972, to three million girls today.

Duncan made a number of important points regarding how Title IX made an impact on girls' and women's participation in high school and college sport; however, while it may have been beyond the scope of his message, Duncan failed to address how the enactment of Title IX in the context of sports has affected girls and women from racially and ethnically marginalized groups.

Girls and women from racially (e.g., Black, Hispanic) and ethnically (e.g., African American, Mexican American) marginalized groups are disproportionately represented in sports as participants (Acosta & Carpenter, 2012; Lapchick, Hoff, & Kaiser, 2011) and leaders (i.e., administrators, coaches; Lapchick et al., 2011). There are a number of factors (i.e., social, historical, legal, economic, religious) that contribute to the underrepresentation of racially and ethnically marginalized girls and women; and understanding these factors is essential to achieving the benefits of sport. Therefore, throughout this chapter we will (a) explain the role of culture in understanding sport and its meaning for racial and ethnic groups in sport;

E. A. Roper (Ed.), Gender Relations in Sport, 73–93.

(b) explicate how theoretical frameworks can address the "intersectionality" of race, ethnicity, and gender in the context of sport; (c) demonstrate how power dynamics (i.e., ideologies, leaders) and politics (i.e., legislation, organizational policies, leaders) can influence and justify participation and representation of racial and ethnic "others" in sport; (d) examine how dominant ideologies, media and legislation can influence and marginalize the experiences of racial and ethnic "others" in sport; and (e) present examples of policies, practices, and organizations which promote social justice for racial and ethnic "others" in sport.

SPORTING CULTURE AND THE "OTHER"

Sport is defined as "institutionalized competitive activities that involve rigorous physical exertion or the use of relatively complex physical skills by participants motivated by internal and external rewards" (Coakley, 2004, p. 21). This definition presents sport as an institution and as an institution it holds a specific place in our society. As such, there are a variety of sports and depending on the group and/ or society participating, the motivation to participate varies in meaning, purpose, organization and cultural significance. Much is discussed on the meaning, purpose, organization, and cultural significance for girls' and women's participation in sport through this text. However, the significance of sport for racial and ethnic groups, similar to gender, has a unique history that cannot be fully expressed in all its complexity within this chapter. Through this chapter, however, we will attempt to provide a general understanding of how race and ethnicity contribute to the gendered experience in sport.

Similar to gender, the conception of race and ethnicity are entrenched within the social fabric of the U.S. and subsequently are deemed sensitive and complex. The terms, race and ethnicity, are often used interchangeably but there is a difference. Race is based on the notion of having shared biological traits, while ethnicity is based on shared cultural traditions. To be more specific, race, in this chapter, is defined as a socially constructed category that comprises a group of people with distinct biological and physical traits (Coakley, 2004; Eitzen & Sage, 2009). Historically, racial categorization has been used as an expression of power most commonly exhibited by European immigrants to establish whiteness, or being white, as the superior race (McDonald, 2005; Smedley, 1999). Thus, while the term "race" signifies biological distinctions between groups, it has also been used as a social construction that has aided in the perpetuation of hegemonic ideologies that promote racism and race-based discrimination.

Ethnicity is different from race, as it is defined by a person's cultural heritage, way of life, shared beliefs, and cultural norms (Coakley, 2004; Cunningham, 2011; Eitzen & Sage, 2009). For example, ethnicity encompasses a person's cultural traditions (i.e., language, customs) that are often connected to her/his nationality such as African American, Japanese American, or Mexican American. Understanding racial categorization and ethnic distinctions is important because they comprise our social fabric and aid our cultural understanding. The meaning held within these social categories often evolves into socially constructed stereotypes that promote and reinforce hegemonic, or dominant, ideologies. In other words, the purpose of racial and ethnic categorization was established to affirm the high value placed on whiteness, and as a result, justify limited opportunities, access, and protection to those who are not white (Ladson-Billings, 1998).

Race and ethnicity are a foundational, historical and cultural abstraction of the U.S. formation. These very abstractions, or components, influence the ways in which people live in society and interact with each other, and thus contribute to defining a group's culture. Within cultures, and the creation of culture, power hierarchies were developed in the social and cultural institutions to express dominance over people based on sociohistorical constructs such as race, gender, social class, age, sexual orientation, and religious affiliation. Thus, if you were not white, male, upper class, able-bodied and of Protestant religion (Cunningham, 2011) you were relegated to the bottom of the respective power hierarchies. Acknowledging this social reality, sport has played a significant role for various social groups that include women and people of color. However, the representation, participation, and experiences of these two social groups are often marginalized due to power hierarchies and hegemonic ideologies that situate them as the "other."

The concept of the "other" is rooted in hegemonic ideologies and binary categorization that justify marginalization of people and groups. According to Collins (1986, 2000), binary categorizations are based on dichotomous oppositional differences, or more plainly, opposites. For example, male/female, white/black, and rich/poor are opposites and require the other to establish meaningfulness. As such, all racial groups categorized as non-white and females are thus "othered" (Collins, 2000; Crenshaw, 1993; Tate, 1997). The culminating effect of being identified as the "other" is to be placed on the margins of society, and in the context of sport these margins consist of (a) limited access, opportunity, and experiences as participants and administrators (Abney, 2007; Bruening, Armstrong, & Pastore, 2005; McDowell, 2009; McDowell & Cunningham, 2009), and (b) limited and stereotypical media coverage (Creedon, 1994; Duncan & Messner, 1998; Eastman & Billings, 2001; Kane & Creedon, 1994; van Sterkenburg & Knoppers, 2004).

INTERSECTIONALITY

So far, we have established that women and people of color have historically been identified as the "other," which situates them on the margins of society. In the context of sport and in the broader society, being placed on the margins often leaves women of color silenced and invisible. Being placed on the margins, or to exclude those who are deemed different, is an expression of social power, bias, and domination. There are historical and on-going contemporary practices of exclusion occurring in the sporting context. Often times, these exclusionary practices are explained and/ or framed in terms of a race-only issue or gender-only issue, thus rationalizing the experience based on one or the other. However, rationalizing issues in only one way can be problematic for people who embody more than one marginalized identity. As McCall (2005) stated, "Interest in intersectionality arose out of a critique of gender-based and race-based research for failing to account for lived experience at neglected points of intersection" (p. 1780). Therefore, there is a need to identify a way in which the experiences of women and people of color (to include those that identify as lesbian, gay, bisexual and transgender (LGBT) and "othered" groups) are understood based on their intersecting identities. One such theoretical framework that aims at addressing people who have been placed on the margins of society and excluded based on their social identity is intersectionality theory.

Intersectionality theory, or intersectionality, examines marginalized people and groups' identity intersections *simultaneously* within various institutions, or systems of domination, that promote oppression, discrimination, and social inequities. Intersectionality associates contemporary issues with postmodern theory, and thus recognizes that knowledge is socially constructed and that there are many truths. As such, Crenshaw (1993) contextualizes the experiences for women of color as (a) structural intersectionality, or overlapping structures of marginalization; (b) political intersectionality, or political practices of marginalization; and (c) representational intersectionality, or implicit and explicit representations of marginalization. These three constructs delineate how the experiences and representations of women of color are often based on stereotypes which trivialize experiences of discrimination and often situate their race and gender categorization as mutually exclusive.

Intersectionality as a critical theory is used to examine and illuminate "fairness and desires to understand, confront, and transform systems of exploitation and oppression in social life" (Coakley, 2004, p. 49). Thus, for the purpose of this chapter, Crenshaw's (1991, 1993) conceptualization of intersectionality serves as an important analytic tool for *identifying, analyzing,* and *transforming* the cultural, political, and structural dynamics of women of color within the institution of sport. Understanding the representation, participation, and experiences of women of color has the potential to not only transform their cause, but to transcend race and gender categorization and use sport as a platform to address the challenges of others who experience oppression, discrimination, and social injustices within and outside the context of sport.

PARTICIPATION AND REPRESENTATION OF THE "OTHER"

The ability of women of color to navigate the hegemonic terrain in society and sport are complex. These complexities arise from the historical and contemporary hegemonic power structures and political dynamics that situate women of color as the "other" based on their race, gender, and class, and other social categorizations (i.e., sexual orientation, religion, political affiliation). Utilizing intersectionality as a theoretical framework, or lens, is important when addressing historically marginalized people and/or groups in society and in sport. In the context of sport, the manifestation of power and political action can be found at the intersections of people's social life (i.e., race and ethnicity, gender and sex, religion, mental and physical ability, sexual orientation; see Carter-Francique & Regan, 2012).

According to scholars, African American women are viewed as the "most oppressed group in America" (Smith, 1992, p. 235) due to their social location and unique historical journey (Allen, 1990; Collins, 1990, 2000; Leonard, 1988). In the context of sport, African American women have also faced the most (in) visible journey as participants (Bruening, Armstrong, & Pastore, 2005; Carter, 2008; Carter & Hawkins, 2011; Wythecombe, 2011) and administrators (Abney, 2007; McDowell, 2009; McDowell & Cunningham, 2009), and have been marred by their omission and/or "re"presentation in the texts and media (Bruening, 2005; Gill, 2011). Therefore, African American women's prominent representation for women of color in the sporting context, and in this chapter, is not intended to devalue the contributions of other racial and ethnic women of color, but to understand how marginalization of people based on their race, gender, and class intersections are influenced by the perpetuation of hegemonic ideologies. In the following subsections, and when information is available on racial and ethnic others, we will illuminate their (a) participation in sport; (b) representation as leaders (e.g., administrators, coaches); and (c) representation in research, literature, and media.

Participation in Sport

Sport participation for girls and women is on the rise, as is that of girls and women of color. Arne Duncan's iteration on the impact Title IX has had on girls and women's sport participation; particularly at the college level, is significant. Examining the rates of participation since the inception of Title IX is important, but understanding when and where girls and women of color as youth, high school, college, and professional participants fit into these rates is of interest.

Youth and high school level. The National Council of Youth Sports' (NCYS) *Report on Trends and Participation in Organized Youth Sports* (2008) indicates that young girls are beginning to participate at a younger age in organized youth sport. Accordingly, they attribute a portion of the rise in participation to Title IX legislation (NCYS, 2008). Young girls of color, however, exhibit less interest than their male and white female counterparts. Sabo and Veliz (2008) conducted a nationwide study to measure the participation rates of girls and boys in exercise and organized team sports. The central focus of their investigation was on how the intersections among families, schools and communities are related to children's involvement and interest in athletics and physical activity. Sabo and Veliz reported the sport participation entrance rates for girls of color for ages six and younger (Black – 29%, Hispanic – 32%), seven through ten (Black – 51%, Hispanic – 47%), and eleven and older (Black – 20%, Hispanic – 21%). According to this data, Black and Hispanic girls' greatest point of entrance was between the ages of seven and ten compared to their white female counterparts that entered sport at a younger age and a higher rate (53% for age six and younger). Sabo and Veliz (2008) indicate that sport participation patterns of girls of color are influenced by each of the following: (a) economics (e.g., parental annual income, cost of the sport to include equipment and travel), (b) community resources (e.g., number of public parks, community-based athletic leagues), and (c) cultural values (e.g., gender traditions or religious beliefs).

In examining girls' participation rates, it is important to incorporate discussion of their athletic involvement, levels of physical activity, and parental perceptions of their child's sport participation (Sabo & Veliz, 2008). For the purpose of this chapter, understanding the athletic involvement rates for girls of color is significant. Sabo and Veliz (2008) provide disaggregate statistical rates for athletic involvement at three different levels of involvement including non-athlete (or not involved), moderately involved, and highly involved. The corresponding percentages of athletic participation rates for girls of color are, respectively, (a) Black girls – 36%, 47%, and 17%; (b) Hispanic girls – 36%, 50%, and 14%; and (c) Asian girls – 47%, 44%, and 9%. For white girls, the rates of involvement are 24%, 54%, and 22%, respectively. Therefore, for girls of color, Asians had the highest rate of "not being involved" in sport followed by Blacks and Hispanics. Conversely, Asian girls had the least rate of involvement at the "highly involved" level. The relevance of the statistical data for girls of color who are "highly involved" becomes more apparent when considering the level of family income.

Again, Sabo and Veliz (2008) provide disaggregate data which compare and contrast white children and children of color. Extracting girls of color that are "highly involved" in sport based on family income reveals the following percentages: 15% for $35,000 and lower, 16% for $35,001 to $50,000, 7% for $50,001 to $65,000, and 13% for $65,001 and higher. Reviewing the same income levels, white girls (e.g., 9%, 18%, 23%, 38%) and boys of color (e.g., 25%, 38%, 18%, 34%) each had higher rates of participation. Thus, while it is important to understand youth sport participation at the juncture of gender and race, providing further analysis based on the aforementioned constructs and their intersection with social class presents the multilevel operation of the "matrix of domination" in the context of sport (Collins, 2000). This notion is also better understood when correlating high school, college, and professional participation rates.

Ultimately, the aforementioned numbers are significant with regard to acknowledging the intersections of race, ethnicity, and class; but even more noteworthy are the implications with regard to the health and well-being for women and girls of color. Therefore, while it is beyond the scope of this chapter, sport *and* physical activity participation have been identified as modifiers to address and decrease percentages of greater social ills such as obesity, teenage pregnancy, and high school dropout rates for women of color (Women's Sports Foundation, 2011). Nevertheless, discerning how these distinctions and rates of participation manifest at the college level is also significant.

College level. At the collegiate level, patterns of participation based on race and gender become more apparent. Research conducted at the University of Central Florida provide an aggregate and disaggregate breakdown of sport participation in which women of color represent 28.6% of women compared to 70.6% of white women participants. More specifically, the disaggregate of women of color was 16.0% Black, 4.2% Hispanic, 0.4% American Indian/Alaskan Native, 2.4% Asian/Pacific Islander, 1.1% two or more races, and 5.2% represented women whom classified themselves as other (Lapchick, Hoff, et al., 2011). When examining women of color on sport teams, they are represented at varying percentages across all teams. However, examining the most prominent sport teams at the division I level, women of color represent 59.7%, 40.4%, and 22.5% in the sports of basketball, outdoor track and field, and softball, respectively (Lapchick, Hoff, et al., 2011). It must be noted that Black women have the greatest representation among women of color on all three sport teams with 51.0% in basketball, 29.1% in outdoor track and field, and a mere 7.7% in softball. These statistics are important as they provide a greater context on the transference of sport participation from the high school to the college level. For more detailed information across sports see the 1999–2000 – 2009–2010 NCAA Student-Athlete Ethnicity Report (NCAA, 2010). Based on these statistics, women of color are highly concentrated, or segregated (see Bebea, 2009), in the sports of basketball and track and field, and their involvement is reflective on the professional level.

Professional level. Examining the participation rates for women of color at the professional level, the numbers reveal greater opportunity limitations. This is consistent for all women but is most significant for women of color in certain sports. As indicated by the college statistical data, women of color (e.g., Black) are highly concentrated in the sports of basketball and track and field. For example, Lapchick, Florzak, and Gearlds' (2011) *Women's National Basketball Association (WNBA) Racial and Gender Report Card* revealed Black and Latina women comprise 69% and 3% of players respectively, compared to 21% of white females. In the sport of track and field, while no official reports have been compiled, reviewing the United States of America (USA) Track and Field website for athlete biographies and photos, one can discern that Black women are greatly represented as participants (USA Track and Field, n.d.).

The statistical data on the participation rates for women of color, again, is significant. Thus, while the data and organizations presented are by no means an exhaustive list, it is our hope to provide an example of the realities of where women of color are competing at the professional level. In addition, the data presented (youth through professional) reveal patterns based on the intersection of gender, race, social class, as well as, access and opportunity in sport. Connections can be discerned from these statistics, but as explicated by Sabo and Veliz (2008), the data should be contextualized based on societal constraints (e.g., school and community resources) and cultural dynamics (i.e., gender traditions, religious beliefs). Likewise, one should consider how societal constraints and cultural dynamics affect women of color's ability to obtain access to leadership positions in the sporting context.

Again, each culture valuation of sport is different and this can contribute to the initial interest to participate as well as to continue sport beyond high school and college. For example, in the African American community, the notion of physical activity and sport participation is valued and welcomed for both males *and* females (Hanks, 1979; Smith, 2000). As Sheldon, Jayaratne, and Petty (2007) stated, "Athleticism is a culturally valued behavior, and a belief in an inherent race difference in this characteristic, unlike other human characteristics that have been discussed in the scientific and public spheres (e.g., intelligence, violence), reflects positively on Blacks" (p. 45). Moreover, they suggest that "the belief in a genetic race difference in athleticism may function to sustain racist ideologies by implying the inferiority of Blacks' intelligence and work ethic" (p. 32). This observation has the potential to contribute to power dynamics, and access and opportunities for Black women and other women of color as leaders in sport.

Representation as Sport Leaders

Power dynamics in sports are not equal and this is evident through the lack of minority coaches, owners, and executives. The Institute for Diversity and Ethics in Sports (TIDES) provide racial and gender statistics on the hiring practices within top sport organizations to include, but not limited to, NCAA institutions, the Women's National Basketball Association (WNBA), and the Associated Press (AP). For example, the 2010 *Racial and Gender Report Card on College Sport* also provides statistics for administrators (e.g., conference commissioner, athletic director, senior women administrator), coaches (i.e., head coach, assistant coach), and staff (i.e., academic advisor, sport information director) (Lapchick, Hoff, et al., 2011). The aggregated statistical data reveals that women of color as a collective group represent a small percentage of administrators and staff at the division I level when compared to white men and white women; and thus, received a grade of B for race and B for gender (see table 1). Conversely, when extracting statistical data from the *Associated Press Sports Editors Racial and Gender Report Card (*Lapchick et al., 2011), women of color in the media represent a significantly smaller percentage of administrators and staff, receiving a grade of C+ for race and F for gender (see table 2). The race and gender demographics and resultant grades of the two organizations indicate that one organization is doing well and the other is doing poorly. But when the statistical data is disaggregated for women of color, to include Black, Hispanic, Asian, Native American and other women of color, the disproportionality becomes readily apparent when compared to white men and white women.

In addition to these report cards, Lapchick and his colleagues have analyzed the representation of racial and gender minorities compared to whites (e.g., men and women) in other sport organizations such as Major League Soccer (MLS), Major League Baseball (MLB), the National Football League (NFL), the National

Table 1. 2008–2009 College Professional Administration by Position*

	White		Black		Asian		Hispanic		Native American		Other Minority		Totals for Women of Color
	Men	Women	Men	Women	Men	Women	Men	Women	Men	Women	Men	Women	Women of Color
Academic Advisor/Counselor	25.4	47.6	10.7	10.2	0.3	0.8	1.0	1.5	0.0	0.1	1.1	1.4	14
Compliance Coordinator/Office	42.0	44.3	3.6	5.3	0.2	0.5	0.9	2.5	0.0	0.0	0.2	0.6	8.9
Fundraiser/Development Manager	58.3	31.8	5.1	1.7	0.3	0.6	0.8	0.8	0.0	0.0	0.7	0.1	3.2
Life Skills Coordinator	16.6	60.6	8.3	11.4	0.0	0.0	0.7	1.4	0.0	0.0	0.3	0.7	13.5
Promotions/Marketing Manager	59.5	31.0	3.5	1.8	0.9	0.4	0.7	0.7	0.0	0.0	0.9	0.6	3.5
Sport Information Director	85.1	10.3	1.1	0.3	1.1	0.3	1.6	0.3	0.0	0.0	0.0	0.0	0.9
Strength Coaches	74.0	10.7	10.3	1.1	0.8	0.1	1.3	0.2	0.1	0.0	1.0	0.2	1.6
Senior Women's Administrator	0.0	85.1	0.0	10.1	0.0	1.0	0.0	2.3	0.0	1.0	0.0	0.5	14.9

*Data extracted from the Racial and Gender Report Card: College Sport (Lapchick et al., 2011).

Table 2. 2010–2011 Associated Press Sports Editors Racial and Gender Report Card**

| | White | | Black | | Asian | | Hispanic | | Other Minority | | Totals for Women of Color |
	Men %	Women %	Men %	Women %	Men %	Women %	Men %	Women %	Men %	Women %	Women of Color
Sports Editors	90.58	6.28	1.35	0.00	.45	0.00	1.35	0.00	0.00	0.00	0
Assistant Sports Editors	77.95	7.35	5.25	1.57	1.57	1.05	3.94	0.26	0.79	0.26	3.14
Columnists	76.80	8.84	10.22	1.10	1.38	0.00	1.38	0.00	0.28	0.00	1.1
Reporters	76.81	8.83	6.78	1.17	1.60	0.15	3.57	0.44	0.66	0.00	1.76
Copy Editors/ Designers	76.14	13.98	2.13	1.82	2.13	0.30	3.04	0.00	0.46	0.17	2.29
Entire Staff Totals	77.83	9.58	5.58	1.27	1.60	0.27	3.07	0.23	0.53	0.03	1.8

**2010 Data has been extracted from the Total APSE Staff Data

Basketball Association (NBA), and the WNBA (TIDES, n.d.). While these report cards do not provide the disaggregate data for the race-gender element, Lapchick and his colleagues do provide an assessment of the progress being made on race and gender diversity representation and diversity efforts over the years by each of these organizations. The aforementioned organizations have the following grades for race and gender, respectively: MLS = A/C+, MLB = A/B, NFL = A/C, NBA = A+/A-, WNBA = A+/A (Lapchick, et al., 2011).

Some scholars have controversially contended that the lack of racial minorities in high-ranking sport positions has been due to racial stereotypes related to "intelligence" (e.g., African American male athletes). Abney (1988, 2007) denotes that cultural stereotypes associated with intelligence may limit Black women's ability to obtain leadership positions (i.e., coaches, athletic administrators). Concomitantly, "othered" groups, including women of color, men of color, and LGBT persons may experience similar barriers obtaining leadership positions within sport organizations. These barriers include (a) societal attitudes toward women and racial minorities (e.g., not trustworthy, intelligence), (b) stereotypes (e.g., lazy, angry), (c) poor media images (e.g., violent, non-professional), (d) structural barriers (e.g., access to formal and informal networks), (e) dead-end positions and the glass ceiling effect, (f) politics, (g) limited career resources and networks, (h) absence of role models and mentors, (i) stacking, and (j) position clustering (e.g., assistant coach) (Abney, 2007). Again, the notion of intersectionality and experiential oppression based on gender, race, ethnicity, and social class each play a role for women of color. Due to the sociohistorical and sociocultural barriers, limited access and limited opportunities ultimately limit the career development for women of color. Thus, women of color remain on the margins with respect to athletic participation, leadership, and mass media representation in the context of sport.

INFLUENCE OF DOMINANT IDEOLOGIES

While the rates of participation and administrative representation provide a statistical illustration for women of color in the sporting context, the statistics do not provide an understanding of their experiences in the sporting context. Understanding the nature of the experiences (i.e., feelings, treatment) and the media's characterization of women of color in the sporting context is important as they are often reflective of their marginalization in the greater society. Again, sport is a microcosm of society (Eitzen & Sage, 2009); thus, dominant ideologies and cultural hierarchies in society are often reaffirmed in the sporting context leaving women of color marginalized, stereotyped, and silenced (Bruening, 2005). This section will explore how the ideologies of intelligence, disparity of wages, femininity versus athleticism, and masculinity of sport each play a role with women of color as it relates to the power dynamics in sport.

The statistical underrepresentation of racial, ethnic, and gender minorities is significant when discussing the marginalized experiences of these groups. Thus, the underrepresentation of women of color as participants at the aforementioned levels of play, as representatives in media, and representatives in college and professional sport organizations warrants the need to understand their experiences within the respective institutions. For instance, upon receiving positions of leadership, African American women typically face marginalization of their leadership styles, organizational roles (McDowell, 2009), and are even characterized unfavorably or subjectively by the media (Azzarito & Harrison, 2008; Gill, 2011). The controversial comments made during the 2007 television broadcast of *The Imus in the Morning Show* about the Rutgers women's basketball team is one such example. On April 4, 2007, radio host Don Imus, executive producer Buddy McGuirk, and sports announcer Sid Rosenberg all made racially demeaning comments about the Rutgers women's basketball team during the broadcast of *The Imus in the Morning Show*. When reviewing the national basketball championship game between the University of Tennessee and Rutgers University, Don Imus was quoted as stating:

> That's some rough girls from Rutgers. Man, they got tattoos....That's some nappy-headed hos there. I'm gonna tell you that now, man, that's some–woo. And the girls from Tennessee, they all look cute, you know, so, like–kinda like–I don't know. (Media Matters, 2007, para 2)

Additionally, Buddy McGuirk was quoted as stating "A Spike Lee thing.... The Jigaboos vs. the Wannabes – that movie that he had" (Media Matters, 2007, para 2). Last, Sid Rosenberg was quoted as stating "It was a tough watch. The more I look at Rutgers, they look exactly like the Toronto Raptors" (Media Matters, 2007, para 2).

Although the eight African-American and two white Rutgers college athletes did not defeat the Tennessee Lady Volunteers in the DI NCAA national basketball championship, each were engulfed by the media frenzy surrounding the comments and sadly their athletic abilities remained invisible to the media. This incident may seem to be an isolated event only impacting women of color; however, it expressively shows how subjectivity can impact participation in sport. Moreover, Don Imus' comments may appear trivial to some due to his position as a "shock" jock; however, research shows that the media holds a powerful key in influencing the portrayal and adorations of minorities in sport (Coakley, 2004). An example of this perception can be viewed in the media portrayal of tennis champion Serena Williams.

Ranked number one in the U.S. by the Women's Tennis Association (WTA) in 2013, media attention on Serena Williams typically focuses on her physique and less on her athletic ability (Coleman-Bell, 2006). The media's depiction of her being "too curvy" sends a disparaging message to young women of color that their body type is not accepted in the world of sports and should be discussed in the media. The emphasis placed on Williams' clothes, attitude (on and off the court), hair style, and language demonstrate how women of color are treated differently and often compared to their white female counterparts. This example also lends itself to explaining the challenge women of color face with the cultural conflict of femininity versus athleticism, which will be discussed later in this section.

Intelligence

The concept of intelligence also plays a role in the perception of and experiences for women of color. For example, as Sheldon, Jayaratne, and Petty (2007) stated, "the belief in a genetic race difference in athleticism may function to sustain racist ideologies by implying the inferiority of Blacks' intelligence and work ethic" (p. 33). This notion of genetics was supported through the controversial book, *The Bell Curve*, which examined intelligence between races. In this book, Richard Herrnstein and Charles Murray (1994) argued that human intelligence is influenced by both inherited and environmental factors. These factors consequently impact a person's job performance, socioeconomic status, and educational attainment, hypothesizing that genes and environment directly correlate with racial differences. Due to this link between race and intelligence, controversy still surrounds this book and its claims regarding racial hierarchy, the dominance of whites, and the inferiority of people of color.

The notion of intellectual inferiority also translates into the inferiority of racial and ethnic others in leadership positions. Juxtapose this notion to that of athletic superiority, as racial and ethnic others are often viewed as superior with physical skills and ability (Azzarito & Harrison, 2008; Sheldon, Jayaratne, & Petty, 2007). The perception of athletic superiority of people of color was captured in the 2007 study conducted by Sheldon, Jayaratne, and Petty. They found that 74% of men and 65% of women perceived African Americans as genetically superior athletes. In addition, 33% of the men and 26% of the women stated that genes explained much, if not all, of the difference between whites and Blacks in athleticism. Hence, racial and ethnic "others," or minority, athletes are "classified" as superior athletes, which is confirmed with their underrepresentation or lack of representation in power positions in sport. Furthermore, the classification as superior athletes has been articulated using negative condemnations. Examples can be found in the media coverage of racial and ethnic minority and female athletes (Billings & Eastman, 2002). Moreover, the media habitually portrays racial and ethnic minority athletes using a narrow view typically encompassing these "genetic" ideologies of being superior athletes (Billings & Eastman, 2002).

Disparity of Wages

Disparity of wages, or pay gap, of women has been a controversial topic in the U.S. for some time. The American Association of University Women (AAWU) defines pay gap as "the difference in men's and women's typical earnings, usually reported as either the earnings ratio between men and women" (2013, p. 5). The U.S. governmental agencies that report wage statistics include the Department of Labor, Department of Education, Bureau on Labor Statistics, and the Census Bureau. Currently there is not a sporting agency that solely reports sports-based statistics about wages, but some scholars and organizations have tackled this subject and provided helpful data to support this issue. In 1996, the Women's Sports Foundation and Evian reported that although opportunities for women in sport have increased, there remains a disparity in prize winnings for women when compared to men. More specifically, they found that women only net 50% of what their male counterparts net in prize winnings. Additionally, they reported that Division I (DI) head coaches for a women's team on an average earn $850,400 whereas head coaches for men's teams average $1,783,100 in earnings. In 2007, the Women's Sports Foundation published an article titled *"Pay Inequities in Sport"* and reported that male athletes receive 55% of college athletic scholarships while females only receive 45%. Flake, Dufur and Moore (2013) examined publically accessible data for professional tennis players ranked in the top 100 at the end of the 2009 season to determine to what extent a pay gap exists between men and women. The researchers found that the median earnings, both in 2009 and over a player's career, were significantly higher for men than for women. While prize money is now equal in prestigious tournaments (e.g., Grand Slam events), prize money is significantly lower for women participating in less publicized tournaments.

Femininity versus Athleticism

Racial and ethnic cultural dynamics and their relationship with dominant gender norms have the potential to influence the patterns of sport participation among women of color (Azzarito & Harrison, 2008; Dworkin & Messner, 2002; Hall, 1988; Sheldon, Jayaratne, & Petty, 2007). The conflict between femininity versus athleticism can be described as the female/athlete paradox (Krane, Choi, Baird, Aimar, & Kauer, 2004). The paradox defines the struggle of attempting to maintain the mental and physical characteristics of what society has labeled as the essential elements of being a woman, or the hegemonic feminine ideal, while attempting to increase their hegemonic masculinity to achieve athletic superiority (Krane et al., 2004). Moreover, the female/athlete paradox involves the struggle women face with attempting to balance femininity versus athleticism.

Azzarito and Harrison (2008) indicated that "race, like gender and class, shapes young people's ways of thinking about athleticism, sport, and society and their performance of sporting bodies" (p. 360). Thus, athleticism can be defined as culturally-based values and behaviors rooted in a person's racial and ethnic background; and not a biological or trait-based characteristic (Sheldon, Jayartne, & Petty, 2007). Hence, athleticism typically reflects positively on Blacks more specifically due to their classification of being physical and naturally superior athletes.

In 2008, findings from Azzarito and Harrison's study supported this theory of Blacks being categorized as genetically superior athletes. The purpose of their study was to examine high school students' perceptions of race and genetics in physical education. The researchers conducted interviews and observed two high school physical education classes. In total, 28 high school students and two physical education teachers were interviewed. The interview questions focused on the students' participation in physical education activity in and out of the classroom, the overrepresentation of Black people in certain sports, and the film and common phrase – 'white men can't jump' and the 'natural black athlete.' Azzarito and Harrison found that white boys were complicit with the notion of Black physical superiority, while the girls, in general, rejected the black genetic edge discourse, adopting a liberal humanistic position (Azzarito & Harrison, 2008). In contrast, Black boys held an "ambiguous position within dominant discourses of race and natural athleticism" (p. 347) which was based on the idea that "natural" athleticism meant more than physical superiority, but also includes the mental drive and fortitude to succeed at sport.

The aforementioned debate and study demonstrates the dramatic difference in ideology between female and male perceptions of overall experience and identity in sport. Consequently, this also exemplifies the characterization and subjectivity that impact women of color, as well as lends itself to explain how the hegemonic concept of "masculinity" contributes to sport.

Masculinity of Sport

As stated previously in this chapter, the female/athlete paradox signifies the struggle of women to balance their femininity and athleticism. Moreover, female athletes are forced to live in two worlds – their sport world, which expects aggressiveness and masculine traits, and the Western driven culture, which expects femininity (Krane et al., 2004). Bordo (1993) defines femininity as "a socially constructed standard for women's appearance, demeanor, and values" (as cited in Krane et al., 2004, p. 316). Female athletes are expected to successfully balance both worlds, but tragically when this balance is not achieved and masculine traits are more apparent these women suffer negative connotations. The masculine references made by Don Imus and his colleagues about the Black female athletes at Rutgers (*"That's some rough girls from Rutgers. Man, they got tattoos.... That's some nappy-headed hos there.* Media Matters, 2007*)* furthered this notion of the complexity surrounding the female/athlete paradox. As a woman, if you show exemplary athletic skills, those attributes might be perceived as attempting to be masculine and therefore viewed as negative due to the loss of female characteristics. Through examples like this, one can hypothesize that the subjectivity of being too masculine is a typical label placed upon Black female athletes. With masculinity being linked to superiority in athleticism, this notion could even be construed as a positive characterization, but when this characterization is attached to the lesbian label, a negative aura traditionally follows African American female athletes. The case *of Jennifer E. Harris v. Maureen T. Portland and Pennsylvania State University* further explains this theory.

In this case, Harris, an African American athlete was dismissed from the Pennsylvania State University (PSU) women's basketball team by head coach Maureen T. Portland due to her alleged defiance against Portland's anti-gay team policies. Portland, who publicly stated she would not allow any lesbian players on her team, harassed Harris privately and publicly for being too masculine. Due to Harris' appearance, she was labeled a lesbian by the coach and was deemed to be a "bad influence" on the team. Harris was also racially discriminated against by the coach. Along with two of her teammates who were also African American, Harris, who led the team in points and had not broken any PSU, NCAA, or conference rules was released from the team. As a result of her dismissal, all returning players from the 2004–2005 season were white. Similar to the Rutgers women's basketball team, the media played a significant role in skewing the focus of this case. The media centered on Harris' sexuality rather than the racial and homophobic discrimination demonstrated by coach Portland. This case reaffirms Crenshaw's (1991) notion of intersectionality, and the either/or consequences to having more than one subordinate characteristic.

TRANSFORMING VALUE OF POLICIES AND PRACTICES

Although Title IX recently turned 40 years old, the struggle of building and providing equity in sports is far from over. Hattery (2012) suggests Title IX has impacted women's sports in many different ways. After the passing of the law, women's athletic organizations like the Association of Intercollegiate Athletics for Women (AIAW) became obsolete and organizations like the NCAA became the premier organization for sport catering to both men's and women's sports. Title IX also has significantly impacted participation and leadership opportunities for women of color. While Black females hold a huge presence in DI basketball as athletes, this existence is not mirrored in coaching positions.

More specifically, white women in DI basketball hold 166 coaching positions whereas Black women hold 35 DI basketball coaching positions (Hattery, 2012). To better understand the negative impact experienced by women of color due to Title IX, Drago (2005) reported that prior to the enactment of Title IX, women held 90% of the collegiate coaching positions in women's sports and after 1972 when the law was passed this percentage radically dropped. In 2005, women only held 44% of the collegiate coaching positions in women sports (as cited in Acosta & Carpenter, 2004). Moreover, once Title IX was enacted, opportunities for participation and employment in women's sports grew tremendously. Consequently, this growth encouraged not only females to coach women's sports, but also men. Historically, sport opportunities for women (employment and participation) were typically volunteer or part-time positions, but the passing of Title IX changed this volunteer culture to full-time employment opportunities (Drago, 2005). Hence the change from volunteer to full-time opportunities made sport positions for women's sport desirable not only to women, but also to men. This greatly impacted coaching opportunities for women, and unfortunately almost demolished the opportunities for women of color who historically have had less athletic employment opportunities than their white female counterparts as represented in the above DI basketball example.

Title IX is not the only legislation impacting minority women in sport. There are numerous laws and policies that impact employment and participation in sport contexts. One commonality of these laws and policies is the lack of coherent principles exemplified by the intersection of gender equity with racial justice (Mathewson, 1996). Historically, the court system uses a single axis framework[1] to examine discrimination in cases. This is a controversial practice because it allows the court to resolve cases and make decisions without delineating the cultural implications surrounding the case as it relates to the experiences of women of color (i.e., intersecting oppressions). Moreover, Crenshaw (1989) argues that the single axis approach excludes the experience of Black women. For instance, the *Equity in the Athletics Disclosure Act* is an example of a single axis approach because it requires institutions to disclose data regarding financial statistics along gender lines, but not other identity lines. On the other hand, the *Women's Educational Equity Act* employs a multidimensional approach because it focuses on women who suffer from multiple forms of discrimination (e.g., sex, race, disability, age) (Mathewson, 1996).

Civil Rights Act of 1964

According to Collins (2000), some of the same laws used to protect minorities from discrimination have been used against them. The concept of "color-blindness" is a reformulated discrimination concept that encompasses treating all people equally and ignoring their surface-level characteristics (i.e., skin color, sex, language), sociocultural characteristics and sociohistorical contexts, and the structural dynamics which marginalize their daily experiences (Collins, 2000). The ideology of color-blindness could have major implications on the sports world. More specifically, it could impact employment opportunities and salaries. As an example, the Civil Rights Act of 1964 prohibits discrimination on the basis of race, color, religion, sex or national origin, but a sport organization that employs a color-blind hiring policy could possibly be made up of leadership and coaches that were not diverse. Consequently, the organization's policies, regulations, and structure would be representative of this limited view and only reflect the ideology of the people within the organization.

CHAPTER SUMMARY

In this chapter, we proposed to explain the relationship between race, ethnicity, and gender in the context of sport. In doing so, we defined race and ethnicity and explained how culture manifests based on racial categorization and ethnic identification. This clarification provided greater insight to the role of sport within racial and ethnic cultures that have been marginalized, or "othered," in the American context. Next, we explained the theoretical framework of intersectionality. Utilizing intersectionality, the remainder of the chapter reflects the various ways that the intersecting categorizations of race, ethnicity, and gender impact women of color in sport. The participation rates and patterns, representation of college and professional sports leaders, and media portrayals all reflect how women of color are marginalized. Despite these statistics and experiences, legislation, legislative practices, and organizations in sport and the greater society are taking steps to understand and acknowledge the barriers and challenges faced by women of color in sport.

NOTE

[1] Single axis framework, defined by American based law, requires a claimant to identify the category to which they claim protection from discrimination (Sargeant, 2011); therefore, the single axis framework further expresses this idea of unjust discrimination due to this classification.

REFERENCES

Abney, R. (1988). The effects of role models and mentors on career patterns of Black women coaches and athletic administrators in historically Black and historically white institutions of higher education. *Unpublished doctoral dissertation*, University of Iowa.

Abney, R. (2007). African American women in intercollegiate coaching and athletic administration: Unequal access. In D. Brooks & R. Althouse (Eds.), *Diversity and social justice in college sport: Sport management and the student athlete* (pp. 51–75). Morgantown, WV: Fitness Information Technology, Inc.

Acosta, R. V., & Carpenter, L. J. (2012). *Women in Intercollegiate Sport: A Longitudinal National Study – Thirty-five year update*. Retrieved March 3, 2013, from http://acostacarpenter.org/AcostaCarpenter2012.pdf

Allen, W. (1990). Family roles, occupational statuses and achievement orientations among Black women in the United States. In M. R. Malson, E. Mudimbe-Boyi, J. Barr, & M. Wyer (Eds.), *Black women in America: Social science perspectives* (pp. 79–96). Chicago, IL: The University of Chicago Press.

American Association of Women of University Women (2013). *The Simple Truth about the Gender Pay Gap*. Retrieved April 22, 2013 from, http://www.aauw.org/files/2013/02/The-Simple-Truth-2013.pdf

Azzarito, L., & Harrison, L. (2008). White men can't jump:' Race, gender and natural athleticism. *International Review for the Sociology of Sport, 43*(4), 347–364.

Bebea, I. (2009 February). Female athletes of color. *The Network Journal: Black Professionals and Small Business News*. Retrieved from http://www.tnj.com/%20female-athletes-of%20-olor

Billings, A. C., & Eastman, S. T. (2002). Selective representation of gender, ethnicity, and nationality in American television coverage of the 2000 summer Olympics. *International Review for the Sociology of Sport, 37* (3–4), 351–370.

Bordo, S. (1993). *Unbearable weight: Feminism, Western culture, and the body*. Berkeley: University of California Press.

Bruening, J. (2005). Gender and racial analysis in sport: Are all the women white and all the Blacks men? *Quest, 57,* 340–359.

Bruening, J., Armstrong, K., & Pastore, D. (2005). Listening to the voices: The experiences of African American female student-athletes. *Research Quarterly for Exercise and Sport, 76*(1), 82–100.

Carter, A. F. (2008). Negotiation identities: Examining African American female collegiate athlete experiences in predominantly white institutions. *Unpublished Dissertation,* University of Georgia.

Carter, A. R., & Hawkins, B. J. (2011). Coping strategies among African American female collegiate athletes' in the predominantly white institution. In K. Hylton, A. Pilkington, P. Warmington, & S. Housee (Eds.), *Atlantic crossings: International dialogues in critical race theory* (pp. 61–92). Birmingham, United Kingdom: Sociology, Anthropology, Politics (C-SAP), The Higher Education Academy Network.

Carter-Francique, A. R., & Reagan, M. (2012). Power and politics. In G. B. Cunningham & J. N. Singer (Eds.), *Sociology of sport and physical activity* (2nd ed., pp. 373–396). College Station, TX: Center for Sport Management Research and Education.

Coakley, J. (2004). *Sports in society: Issues and controversies* (8th ed.). Boston, MA: McGraw-Hill.

Coleman-Bell, R. (2006) Droppin' it like it's hot: The sporting body of Serena Williams. In S. Holmes & S. Redmond (Eds.), *Framing celebrity: New directions in celebrity culture*. New York: Routledge.

Collins, P. (1986). Learning from the outsider within: The sociological significance of Black feminist thought. *Social Problems, 33*(6), S14–S31.

Collins, P. (1990). *Black feminist thought: Knowledge, consciousness and the politics of empowerment*. Boston, MA: Unwin Hyman.

Collins, P. (2000). *Black feminist thought: Knowledge, consciousness, and the politics of empowerment* (2nd ed.). New York: Routledge.

Creedon, P. J. (Ed.) (1994). *Women, media, and sport: Challenging gender values*. Thousand Oaks, CA: Sage Publications.

Crenshaw, K. (1989). Demarginalizing the intersection of race and sex: A Black feminist critique of antidiscrimination doctrine, feminist theory, and antiracist politics. *University of Chicago Legal Forum, 139–167.*

Crenshaw, K. (1991). Mapping the margins: Intersectionality, identity politics, and violence against women of color. *Stanford Law Review, 43*(6), 1241–1299.

Crenshaw, K. (1993) 'Beyond racism and misogyny.' In M. Matsuda, C. Lawrence & K. Crenshaw (Eds.), *Words that wound*. Boulder, CO: Westview Press.

Cunningham, G. B. (2011). *Diversity in sport organizations* (2nd ed.). Scottsdale, AZ: Holcomb Hathaway Publishers.

Drago, R., Hennighausen, L. Rogers, J. Vescio, T., & Stauffer, K. D. (2005, August 19). *Final report for CAGE: The coaching and gender equity project*. Retrieved April 23, 2013 from http://lsir.la.psu.edu/ workfam/CAGE.htm

Duncan, M. C., & Messner, M. A. (1998). The media image of sport and gender. In L. Wenner (Ed.), *MediaSport* (pp. 170–185). London: Routledge.

Dworkin, S. L., & Messner, M. A. (2002). Just do … what? Sport, bodies, gender*. In S. Scranton & A. Flintoff (Eds.), *Gender and sport: A reader* (pp. 17–29). London: Routledge.

Eastman, S. T., & Billings, A. C. (1999) 'Gender parity in the Olympics: Hyping women athletes, favoring men athletes.' *Journal of Sports and Social Issues, 23*(2), 140–70.

Eastman, S. T., & Billings, A. C. (2001). Biased voices of sports: Racial and gender stereotyping in college basketball announcing. *Howard Journal of Communications, 12*(4), 183–201.

Eitzen, S., & Sage, G. (2009). *Sociology of North American sport* (8th ed.). Boulder, CO: Paradigm Publishers.

Flake, C., Dufur, M., & Moore, E. (2013). Advantage men: The sex pay gap in professional tennis. *International Review for the Sociology of Sport, 48*, 366–376.

Gill, E. (2011) Rutgers women's basketball & Don Imus controversy (RUIMUS): Privilege, new racism, and the implications for sport management. *Journal of Sport Management, 25*, 188–130.

Hanks, M. (1979). Race, sexual status, and athletics in the process of educational achievement. *Social Science Quarterly, 60*, 482–496.

Hattery, A. J. (2012). *They play like girls: Gender and race (In) equity in NCAA sports*. Retrieved March 3, 2013 from, http://lawpolicyjournal.law.wfu.edu/files/2012/05/Vol.2-1-Article-Hattery.pdf

Herrnstein, R., & Murray, C. (1994). *The bell curve*. New York: The Free Press.

Kane, M. J., & Creedon, P. J. (1994). The media's role in accommodating and resisting stereotyped images of women in sport. In P. J. Creedon (ed.), *Women, media, and sport: Challenging gender values* (pp. 28–44). Thousand Oaks, CA: Sage Publications, Inc.

Krane, V., Choi, P. Y. L., Baird, S. M., Aimar, C. M., & Kauer, K. J. (2004). Living the paradox: Female athletes negotiate femininity and muscularity. *Sex Roles, 50*, 315–329.

Ladson-Billings, G. (1998). Just what is critical race theory doing in a nice field like education? *Qualitative Studies in Education, 11*(1), 7–24.

Lapchick, R., Aristeguieta, F., Bragg, D., Clark, W., Cloud, C., Florzak, A., Frazier, D., Gearlds, A., Kuhn, M., Lilly, A., Record, T., Sarpy, C., Schulz, E., Spiak, & Vinson, M. (2011). The complete racial and gender report card. The Institute for Diversity and Ethics in Sport with the DeVos Sport Business Management Program in the College of Business of the University of Central Florida. Retrieved from http://dl.dropbox.com/u/11322904/ RGRC/ 2011_RGRC_FINAL.pdf

Lapchick, R., Florzak, A., Gearlds, A. (2011). The 2011 Women's National Basketball Association Racial and Gender Reports Card. Retrieved from http://web.bus.ucf.edu/documents/sport/ WNBA_RGRC_ FINAL.pdf

Lapchick, R., Hoff, B., & Kaiser, C. (2011, March 3). *The 2010 Racial and gender report card: College Sport*. The Institute for Diversity and Ethics in Sport, University of Central Florida: Orlando, Florida.

Lapchick, R., Moss, A., Russell, C., & Scearce, R. (2011). The 2010–11 Associated press sports editors racial and gender report card. Retrieved from: http://web.bus.ucf.edu/documents/sport/2011_ APSE_ RGRC_FINAL.pdf

Leonard, W. (1988). *A sociological perspective of sport* (3rd ed.). New York: Macmillan.

Mathewson, A. D. (1996). Black Women and gender equity and the function at the junction. *Marquette Sports Law Journal, 6*(2), 239–266.

McCall, L. (2005, Spring). The complexity of intersectionality. *The University of Chicago Press, 30*(3), 1771–1800.

McDonald, M. G. (2005). Mapping whiteness and sport: An introduction. *Sociology of Sport Journal, 22,* 245–255.

McDowell, J. (2009). What can we learn from ADs who are Black females? *Women in Higher Education, 18* (5), 19–20.

McDowell, J., & Cunningham, G. B. (2009). Personal, social, and organizational factors that influence black female athletic administrators' identity negotiation. *Quest, 61,* 202–222.

Media Matters. (2007). *Imus called women's basketball team "nappy-headed hos".* Retrieved on March 15, 2013, from www.mediamatters.org.

National Collegiate Athletic Association (2010). 1999–2000 – 2009–10 NCAA Student-Athlete Ethnicity Report. *NCAA.* Retrieved from http://www.ncaapublications.com/ product downloads/SAEREP11. pdf

National Council of Youth Sports (2008). *Report on trends and participation in organized youth sports: Market research report.* Retrieved from http://www.ncys.org/pdfs/2008/2008-ncys-market-research-report.pdf

Sabo, D., & Veliz, P. (2008, October). Go out and play: Youth sports in America. Retrieved from http://www.womenssportsfoundation.org/home/research/articles-and-reports/mental-and-physical-health/go-out-and-play

Sargeant, M. (2011). *Age discrimination and diversity.* New York: Cambridge University Press.

Sheldon, J. P., Jayaratne, T. E., & Petty, E. M. (2007, September). White Americans' genetic explanations for a perceived race difference in athleticism: The relation to prejudice toward and stereotyping of blacks. *Athletic Insight: The Online Journal of Sport Psychology, 9*(3).

Smedley, A. (1999). *Race in North America: Origin and evolution of worldview* (2nd ed.). Boulder, CO: Westview Press.

Smith, Y. (1992). Women of color in society and sport. *Quest, 44*(2), 228–250.

Smith, Y. (2000). Sociocultural influences of African American elite sportswomen. In D. Brooks & R. Althouse (Eds.), *Racism in college athletics: The African American athlete experience,* (2nd ed., pp. 173–197). Morgantown, WV: Fitness Information Technology, Inc.

Tate, W. (1997). Critical race theory and education: History, theory, and implications. *Review of Research in Education, 22,* 195–247.

The Institute for Diversity and Ethics (TIDES) (n.d.). The racial and gender report card. *University of Central Florida: DeVos Sport Business Management.* Retrieved from http://web.bus.ucf.edu/ sportbusiness/?page=1445

United States of American Track and Field (n.d.). Athlete bios: Archived bios. *USA Track and Field.* Retrieved from http://www.usatf.org/Athlete-Bios/Archive.aspx

U.S. Department of Education (2012, June 20). Remarks of the U.S. Secretary of Education Arne Duncan on the 40 anniversary of Title IX. *The White House.* Retrieved from http://www.ed.gov/news/ speeches/remarks-us-secretary-education-arne-duncan-40th-anniversary-title-ix

van Sterkenburg, J., & Knoppers, A. (2004). Dominant discourses about race/ethnicity and gender in sport practice and performance. *International Review for the Sociology of Sport, 39*(3), 301–321.

Women's Sport Foundation (2007, March). Pay Inequity in Athletics. Retrieved April 22, 2013, from http://www.womenssportsfoundation.org/home/research/articles-and-reports/equity-issues/pay-inequity

Women's Sports Foundation (1996) Evian pay Equity Study: 1996. Retrieved April 22, 2013, from http://www.womenssportsfoundation.org/home/research/articles-and-reports/equity-issues/evian-pay-equity-study-1996

Withycombe, J. L. (2011). Intersecting selves: African American female athletes' experiences of sport. *Sociology of Sport Journal, 28*(4)

AFFILIATIONS

Akilah R. Carter-Francique, PhD
Department of Health and Kinesiology
Texas A&M University

Courtney L. Flowers, PhD
Department of Health, Physical Education and Sports Studies
University of West Georgia

THERESA A. WALTON

6. FRAMING TITLE IX

Conceptual Metaphors at Work

INTRODUCTION

The passage of Title IX of the Education Amendments of 1972 was a pivotal moment in the history of women in education. Yet, rather than focus on the dramatic expansion in educational opportunities for women, public discourse over the last four decades deals almost exclusively with the profound influence of Title IX on scholastic athletics. Title IX and athletics are intrinsically linked in the public imagination.

Title IX can be considered one of the most successful federal civil rights laws, when considering its impact on its purpose – gender equity in education. In 1970, women earned 1% of dental, 8.4% of medical, 5.4% of law, and 14% of doctoral degrees. Most colleges and universities had higher admissions standards for women and quota limits on the number of women allowed in professional degree programs. In 2009, women earned 46.4% of dental, 48.9% of medical, 45.8% of law, and 52% of doctoral degrees (US Census, 2012). Immediately after the passage of Title IX, universities and colleges changed their admissions standards and policies and the impact was swift.

However, athletics proved unique. First, sport is gender segregated and second, sport has historically been considered a male domain, literally a space for affirming masculinity. Thus, the equal inclusion and treatment of girls and women has proven difficult and controversial. Since the 1970s, the idea that giving girls and women sport opportunities denies them to boys and men is one of the most consistent fears. This fear rests on cultural understandings of sport as a masculine activity. It is also framed as a question of who deserves sport opportunities. Since sport is thought to be a masculine activity, boys and men are considered more "naturally" interested in sport, thus more deserving of opportunities in sport.

In my previous work analyzing media coverage of Title IX (Walton, 2003, 2010), I examined the inconsistencies in the logic used to hold Title IX accountable for cuts in particular men's collegiate sports, especially wrestling, and relied heavily on data and facts to demonstrate these inconsistencies in a non-polemic way. These data clearly demonstrate that women consistently get less opportunity and potentially lower quality opportunities across the country in collegiate athletics (see

E. A. Roper (Ed.), Gender Relations in Sport, 95–118.
© *2013 Sense Publishers. All rights reserved.*

the National Collegiate Athletic Association's (NCAA) report on Gender Equity, NCAA participation reports and Equity in Athletics Disclosure Act for extensive data). Yet the publication or presentation of these facts seems to have no impact on the underlying logic, which supports the idea that Title IX is "killing" men's "minor" sport. So this debate continues to rage. Consequently, I have come to realize it is not a matter of fact or logic, but rather a matter of worldviews. In media accounts and public discussion, certain frameworks have been deployed to understand Title IX, and sport more generally, and maintain the perception that sport is the 'natural' domain of men.

Indeed, nearly all public discourse of Title IX starts from the premise that Title IX is killing men's sport. Title IX is commonly described as a "death knell" for, and "killer" of, men's minor sports which are "cut," "dropped," "benched, "lost" and "eliminated" in the "Pyrrhic victory" that women have gained on the playing fields and gyms. When that is the "the problem" to be solved, solutions focus on how to change policy to protect unfortunate male victims. As C.L. Cole (2003) states: "Although anti-Title IX complaints identify the guidelines as the principle problem, these guidelines are routinely glossed over in the hysterical, anti-Title IX narratives. Indeed, the truth-effects of these popular narratives depend on this gloss" (p. 87). Therefore, pointing out statistics and information that do not fit with the way Title IX is framed, does nothing to mitigate popular misunderstandings of Title IX enforcement or to challenge male hegemony within sporting spaces.

Faced with this dead end, I have looked for alternative ways of understanding the cultural importance of maintaining this seemingly unshakable concept of sport, as well as public discourse over Title IX within this framework. Most helpful has been the work of cognitive scientist George Lakoff (Lakoff, 1995, 2002, 2009; Lakoff & Johnson, 1987) to understand how we make sense of the world through conceptual metaphors. Lakoff (1995) argues that:

> We may not know it, but we think in metaphor. A large proportion of our most commonplace thoughts make use of an extensive, but unconscious, system of metaphorical concepts, that is, concepts from a typically concrete realm of thought that are used to comprehend another, completely different domain. (p. 177)

Importantly, examining metaphorical thought is not simply a matter of naming something. Instead, it is one of the main ways we understand our experiences, and therefore how we reason based on that understanding. Moreover, "to the extent that we act on our reasoning, metaphor plays a role in the creation of reality" (Lakoff & Johnson, 1987, p. 79). Thus, I use Lakoff's work to uncover the conceptual metaphors within political discourse to examine the ongoing debates surrounding Title IX.

In this chapter, I begin by giving a brief overview of Title IX policy, which helps ground the discussion on what is really required by the law, rather than the often inaccurate public understandings of the law. I then give a decade-by-decade overview of the framing of the law to flesh out the conceptual metaphors through which the law has developed and been debated. This leads to a fuller understanding of the cultural meaning of Title IX and why it continues to be a lightning rod for debate.

POLICY

Congress passed Title IX and President Richard Nixon signed it into law in 1972. At the time Title IX was passed, the Department of Health, Education and Welfare (DHEW) of the Executive Branch was responsible for the creation of policy. The oversight of Title IX was passed onto the Department of Education (DOE) when it was created in 1980 and DHEW was eliminated. Within the DOE, the Office for Civil Rights has oversight responsibilities for Title IX. In the Code of Federal Regulations (CFR) Title 34 on Education, Section 106 deals with implementing Title IX of the Education Amendments of 1972. Section 106.41 Athletics (a) reads that:

> No person shall on the basis of sex, be excluded participation in, be denied the benefits of, be treated differently from another person or otherwise be discriminated against in interscholastic, intercollegiate, club or intramural athletics offered by a recipient, and no recipient shall provide any such athletics separately on such basis.

Part b allows, however, that separate teams are permissible for members of each sex "where selection for such teams is based upon competitive skill or the activity involved is a contact sport" (Education Amendments of 1972, 1979). However, for those of the historically under-represented sex (women), the provision states that they are to be allowed to try out for men's teams when there is no equivalent women's team – with the exception of contact sport.

Part c of Section 106.41 outlines what is meant by 'Equal Opportunity.' This includes effective accommodations of students' interests and abilities, which has garnered the lion's share of attention to Title IX. It also includes equipment and supplies, travel and per diem, scheduling of games and practices, publicity, facilities, coaching and academic tutoring, medical and athletic training support, dining and housing, and publicity. Scholarships are addressed in 34 CFR 106.37(c).

Part d of Section 106.41 allows for an adjustment period, which was optimistically set at three years from the time that the regulation was written in 1975. Not only was sporting equality not reached in those three years, but further clarification was provided in 1979 with the Intercollegiate Athletics Policy Interpretation (44 Federal Register 71413, December 11, 1979). This policy interpretation created the three-part test for effective accommodations of students' interests and abilities and gave further clarifications for what became known as 'benefits, opportunities and treatments' including those areas previously noted.

The three-prong test for effective accommodations of students' interests and abilities gives institutions flexibility in showing compliance. The policy itself was heavily influenced by public commentary, including the NCAA, men's athletic administrators, football coaches associations, university administrators, and women's rights groups. DHEW received over 700 comments on the proposed policy and addressed how the comments influenced the final regulations (44 Federal Register 71413, December 11, 1979). The standard allows that collegiate athletic programs need only meet one of the standards to be in compliance with this area of Title IX: 1) the proportion of male and female athletes matches undergraduate enrollment, or 2) the institution shows a history and continuing practice of program expansion for the under-represented sex, or 3) where neither of the first standards is met, the institution can argue that it has fully accommodated the interests of the under-represented sex.

At the time this policy was written, a majority of undergraduates were men, so there was resistance to the idea that women should receive half of the athletic opportunities and benefits. This policy also allows that it would take programs time to get women's benefits and opportunities similar to men's when they had been given such sub-par resources and opportunities to this point, while men's athletics had been fostered for nearly 100 years. The third provision gets to the heart of the debate over Title IX, which allows for the argument that males are just more inherently interested in sport than females.

Now that women are the majority of undergraduates, prong one is no longer viewed favorably by many who argue for Title IX policy change, typically those representing men's nonrevenue producing sport, referred to as 'minor' sport – often the same groups that argued for option one when men were a majority of undergraduate students. Meanwhile, as women have been offered more sporting opportunities, they have jumped at the chance. As Kennedy (2010) noted, "Female athletic participation has increased by 904% in high schools and 456% in colleges, since the enactment of Title IX in 1972" (p. 79). However, women still are not allowed participation in the most populated sport – football – which heavily skews participation numbers to favor men and to create a situation where other men's teams may be sacrificed to keep football as a male domain. A sport structure that continues to deny women full participation opportunities works to both maintain the ideology that men are more interested in sport than women, and at the same time keep one of the most culturally significant sports, football, as a male preserve.

LAKOFF: CONCEPTUAL METAPHORS

George Lakoff examined the different ways that conservatives and liberals conceptualize the world by systematically analyzing "everyday conceptualization, reasoning, and language" (Lakoff, 2002, p. 3). In general, Lakoff argues that rather than assess facts and information on a case-by-case basis, we have deeper frameworks through which we understand the world and we then fit facts and information into our frameworks. One of the complex frameworks we use, on a mostly unconscious level, is conceptual metaphor.

Conceptual metaphors are made up of simpler metaphors and at the most basic level, primary metaphors. Primary metaphors "are motivated by embodied experiences coming together regularly" (Lakoff, 2012, p. 777). For example, when parents hold their children affectionately, children correlate experiences of warmth and affection, creating a primary metaphor of Affection as Warmth. Importantly for this chapter, "political ideologies are structured around metaphors for morality" (Lakoff, 2012, p. 778). Thus, we will look to Lakoff's work on morality in political metaphors to shed light on debates over Title IX law and policy. These political metaphors help us to understand how seemingly disparate issues – Title IX, affirmative action, gay rights, etc. – are linked conceptually and metaphorically through divergent notions of morality and more specifically, 'family values.'

At its root, "much of moral reasoning is metaphorical reasoning" (Lakoff, 2002, p. 5). These conceptual metaphors, Lakoff (2002) argues, are a central component of ideological systems and offer a way of "conceptualizing one domain of experience in terms of another, often unconsciously" (p. 4). In order to systematically understand conceptual metaphors and how they apply in political language, Lakoff (2002) attempted not just to categorize them, but to analyze the modes of reasoning; show how they relate across issues and are understood as fitting together; demonstrate the links between the forms of political reasoning and moral reasoning; "show how moral reasoning in politics is ultimately based on models of the family;" and finally explain why the models fit together as they do (p. 17). Thus,

> the link between family-based morality and politics comes from one of the most common ways we have of conceptualizing what a nation is, namely, as a family. It is the common, unconscious, and automatic metaphor of the Nation-as-Family that produces contemporary conservatism from Strict Father morality and contemporary liberalism from Nurturant Parent morality. (Lakoff, 2002, p. 13)

The conceptual metaphors present in the debates surrounding Title IX tap into these underlying understandings of morality by seeming to be common sense. Therefore, a lot of the work in shaping opinion over Title IX has nothing to do with the facts of whether or not women are still facing discrimination in the athletic realm or whether men are losing opportunities *because of* Title IX. Rather, it has everything to do with the way people understand the world and the frames through which they communicate that understanding. In my ongoing work on this topic, I have often puzzled over the lack of interface between those who support the enforcement of Title IX and those who see Title IX as the "death knell" for men's minor sport. Lakoff's work helps me to see why these two sides can look at the same information and come to such wildly different conclusions. While I once believed that just showing people the facts, as it were, would make them realize the realities of capitalism within collegiate athletics, it has become increasingly clear to me that the fight over resources is just the factor that brings the issue to the surface; it is not the core struggle, nor the most useful tool for analysis. The conceptual metaphors Lakoff advances for understanding much of our political framings come from the over-arching "nation as a family" metaphor. Thus, the frames relate to metaphors of different family structures and parenting models, which help to more clearly understand debates over Title IX.

FRAMES

Family Values

Lakoff (2002) argues that the differences between Americans which creates the visual mapping of the "red" states versus the "blue" is not just a difference of political beliefs, but instead a difference of "two ways of understanding the world" (p. ix). Lakoff argues: "the political division is personal" (2002, p. x). Yet this division remains largely unexamined and unvoiced in the public domain because, Lakoff argues, it is largely unconscious. While it is "difficult to engage in public discourse about things that most people have no public access to" it is not impossible (Lakoff, 2002, p. x). Thus, a seemingly endless supply of issues that link those who belong to the camps of "conservative" or "liberal" are "manifestations of a single [unconscious] issue: strictness versus nurturance" (Lakoff, 2002, p. x). For these particular metaphors to be useful in understanding liberal and conservative world views and the impact of those views on public debate and policy, they must meet the adequacy condition of explaining the "topic choice, word choice, and discourse forms of conservatives and liberals" (Lakoff, 2002, p. 28). Lakoff (2002) argues that the two opposing models of the family "explain why certain stands on issues go together," and "why the puzzles for liberals are not puzzles for conservatives" and vice versa (pp. 32–33).

At the root of these conceptual metaphors of family, are different conceptualizations of morality. While Lakoff (1995) argued that there are about two dozen metaphors that structure our thoughts on morality, one of the most important is conceptualizing morality in terms of accounting. In this way we 'keep moral books' and think of well-being as wealth. Thus, "just as it is important that the financial books be balanced, so it is important that the moral books be balanced" (Lakoff, 1995, p. 179). In terms of morality, then, it is moral to pay your debts and immoral not to pay them.

There are some basic schemes of how the conceptual metaphor of morality works in this instance. First is reciprocity, whereby if I do something good for you, then you *owe* me something, or have a moral debt. If you do something equally good for me, then you have *repaid* your debt (reciprocity) and we are even – balanced books. We can see the financial metaphor at work here with concepts like *owe, debt, repay*, and so on when we speak of morality. Thus with reciprocity, there are two principals of moral action: first, adding positive value; second, paying one's moral debts. So, when you did something good for me, you engaged in both forms of moral action together, adding positive value and re-paying your moral debt.

Another moral accounting scheme is retribution. In the case of negative action, moral accounting gets more complicated. Retribution is governed by a moral version of math whereby "giving something negative is equivalent to taking something positive" (Lakoff, 1995, p. 180). Thus, if I harm you, I have taken something positive. In causing you harm, I cause you a moral dilemma with respect to the first and second principals of moral accounting. If you do something equally harmful to me, in terms of morality, this can be interpreted two different ways. By the first principal you have acted immorally since you did something harmful and you should be adding positive value. By the second value, you acted morally since you were repaying your moral debts. On the other hand, had you not caused me harm, you would have been acting morally by the first principal and immorally by the second principal by not 'making me pay' for the harm I had done. In this accounting, then, you must make a choice and give priority to one of the principals. The Morality of Absolute Goodness puts the first principal first. The Morality of Retribution puts the second principal first.

As might be expected, different groups of people favor different solutions to this moral dilemma. In this we can see a root difference in conceptual metaphors for conservatives and liberals. For example, with the death penalty, liberals rank absolute goodness over retribution, while conservatives prefer retribution.

This example illustrates what Lakoff means when he speaks of 'conceptual metaphor.' It is an unconscious, automatic mechanism for using inference patterns and language from a source domain (in this case, the financial domain) to think and talk about another domain (in this case, the moral domain) (Lakoff, 1995, p. 182). While this is just one example to understand differences in conceptual metaphors between liberals and conservatives, I will use others as appropriate. I will first start with two broad conceptual metaphors of family models for conservatives and liberals.

Strict Father

Central to the conservative worldview, according to Lakoff, is the metaphor of the strict father model of morality. To give the nutshell version, the strict father is the head of a traditional nuclear family,

> with the father having primary responsibility for supporting and protecting the family as well as the overall authority to set overall policy, to set strict rules for the behavior of children, and to enforce the rules. The mother has the day-to-day responsibility for the care of the house, raising the children, and upholding the father's authority. Children must respect and obey their parents; by doing so they build character, that is, self-discipline and self-reliance. (Lakoff, 2002, p. 33)

Once children become adults they are to set their own discipline and authority. So, a central component to this worldview is the idea that the exercise of authority is itself moral – "that is, it is moral to reward obedience and punish disobedience" (Lakoff, 2002, p. 67). The role of sport for boys can clearly be understood in this model as it has traditionally been the 'natural' domain for learning the necessary discipline for success. From this perspective, "the world is difficult and people have to be self-disciplined to be able to survive in a difficult world" (Lakoff, 2002, p. 68). Consequently, the metaphors of sport as a battlefield or training ground for life fit aptly here.

Nurturant Parent

The dominant liberal metaphor is built around the ideal nurturant parent family model. To give an abbreviated version of this model, the main ethic is that of caring. In this framework, rather than developing through discipline, "children become responsible, self-disciplined, and self-reliant through being cared for and respected, and through caring for others" (Lakoff, 2002, p. 108). "Protection is a form of caring, and protection from external dangers takes up a significant part of the nurturant parent's attention" (Lakoff, 2002, p. 109). These dangers include environmental concerns, harm from other people, unsafe toys, food, diseases, etc. Thus, civil rights laws like Title IX make sense within this model because they protect constituencies who have not been treated fairly, cared for, and protected in the past. This fits particularly well with the idea that nurturance carries importance not just within the family, but also in the larger community. As Lakoff (2002) notes, in this model, "self-fulfillment and nurturance of others are seen as inseparable" (p. 109). The ideal world within this moral system then is "governed maximally by empathy, where the weak who need help get it from the strong" (Lakoff, 2002, p. 112).

Title IX debate and policy creation can be more clearly understood if we look for how these metaphorical frameworks are invoked. As Lakoff states, "there are no neutral concepts and no neutral language for expressing political positions within a moral context" (2002, p. 385). Moreover, political leaders and intellectuals have systematically created frames to try to bring all issues in line with their idealized moral position, creating "their own partisan moral-political concepts and partisan moral-political language" (Lakoff, 2002, p. 385).

Even though people see language as neutral and believe in their own ability to make up their own mind, the ways we make sense of the world are largely impacted by our conceptual systems or ideologies. When issues are framed in ways that resonate with our conceptual framings, they 'make sense.' Isolated facts presented to people do not make them restructure their conceptual frames; rather they tend to bounce off these frames. Facts need to be framed systematically to fit within larger worldviews for people to make 'common sense' of them. As cognitive science has demonstrated, "most people don't even know that they have conceptual systems, much less how they are structured" (Lakoff, 2002, p. 388). As a result, even having conversations about these worldviews is difficult. Analyzing public debate and media coverage of Title IX gives us a concrete example of how these conceptual metaphors have been invoked in political discourse, legal history and policy debate.

IN THE BEGINNING: THE 1970s

1972, the year Title IX quietly slipped through Capital Hill and was signed into law by President Richard Nixon, the women's liberation movement was in full force and women seemed determined to explore every avenue previously closed to them.

While some women tested their endurance by officially running the 26.2 miles of the Boston marathon, other women tested their strength and agility, donning their shoulder pads for a fledgling professional football league. Women entered the inner sanctums in the world of sport in such previously all-male sport occupations as athletic training and facilities maintenance. Many ritzy athletic clubs opened their front doors and membership rosters to women – if not full membership privileges. Meanwhile, the very heart of Americana sport, professional baseball, hired its first woman umpire, Bernice Gera. While clearly impressive, this list remains an unfulfilled promise – a hint at progress that never followed.

Firsts imply an opened door of opportunity with many women standing on the shoulders of their fore-mothers in a move toward cultural equality. Instead, as the debate during that time over the passage of the Equal Rights Amendment reflects, as well as the furor over Title IX and athletics that quickly ensues, the issue of gender equality even now is far from settled. The firsts of the 1970s reflect fields still primarily dominated by men today. During this time, traditional gender roles began to be questioned and to shift. Women's advancements into previously male domains were considered a threat to patriarchal family structures. This was a shift that some people embraced and celebrated, while others viewed it as a threat to social order. Not surprisingly the question of family structure emerges, with the advocacy for the nurturant family model to challenge the strict father model. Central to these debates were notions of men's and women's 'natural' roles in society.

In the era of the second wave of feminism, the 'battle of the sexes,' and debate over the Equal Rights Amendment, many sports writers just plain saw women in certain sports as unnatural. Burly, cigar smoking David Condon (1973) of the *Chicago Tribune* offered this bit of wisdom, "The sad truth is that women are no more equipped to participate in some sports than I am equipped to be a playboy bunny" (p. 3). As proof he pointed out, "You know how many ladies, in 99 years, ever won the Kentucky Derby? Only one. That was in 1915, and the doll's name was Regret, which is a perfect name for a doll" (Condon, 1973, p. 3). Many reporters and editorials shared this uneasiness over women in sport and held suspicion regarding both their femininity and biological sex. These were the dominant cultural attitudes relating to sport as Title IX policy was being crafted.

Not all reporters, however, supported these beliefs. A small group of young female sport reporters, as well as several progressive male writers, offered counter perspectives regarding women and sport. Even in support of women's athletics, though, a typical apologetic stance applied. According to one media source, "a woman can be both tough and aggressive as an athlete and loving and attentive as a mother" (Soifer, 1975, p. 6). Another remarked of professional football players on the Los Angeles Dandelions, these women "were hardly roller derby types. Not one needed a chromosome check. They were generally small, curvy and long-haired" (Liddick, 1973, p. IX:1). Often women athletes made a point of distancing themselves from feminism in an attempt to gain support and legitimacy. One professional football player demurred, "Oh, we're not for women's lib—equal pay, sure—but not that bra burning stuff" (Liddick, 1973, p. IX:1).

By 1975 when it became clear that the courts would uphold girls' right to all educational activities, including sport, many officials sat and waited – hoping no girls would want to play. As then Board of Director of sport and recreation for the Chicago Board of Education put it, "The truth is, we couldn't legally stop any girl from competing on a boys' team. But I don't want to alert the girls to that or they'd start applying to play, and we don't want that to happen" (Preston, 1975, p. 3). He continued,

> You know this lib thing started up only recently, but we've had boys' sports since 1901 or so. We've had sports and teams and coaches for the boys, and if we start taking them away now, the boys are going to yell. (p. 3)

Boys and men were viewed as more deserving of sport opportunities because they were more historically invested. On the flip side, others saw women's exclusion as an issue of historic harm. Clearly each perspective called for different moral answers.

The worries also extended to the damage to men if women were allowed in sport. As one journalist reflected, "Will the trend toward unisex sports shake men's already unsteady psyches?" (Liddick, 1973, p. 1). The coordinator of the men's graduate program in physical education at Ithaca College believed so: "It's been acknowledged that sport is nearly all that many males have with which to identify. What is to happen to them?" (Liddick, 1973, p. 1). He worried that the "unisex push could do serious psychological harm to men" (p. 1). To which clinical psychologist Dr. Ruth Lambert countered, "What we should be concerned about is the crippling and damaging effects upon women's self-esteem caused by segregation, not preserving temples of the masculine mystique" (p. 1). Leaving women on the sidelines, she maintained, "has often left women vulnerable and weak, marked as the perennial victim" (p. 1). Thus, women countered moral concerns about damage to men with pointing out the damage that not having sport opportunities does to women. Clearly, moral accounting is at work in these arguments. The progressive idea of the 1970s maintained that differences between men and women in sport were largely cultural rather than biological.

Given current debates over Title IX pitting men's minor sports against women's sport for apparently scare resources, it is interesting to note the financial issues faced by collegiate athletics even before the passage of Title IX. Debates can be understood with the logic of family models. The question is what type of family is an athletic department: a family that nurtures the needs of all members or a family that rewards the strong and works to maintain their success? Quibbling over the "purpose" of sport and distribution of resources, according to columnist David Condon (1975), only happened because of jealousy – as the less successful child might be of her more successful brother. "These critics place no premium on the athlete's dedication to excellence and to winning. And I'm afraid that those people will use the excuse of economic emergency to curtail the influence that athletics has in academic life"

(p. 4:3). Arguing that the "eggheads of college sport" who wanted to curtail spending in football and basketball were likely the same "bleeding hearts who thunder that there must be increased emphasis on women's sports on the campuses" did so because "they'd really like to tear down sports that emphasize strength, sacrifice, and the development of leadership" (Condon, 1975, p. 4:3). By this measure, the role of sport is not educational development for all participants, but rather to develop particular men for future leadership. This supports the notion that moral strength must be built through self-discipline and self-denial. Thus, denying this to these male athletes fosters moral weakness. And, by this logic, as Lakoff (1995) notes, "moral weakness is nascent immorality – immorality waiting to happen" (p. 185).

Some journalists reported on calls for more meaningful changes to college athletics. These changes were reflective of the growing counter-culture ideology and ongoing civil rights debates playing out across the country, which fit with the morality of the nurturant family model. *New York Times* columnist Neil Amdur (1972) asserted, "It was the death of four Kent State students in May, 1970 that helped trigger the wave of emotional discontent and philosophical rhetoric in athletics" (p. 1:22). College sport – in particular football and basketball – should be changed, these factions argued, not just to share resources more equitably but to put an end to the whole-scale exploitation of the student-athletes involved in big time sport. One of the central tenants of the nurturant parent model is protection from danger, since that protection is a form of caring, thus regulations curbing abuses are important. According to Lakoff (1995), "Just as a nurturant parent must protect his children, a government must protect its citizens—not only from external threats, but also from pollution, disease, unsafe products, workplace hazards, nuclear waste, and unscrupulous businessmen" (p. 200–1).

These debates highlight philosophical issues regarding the purpose of sport. In attempting to understand women's sport participation some reporters focused on the impact on men and women participants while others questioned the viability of women's sports as a business venture. The line between professional sport and supposedly amateur college sport were easily blurred. With spectators understood to be an integral part of the college sport experience, many reporters did not see the possibility for the success of women's sport.

Reflecting and supporting cultural barriers, such as those already mentioned, women faced formidable structural barriers imposed by a business sport model, which gets at the heart of who deserves sport opportunities. In terms of moral accounting, women were seen as being less morally worthy of sport opportunities because they were not paying the same dues to develop as men's sport. Some men in athletics urged women to be patient in their quest for equality. One male physical educator and basketball coach instructed,

One must remember that much of the difference between men's and women's athletic programs is historical. The girls are just getting a late start. What the women sometimes don't see is that the difference is not between men's and women's programs, but between income-producing and non-income-producing sports, period. At many schools, non-income sports literally go begging for money, men or women. (Sandbrook, 1972, III:7)

By this logic, women should pay their dues before expecting opportunities. On the other side, the nurturant parent model would call for a fair chance for everyone to have self-fulfilment, expecting the government to step in and make policy, such as Title IX, to help that to happen for groups that had been historically disadvantaged. Each side is using a different moral accounting to determine who should receive sporting opportunities.

As soon as athletics were mentioned within the same breath as Title IX, male football coaches, athletic directors, and legislators began crying foul and made repeated attempts to alter the course of Title IX. At the legislative level, the Javits Amendment, passed July 1, 1974, mandated that the DHEW regulations must include "with respect to intercollegiate athletic activities, reasonable provisions considering the nature of particular sports" (US Senate, 1974). Many proposals called for rejecting the regulations in their entirety (e.g., Senator Jesse Helms and Representative James G. Martin) or exempting sport altogether or at least exempting revenue producing sport. The Tower Amendment was the first of these in 1974. Others followed in the summer of 1975, after the regulations were created. Senator Helms introduced the last of these in 1977. None of these resolutions passed as most died in committee.

Then president of the NCAA, John Fuzak, exclaimed that applying Title IX to athletics "borders on insanity that threatens to destroy many university athletic programs" ("Fuzak Urges Review of Title IX Issue," 1975, p. III:1). Darrell Royal, then coach and athletic director at the University of Texas and President of the American Football Coaches Association, complained that, "The end result could very well be that we'd have to give up all athletic programs. Eventually, we can see a dying process for all athletics for both men and women" ("End of College Sport Forecast," 1975, p. III:1). He lamented,

I'm not opposed to women's intercollegiate athletics, so help me...but we're going to be so drained and so weakened there won't be enough money to continue...I can't see that they will do anything but eliminate, kill or seriously weaken programs we now have in existence (for men). (p. III:1)

Representative Ronald Mottl, a democrat from Ohio who went to Notre Dame on a baseball scholarship, used interesting logic,

I thank God for football and basketball that supported us or else I never could have gotten my education. The bureaucrats at HEW are all wet on this. We want to be fair to women, but this is not the way to go about it. ("End of College Sport Forecast," 1975, p. III:1)

While most men's sport also does not make money, like most women's sport, there was still a sense that other men's sport had "paid their dues" as women's sport had not.

106

Betty Thompson, the women's athletic director at the University of Texas responded, using the conceptual metaphor of the nurturant family, by noting,

> I think it's a scare tactic. It's terribly unfortunate that women are becoming the scapegoats for problems that were coming into existence long before the push for women's intercollegiate athletics. Darrell Royal has said men's intercollegiate athletics brings in $2.4 million and $1 million goes back into football. Well, it's discriminatory to me when you redistribute the rest of that money to men only. Men's tennis does not generate revenue and neither does women's tennis. ("Women Scapegoats in College Sports," 1975, 4:6)

For her, the issue is more about fairness and duty to each other. Lakoff (1995) writes,

> In a nurturant family, it is the duty of older and stronger children to help out those who are younger and weaker; so in a nation it is the duty of citizens who are better-off to contribute more than those who are worse-off. (p. 201)

Women's ambivalence toward a sport model that placed winning and revenue production as top priorities also created some tension – making it even less clear what equity between men's and women's programs would mean. As former women's athletic director at University of California Los Angeles (UCLA) opined, "I want a program similar to the men's but not the same. I do not want a program that emphasizes winning and the accompanying pressures. Just a program that enables the girls to play" (Sandbrook, 1972, III:1). As a result, the Association of Intercollegiate Athletics for Women (AIAW) initially instituted a no-scholarship, no recruiting policy that smelled of discrimination to many female athletes who felt they were being denied educational opportunities offered to men. In response to the question, "Can't we just play?" one UCLA athlete answered, "If that's your philosophy you're in the wrong program because I'm here to win. I didn't bust my ass for nine years to lose" (Bensten, 1975a, p. III:1). This invokes the same moral logic that men's athletics was using to maintain their moral right to sport opportunities. These issues became more pressing by 1975 as schools were trying to determine what to make of the Title IX guidelines in athletics put forth by then HEW Secretary Casper Weinberger. In recognizing their past discrimination against women and responding to women's growing cultural interest in sport, many schools increased their athletic budgets for women as well as their sport offerings before Title IX regulations were determined.

The example of UCLA illustrates the convergence of these issues. In 1972, one administrator in the recreation department oversaw women's athletics at UCLA with a budget of $20,000. This budget covered ten intercollegiate sports, included the administrator's salary and no paid coaches. Meanwhile the men's athletic department sponsored 18 sports for 811 male athletes on a budget of $2.9 million. While the women received no scholarships, the men enjoyed $498,000 worth of support. The 31 full and part-time coaches earned $408,000 in comparison to the 10 part-time volunteer coaches for the women. In describing the situation, one journalist seems reluctant to admit discrimination, writing that "the women's athletic director is critical of what *she calls* inequality between the men's and women's programs" (Sandbrook, 1972, III:1, emphasis added). This really points to cultural beliefs of men's and women's place in athletics. In the 1970s, if women received any opportunities, that was thought to be enough for them.

A WEAKENING OF CIVIL RIGHTS LEGISLATION: THE 1980S

The 1980s witnessed significant change to the application of Title IX to collegiate athletics. A backlash to the civil rights advances of the 1960s and 1970s was taking shape in the form of an alliance between the religious right and the new right. The election of President Ronald Reagan solidified this shift to the right. For Title IX, the changes came in the form of the 1984 Supreme Court decision in Grove City College v Bell, followed by the legislative response with the Civil Rights Restoration Act (1987), which became effective in 1988.

The Grove City College case centered on whether an institution was beholden to Title IX in its entirety, or only those parts of the institution that received federal funding. To maintain their independence, Grove City College did not receive any federal funding. However, some students at Grove City College received federal funding by way of Pell Grants and subsidized loans. The Supreme Court made a narrow decision stating that only the parts of the college that received federal funding had to comply with the law. In this case, that meant only the admissions office. The effect of this decision was far-reaching. It did not just impact Title IX, but all civil rights laws written in the same language: Title VI of the Civil Rights Act of 1964 barring race discrimination, Section 504 of the Rehabilitation Act of 1973 barring discrimination based on disability, and the 1975 Age Discrimination Act. For most of the 1980s, Title IX did not apply to athletics as virtually no athletic department received federal funding (Walton, 2010).

Congress spent the next few years working to get the broad meaning of these civil rights laws restored. They argued that it was their original intent in passing the laws and that if one part of an institution enjoyed federal funds, then the entire institution benefitted from it. Thus, even if athletics did not directly get federal funding, they enjoyed the benefits of having students on federal financial aid, which decreased the burdens of scholarship costs. Moreover, supporters of Title IX pointed to the harm done to women because of discrimination. As Republican Senator Bob Packwood (1984) argued,

> Sexual discrimination in education is subtle but pernicious, affecting its victims for the rest of their lives. Thus, the absurdity of the Grove City decision: It is of little use to bar discrimination in a school's financial aid program if a woman cannot gain admittance to, or participate in, the institution because of its other discriminatory policies and practices. It is of equally little use to bar discrimination in employment if a woman cannot attain the necessary education to obtain that employment. (A27)

The unification of the religious right and New Right, which coalesced during President Reagan's term, dominated the debates on this issue. As I noted in research which focused on media coverage of Title IX in the 1980s:

> One of the strengths of this coalition building was the ability of the movement to bring together groups of people who cared little for the main agenda of the Republican Party related to economic ideologies, but cared deeply for particular religiously oriented causes, such as abortion or the inclusion of Christian teachings in public schools. Others were drawn in via issues of government interference, such as gun control. The focus was not on convincing constituents of core beliefs, but rather to tap into already deeply held beliefs and to strengthen fears that those ways of life were threatened by the social change brought on by civil rights. (Walton, 2010, p. 15)

The decision to pursue the Grove City College case was part of a larger plan to weaken all civil rights laws, which was part of Reagan's program to "deregulate" the "overly burdensome" federal government. "The ideological importance of sport in this plan, which singled out Title IX for federal review, was part of a push to appeal to a nostalgic (although non-existent) return to 'family values'" (Walton, 2010, p. 16). Thus we see conceptual metaphors of the family continue strongly in the 1980s. The rhetoric of deregulation made sense to those viewing the world from the logic of a strict father metaphor. Once adults become self-reliant, they become authorities of their own lives. Interference with this becomes burdensome 'meddling.' As Lakoff (1995) writes, "Conservatives speak of the government meddling in people's lives with the resentment normally reserved for meddling parents. The very term 'meddling' is carried over metaphorically from family life to government" (pp. 192–3). Not surprisingly, those who supported civil rights laws took issue with this approach. Journalist Judy Mann (1981) said that to remove laws barring discrimination of women "is not an exercise in conservative restraint of the federal government. It is an exercise in conservative irresponsibility toward the well-being of women" (p. C1). As Lakoff (1995) argued, "Nurturant parents want all their children to fulfill their potential, and so it is the role of government to provide institutions to make that possible" (p. 201).

Throughout the 1980s the focus remains on the proper role of government regulation, due to the dominance of the Grove City Supreme Court case and the Civil Rights Restoration Act. Conceptual metaphors of the family are central to these debates. On the one hand there is President Reagan and the conservative attack on "big government." This plays into the conceptual model of the strict father family both in terms, as shown above, of adults being allowed to be self-reliant, as part of their moral obligations of exercising authority and creating their own success. It is also supported through the metaphor of each head of household (ideally the father) being complete authority for his family. According to this thinking, no government authority should overstep this boundary – whether it is what is taught in school, family consumption, access to services, etc. This explains ongoing debates over the teaching of evolution or creationism, sex education, regulations on pesticides, food production, or access to birth control. Here is where we see that the issue is not simply about regulation, but more about the authority central to the strict father conceptual metaphor. Ironically, the Grove City College decision actually made the federal regulation more burdensome to the government, which then had to determine whether federal funds were directly involved in cases of discrimination. If burdensome regulation were the main concern, there would be no regulations to keep teachers from teaching certain subjects, such as comprehensive sex education or to keep women from gaining access to birth control. These are government regulations driven by a metaphorical fight over authority. It goes beyond arguing for a free market economy, toward supporting certain regulations while resisting others. Lakoff (1995) summarized, "It explains why opposition to environmental protection goes with support for military protection, why the right-to-life goes with the right to own machine guns and why patriotism goes with hatred of the government" (p. 195). Idaho Republican Representative George Hansen's introduction of a Family Protection Act in 1981, which would have, among other things, repealed Title IX, provides a clear example of the connection between the metaphor of the nation as a family, and the particular strict father metaphor of conservatism. In this instance, too, the understood 'natural' roles of men and women were at stake.

We see this narrative in support for the Grove City Supreme Court Case and in response to the passage of the Civil Rights Restoration Act of 1987. Playing on the connection between the New Right and the Religious Right, an editorial in the *Washington Post* exclaimed that the bill "will lead to widespread erosion of American freedoms.... Our government is founded upon the principle that freedom is endowed by the Creator, not by the whim of a ruling body.... Indeed, the new bill is a blueprint for disaster" (James, 1988, p. A27). "The Moral Majority," a leading organization of the Religious Right, called the bill "a perverted law" that would make churches victims of "militant gays, feminists and others who have no respect for God's laws" possibly forcing day-care centers subsidized by the government to hire transvestites" ("An Indecent Veto," 1998, p. D2). Both of these quotes highlight the belief of the natural role of men and women within the strict father conceptual metaphor. This metaphor is further invoked to inspire fear that 'meddlesome' government interference could force people to act against their own moral beliefs.

Reagan and his supporters argued that civil rights legislation imposed on the personal liberties of citizens and private groups. Yet, as many editorials pointed out, "The liberty that individuals will lose is the opportunity to discriminate on the basis of race, gender, handicap, or age and to have that discrimination subsidized by the public treasury" (Ellis, 1988, Sec. 1, p. 30). Thus, at the heart of the Civil Rights Restoration Act was the nurturant family conceptual metaphor. These groups are linked legally because any Supreme Court decision on Title IX impacts all other laws written in the same language (thus, those laws relative to race, disability and age discrimination). They are also linked metaphorically through the nurturant family conceptual metaphor as groups that have been historically treated unfairly and should therefore be protected by the government to allow for fair opportunities. As one writer argues, "Compartmentalized discrimination is not neutral. It is wrong. President Reagan may be getting the lawyers he wants, but minorities and women are not getting the civil rights champions they deserve" ("Compartmentalized Discrimination," 1983, Sec. 4, p. 18).

With the Civil Rights Restoration Act, Title IX once again applied to athletics. It had only barely gotten started by the end of the 1970s and was out of commission for athletics for most of the 1980s. So the 1990s were thought to be the time for equality to come to fruition in educational athletics. We did see tremendous growth in women's athletics, both in terms of participation and in terms of increased funding. However, that growth is outpaced considerably by the growth in men's sport on both counts. Yet, the 1990s marked the time when the narrative that Title IX is 'killing' men's minor sport came into full force and by the 2000s it became the dominant narrative.

FAIRNESS, QUOTAS AND 'COMMON SENSE:' THE 1990S AND 2000S

The issue of fairness is one of the basic differences in understanding rhetoric surrounding Title IX. Not surprisingly, fairness is defined differently according to each worldview. According to Lakoff (2002), "one of the most basic conceptions of morality we have conceptualizes moral action as fair distribution and immoral action as unfair distribution" (p. 61). Fairness within the strict father moral system sees scalar distribution to be most important: the harder you work, the more you get. Since success itself is defined as moral, then clearly it is also moral to reward hard work. Moreover, giving someone something they have not earned is not fair and is therefore immoral. Furthermore, because self-discipline is a hallmark of both morality and of success, success itself becomes moral. One's success becomes evidence of one's morality.

Within narratives of Title IX, part of the examination of whether a program *should* be eliminated or not focuses on how successful the program was. For example, when California State, Bakersfield announced they were cutting the men's wrestling program, one journalist wrote,

> It's not that the team wasn't performing. The only Division I sport at CSUB, the program has distinguished itself over the years, winning two PAC 10 championships and finishing in the top 10 in the NCAA finals three out of the previous four years. (Lynch, 2001, para. 2)

One of the most referred to cases to make this point is UCLA, which cut men's swimming and gymnastics in 1994, despite being "programs that consistently produced Olympic medalists" (Lynch, 2001). Because the nature of collegiate athletics is held to be competitive it fits easily within this conceptual metaphor of morality. Through success, athletes are not simply demonstrating their athletic prowess but also their self-discipline and therefore their morality. Clearly, then, it is immoral to cut such teams and deprive athletes of their chance not just for success, but also for morality.

This framework of morality extends to morality as justice, where the metaphor of financial transaction is evoked. In this we see how conceptual metaphors work in complex ways, invoking simpler metaphors. In this instance, morality as justice reasons that, after everything those athletes and coaches did to represent their schools, morally the institutions *owe* it to them not to cut their teams. As one UCLA gymnast said, "For them to drop that team after what they did for the school, it's definitely shitty" (Lynch, 2001). Likewise, when the University of Iowa added women's rowing in 1993, the *Quad City Times* wrote:

> There's going to be some male wrestler at Iowa who has spilled his sweat and blood on the mat for 15 years, practicing and refining his technique over and over, who is rewarded with a fraction of a scholarship. Then there is going to be some young lady who swims a lot and dabbled in the discus in high school, who two months ago didn't know which end of the oar to put into the water, who has her entire education paid for by a rowing scholarship. (Boyne, 1994, p. 36)

The question here, then, is who *deserves* a college scholarship, as well as, what is *owed* to male athletes dedicated to their sport.

Furthermore, the market success of particular men's sports supports the seemingly 'natural' order accepted in this view. In a chicken and egg scenario, success and therefore morality can be measured by coaching salaries and other material support. Thus, the fact that women's programs garner less cultural attention and receive fewer resources offers tautological evidence that women deserve less based on the natural moral order. For example, one rowing coach noted that her sport gained legitimacy when her salary got a 40% boost after an equal pay investigation: "It's like the administration has given us a seal of approval and everyone respects that" (Boyne, 1994, p. 35).

In the strict father moral system, weakness itself is considered immoral, and helping the undeserving weak is viewed as enabling their immorality. Thus, through the lens of the strict father morality, civil rights laws do not help people because they do not teach people to be self-sufficient. So, by this logic, civil rights laws contribute to immorality. Thus, conservatives find fault with all civil rights laws, which they deem no longer necessary, arguing that sexism and racism are problems of the past. Thus, if women do not have equal opportunity it is because they lack desire. Specifically for Title IX, men are understood as 'naturally' being more interested in sport, which follows the 'natural' moral order of the strict father model. This means that Title IX unreasonably requires schools, according to this frame, to offer girls and women sport opportunities they do not even want. Despite court decisions that consistently find that girls and women *are* interested and are not getting the same opportunities or quality of experience, the fact that fewer girls and women participate in sport again provides self-referencing evidence of their lack of interest – even as they are offered fewer opportunities than males, most especially football which has the largest team rosters.

According to message boards, print media and television coverage, it is clearly 'common sense' that boys and men are more interested in sport than girls and women. If not, then Title IX compliance should be easy for schools, as one writer comments, "All they would have to do is offer the same number of teams for women, and the problem would go away" (Lynch, 2005). He cites as evidence that more sports are being offered to women than to men in the NCAA, yet there are still more male athletes. This ignores how many opportunities are offered per team; how much time, effort, and money are spent on recruiting; or the amount of cultural support for male and female athletes. Again, what we see here is the 'strict father' framework to offer a simple 'common sense' view, without reference to the actual facts of male and female sport opportunities or treatment in athletics. It leads to a 'rational' conclusion that Title IX is 'killing' men's sport while forcing opportunities onto girls and women that they do not even want.

However, participation statistics do not support this. Females have jumped at sport opportunities. The last barrier to full participation opportunities remains female exclusion from football. This also skews overall participation numbers toward males because of the high participation numbers on each team and the growth of the number of football teams offered over the decades. This means that more, but smaller, female teams need to be offered to come close to male participation opportunities. Moreover, this does not account for the vast spending differences between men's and women's collegiate sport.

Yet, as Lakoff (2002) argued, "nothing is 'just' common sense. Common sense has a conceptual structure that is usually unconscious" (p. 4). Common sense then is "deep, complex, sophisticated, and subtle…especially in the domains of morality and politics…Much of what we read on the daily op-ed pages of our finest newspapers is metaphorical common sense reasoning" (Lakoff, 2002, pp. 4–5). This reasoning takes the way things are today as evidence for the natural order of things, and disturbing that natural order is viewed as immoral.

The use of language over this debate strongly evokes issues of morality. When Title IX is said to push gender equity onto schools, thereby killing men's sport, and forcing athletic directors to make cuts, and drop or cap teams, metaphors of moral strength are in use. Lakoff (1995) argued that moral strength is "a complex metaphor with a number of parts, beginning with: Being Good is Upright; Being Bad is Being Low" (p. 184). Thus, 'upstanding citizens' are 'on the up and up' and do not 'fall from grace,' like a 'snake in the grass.' Title IX in this instance, then, is framed as immoral because it serves to keep men's sport down, causing them harm, where morality is understood as upright, and immorality as being low. As CSUB wrestler Stephen Neal notes, "We feel we are the last *stand* for wrestling. We are going to keep fighting" (in Lynch, 2001, emphasis added). Title IX is framed in this way as a threat to men's moral wholeness and taking away opportunities to build moral strength.

This plays out clearly when blame for cuts in men's sport is placed with women, but also in the hostility and misogyny directed toward female athletes. While the underlying notion that women are not 'naturally' interested in sport runs throughout public discourse, the lack of respect and antagonism many female athletes, particularly those perceived to be gay, face, is rarely mentioned. As one author notes in *American Rowing*, "However strong the law is, it can't control people's hearts and minds" (Boyne, 1994, p. 35). At the University of New Hampshire, for example, after crew was elevated to varsity status, they began being harassed and an "obscene, misogynous message was left" on the coach's answering machine "referring to the women as 'dykes' and threatening to rape them" (Boyne, 1994, p. 35).

Of course the use of the strict father conceptual metaphor underlying these arguments does not make sense to all people. Those whose thinking falls more in line with the nurturant parent conceptual metaphor, see it as selfish to keep sport opportunities primarily for men and to give more to programs already doing well, while still not giving equal opportunities to women. In this family model, there is a different set of moral priorities at work. First, with Morality as Empathy, "empathy itself is understood metaphorically as feeling what another person feels" (Lakoff, 1995, p. 198). This goes beyond the Golden Rule, what some might call the Platinum Rule, to say "Do unto others as they would have you do unto them." Morality as Nurturance includes seeing the community as a family and that "helping people who need help is a moral responsibility" (Lakoff, 1995, p. 199). This includes self-nurturance and social nurturance. Morality as Fairness means equal distribution, impartial rules, and rights-based distribution. Thus, moral action is to act fairly according to these concepts of fairness. From the nurturant family metaphor, through these versions of morality, one is always striving for moral growth, something that can continue throughout one's life.

The nurturant parent morality considers many models of fairness depending on the situation: equality of distribution, opportunity, procedural distribution, rights-based fairness, and need-based fairness, among others. According to this perspective, Title IX should be enforced because it is the fair, and therefore the moral thing to do. It is the law of the land, and it calls for fair distribution of opportunities based on interest and abilities. As Bob Gardner, the chief officer of the National Federation of State High School Associations notes: "The colleges get all the attention, but Title IX isn't about the nation's elite college athletes. It's about providing a grass-roots gateway to sports that benefit millions" (in Pennington, 2004). Boyne (1994) writes,

gender equity isn't just a women's concern or a feminist crusade, it's a human issue, affecting the lives of us all—fathers, mothers, sisters, and brothers. What we do for each other, we do for ourselves—and for the dignity and quality of the sport of rowing. (p. 37)

This invokes the nurturant parent conceptual metaphor, whereby families take care of each other.

Clearly, the implementation of Title IX fits with the nurturant parent perspective, particularly the focus on equal opportunity. Tina Sloan Green, the co-founder and

President of the Black Women in Sport Foundation noted, "The value of sports is not only the physical and the mental, but it's also valuable in terms of preparing you for an administrative opportunity, especially with sport being a multibillion-dollar business" (Rhoden, 2012, p. D5).

Indeed, from the framework of the nurturant parent, Title IX does not go far enough. There are still glaring inequalities in opportunity, funding, support and facilities. At the same time men's minor sports are being cut and that loss blamed on Title IX and lack of funding, the amount of money in collegiate sport has increased exponentially. One area in need of careful attention is coaching and administrative salaries. As the *New York Times* reported,

> The average salary for the coach of an NCAA Division I men's team in any sport – including universities in the Football Bowl and Football Championship Subdivisions – increased by 67% to $267,007 from 2003 to 2010, according to statistics from the Department of Education. By contrast, the average salary for the coach of a women's team increased by 16% to $98,106. (Gentry & Alexander, 2012, p. B10)

Furthermore, where women previously had opportunities to advance in athletics as coaches and administrators, those positions are now filled by men. In some sports, nearly 50% of the coaching positions for women's teams are held by men – particularly in more lucrative sports such as basketball. On the face, that might seem fair, except that less than 2% of coaches of men's teams are women – and none in the most lucrative and culturally esteemed sports of men's football and basketball. So, while men have opportunities to coach women, women do not have opportunities to coach men. From a nurturant family model, women are not being treated fairly within athletics by any measure. Thus, all 'family members' are not receiving opportunities for self-fulfillment and moral growth.

Moreover, Title IX disproportionately benefits whites over all other Americans. As one writer argued, "Race is by far the most debilitating limitation of Title IX, yet you barely hear discussion of it. This reflects an old way of thinking about inequality, in which gender was the model. The only model" (Rhoden, 2012, p. D5). Black women are underrepresented in every college sport except track and field and basketball, where they are overrepresented at the Division I level. The picture is even worse for Latinas, Native Americans and Asian Americans. Black women's overrepresentation in certain sports and underrepresentation in others also furthers racial stereotypes.

More recently, some media accounts have explicitly used a family metaphor to describe choices facing college administrators. When the University of Maryland was facing a budget crisis, one reporter wrote:

> It's as if [University President] Loh was the patriarch of a family that had grown too large and too costly, and he wanted other relatives to suggest which kids should stay and which should go. Maryland has 27 "kids" (i.e., teams) in

its athletic department. There's no way the school can keep all of them without going broke, as it faces a $4 million deficit this fiscal year and more than $17 million by 2017. So regardless of other suggested remedies for fundraising and lowering spending, the committee was destined to recommend the elimination of some sports. (Snyder, 2011, p. C1)

A subtle shift occurs when administrators are held responsible for the decisions they make. In the previous decades, and still sometimes currently, administrators are not mentioned at all as Title IX is offered as the a priori reason for the elimination of teams. This has created a misunderstanding of the law that it mandates particular teams being eliminated. Some even believe that it mandates equal funding between men's and women's athletics, which even a cursory glance at Equity in Athletics Disclosure statistics, or even NCAA statistics show is widely off the mark.

In a return to ideas from the 1970s, some commentators and scholars see gender segregation as part of the problem that perpetuates women's inequality. Pappano and McDonagh (2008) argue:

When we invest in sports as fans, parents, and recreational players, whether we know it or not, we become complicit in a deeply gendered institution in which male superiority and female inferiority are played out as clearly as HDTV. Ironically, though, we've come to accept this differential treatment of males and females as "normal." It appears to be all right to charge $4 to see the Rutgers women's soccer team play and $7 to see the men's team play, for example. (p. 9)

They argue that Title IX opened the door to opportunity, but not equality. Once again, from a nurturant family model this is unacceptable, as it keeps women from reaching their full potential. From this perspective, it is unfair, not nurturing, and lacks empathy, thus causing harm and is therefore immoral.

CHAPTER SUMMARY

Clearly we can see "that politics is not just about policy and interest groups and issue-by-issue debate" (Lakoff, 2002, p. 19). As this analysis shows, conservatives have set the agenda in the debate over Title IX in public forums. When discussions start with the question of how to 'correct' the 'unintended consequences' of Title IX on men's minor sport, the conservative frame is already in play. Yet, when resources and opportunities are compared using all data available, women are still getting the short end of the stick. This could explain why, like Title IX, liberal political views sometimes win in court cases, but lose voters (Starr, 2005). As a *New York Times* writer laments:

For decades, many liberals thought they could ignore the elementary demand of politics – winning elections – because they could go to court to achieve these goals on constitutional grounds. The great thing about legal victories like Roe

v. Wade is that you don't have to compromise with your opponents, or even win over majority opinion. But that is also the trouble. An unreconciled losing side and unconvinced public may eventually change the judges. (Starr, 2005)

What's more, when one side sets the language and questions of the debate – the conceptual metaphors – a lot of work has already been accomplished in determining the 'common sense' conclusion. In the case of Title IX, one writer gives a clear example of this framing: "no one denies that many men's programs have been cut in the pursuit of gender parity, there's disagreement about the overall numbers" (Lynch, 2005). And, further, "without policy change, Title IX is likely to keep killing men's teams" (Lynch, 2005). Likewise, all civil rights laws are taking common sense hits similar to Title IX. A study released late in 2004 revealed that enforcement of civil rights laws have declined since 1999, even though the number of complaints remained constant, and that trend persisted into George W. Bush's second term in office as a consistent conservative moral conceptual framework continued to be cultivated in public discourse ("Enforcement," 2004). Interestingly, the media has been relatively quiet about shifts toward more enforcement of Title IX during President Barack Obama's two terms, even though enforcement has been more aggressive than at any point in the history of the law.

These issues continue to play out in ongoing debates over Title IX. Individually, and even more so collectively, they yield a comprehensive portrait of the layered nature of the representations of Title IX, the multiple meanings, and the articulations of ever changing perceptions of the intersections of sport and gender. While Title IX continues to open educational doors for women, athletics remains the popular focus of controversy. As a public and traditional domain of masculinity building that serves to maintain the gender hierarchy, sports remain an important cultural site for understanding shifting power relations. Debate over Title IX and athletics offers a useful site for exploring these cultural negotiations.

REFERENCES

Amdur, N. (1972, April 27). 'Individuals, not chattels:' The new mood in athletics. *Chicago Tribune*, sec. 1, p. 22.

An indecent veto. (1998, March 20). *St. Petersburg Times* (Florida), p. D2.

Bensten, C. (1975a, April 22). Women's sports ask the question: Is winning the only way to go? *Los Angeles Times*, sec. III, p. 1.

Boyne, D. (1994, July/Aug). Gender equity comes of age. *American Rowing*, *26*(4), 34–37, 40–41.

Cole, C. L. (2003). On issue: Playing the quota card. *Journal of Sport and Social Issues*, *27*(2), 87–99.

Compartmentalized discrimination. (1983, Aug. 14). *New York Times*, sec. 4, p. 18.

Condon, D. (1973, May 26). When the gals went big time in sports here, *Chicago Tribune*, sec. 2, p. 3.

Condon, D. (1975, Aug. 15). Critics out to cure college sports—or kill them? *Chicago Tribune*, sec. 4, p. 3.

Education Amendments of 1972 § 106.41 Athletics (1979). Available: http://www.gpo.gov/fdsys/pkg / CFR-2012-title34-vol1/xml/CFR-2012-title34-vol1-sec106–41.xml

Ellis, J. (1988, May 14). Letter to the Editor. *New York Times*, Sec. 1, p. 30.

End of college sport forecast: Coaches opposed to equal funding. (1975, June 18). *Los Angeles Times*, sec. III, p. 1.

Enforcement of civil rights law declined since '99, study finds. (2004, Nov. 22). *New York Times*. Retrieved from http://www.nytimes.com/2004/11/22/national/22civil.html

Fuzak urges review of Title IX issue. (1975, Sept. 17). *Chicago Tribune*, sec. 6, p. 3.

Gentry, J. K., & Alexander, R. M. (2012, April 3). Pay for women's basketball coaches lags far behind that of men's coaches. *New York Times*, p. B10.

James, W. (1988, Feb. 11). Taking exception. *Washington Post*, p. A27.

Kennedy, C. (2010). A new frontier for women's sports (beyond Title IX). *Gender Issues, 27*, 78–90.

Lakoff, G. (1995). Metaphor, morality, and politics, or, why conservatives have left liberals in the dust. *Social Research, 62*(2), 177–213.

Lakoff, G. (2002). *Moral politics: How liberals and conservatives think* (2nd ed.). Chicago: University of Chicago Press.

Lakoff, G. (2009). George Lakoff: A presidential commission on parenting and its effects. *Tikkun, 24*(1), 63–64.

Lakoff, G., & Johnson, M. (1987). The metaphorical logic of rape. *Metaphor and Symbolic Activity, 2*(1), 73–79.

Liddick, B. (1973, April 15). Off with the pompons, on with the pads, *LA Times*, sec. IX, p. 1.

Lynch, M. (2001, March 27). Title IX's Pyrrhic victory: How the quest for 'gender equity' is killing men's athletic programs. Retrieved from http://wrestlegirl.com/gnews366.htm

Mann, J. (1981, Oct. 21). Title IX: Senator Hatch aims at Title IX. *Washington Post*, p. C1.

Packwood, B. (1984, April 20). Discrimination aided. *New York Times*, p. A27.

Papanno, L., & McDonagh, E. (2008, Jan. 31). Women and men in sports: Separate is not equal. *Christian Science Monitor*, p. 9.

Pennington, B. (2004, June 29). Title IX trickles down to girls of generation Z. *New York Times*. Retrieved from http://www.nytimes.com/2004/06/29/sports/othersports/29title.html

Preston, M. (1975, Jan. 30). It'll take real teamwork to beat local biases, *Chicago Tribune*, sec. 3, p. 3.

Rhoden, W. (2012, June 11). Black and white women far from equal under Title IX. *New York Times*, p. D5.

Sandbrook, J. (1972, May 31) Campus revolution: Women's athletics. *Los Angeles Times*, sec. III, p. 1.

Snyder, D. (2011, Nov. 16). UMd. President Loh has hard judgment call. *Washington Times*, p. C1.

Soifer, J. (1975, May 9).Mother runs best…some of the time. *Los Angeles Times*, sec. III, p. 6.

Starr, P. (2005, Jan. 26). Winning cases, losing voters. *New York Times*. Retrieved from http://www.nytimes.com/2005/01/26/opinion/26starr.html

US Census. (2012). Retrieved from http://www.census.gov/compendia/statab/cats/education/higher_education_degrees.html

US Senate Conference Report No. 1026, 93rd Cong., 2nd Sess. 4271 (1974). Washington, Government Printing Office.

Walton, T. (2003). Title IX: Forced to wrestle up the backside. *Women in Sport and Physical Activity Journal*, 12(2), 5–26.

Walton, T. (2010). Reaganism and the dismantling of Civil Rights: Title IX in the 1980s. *Women in Sport and Physical Activity Journal,* 19(1), 14–25.

Women scapegoats in college sports. (1975, July 17). *Chicago Tribune*, sec. 4, p. 6.

AFFILIATION

Theresa A. Walton, PhD
School of Foundations, Leadership and Administration
Kent State University

CHRISTY GREENLEAF & TRENT A. PETRIE

7. STUDYING THE ATHLETIC BODY

INTRODUCTION

The athletic body, like all bodies, is subject to social construction and interpretation. The nature of sport places the athlete's body on display for judgement, evaluation, and critique. Athletes' physiques and physical characteristics not only contribute to their athletic performance, but also are assumed to represent personal attributes often associated with gender. In this chapter, the gendered nature of athletic bodies, body image(s) and eating attitudes and behaviors are addressed.

BODIES ON DISPLAY

Gendered Constructions of Bodies and Body Images

In Western society, socially constructed gender ideals are commonly prescribed and ascribed to bodies; in other words, gender is mapped onto and represented by the physical appearance of the body (Grogan, 2008; Lorber & Martin, 2003). Boys and men are expected to have lean, muscular, and powerful physiques that represent assumed masculine qualities, such as autonomy and aggressiveness. Girls and women, on the other hand, are expected to have more diminutive physiques – thin and sylphlike – presumed to represent feminine characteristics, such as passivity and dependence. As such, physical body characteristics like muscularity, leanness, adiposity, and height have gendered meanings. Being muscular and having a large physical size and stature are typically thought to symbolize masculinity and therefore are considered to be "appropriate" and expected physical characteristics for boys and men. For women, there appears to be two prevailing bodies that are thought to represent feminine ideas – a thinner, tall, and tubular body type that represents the physique associated with fashion models and a lean, toned, athletic, yet curvaceous physique that is associated with the models that grace the pages of Victoria's Secret catalogues or *Sports Illustrated* swimsuit issues.

In general, conformity to socially prescribed physical or body-shape characteristics is highly valued and rewarded. Social status and capital (e.g., popularity, prestige, salary) are often afforded to individuals who have or develop bodies consistent with gendered body ideals. Deviance from socially acceptable body shapes often results in social stigma (Judge & Cable, 2011; Kwan & Trautner, 2009). Having a body or physique that is inconsistent with body ideals is associated with teasing,

E. A. Roper (Ed.), Gender Relations in Sport, 119–140.

bullying, and social rejection. For example, overweight and obese individuals, both adults and children, report being teased by family and friends, mistreated by medical and health professionals, and excluded from social relationships (Puhl & Heuer, 2009). Historically, girls and women have experienced greater pressure to conform to gendered body ideals than boys and men, likely because of the high social value placed upon appearance for them (Kwan & Trautner, 2009). More recently, however, the social expectations and pressures for boys and men regarding male body ideals have become more pervasive (Grogan, 2008; Grogan & Richards, 2002).

Social body ideals (e.g., muscular for men and thin for women) in Western society are ubiquitous and are communicated and reinforced through media, such as magazines, television, and movies. And in sport, bodies play the central role, being in the spotlight and on display for all to evaluate and scrutinize, both in terms of functionality and appearance. Moreover, because participation and competition are commonly segregated by sex, an assumed dichotomy is highlighted. The segregated structure and organization of sport environments suggests differences between male and female athletes, their performance and their bodies, as well as reinforces socially prescribed expectations of masculinity and femininity.

Social Constructions of Athletes' Bodies

With the commercialization of sports during the past 50 years, athletes' bodies have taken on greater social significance and have come to represent, for both men and women, the "ideal type" (i.e., the idealized physique that all should strive to achieve). Further, mass media representations of athletes' bodies tend to highlight and exaggerate gendered body ideals and, for female athletes, often present them in ways (e.g., photos) that highlight their status as sexual objects as opposed to their performances in sport (Kane, LaVoi, & Fink, 2013). When female athletes are presented in this hypersexualized way, they are more likely to be viewed as sex objects, where the focus is on their appearance (e.g., being attractive) as opposed to their abilities as performers (Daniels & Wartena, 2011). In fact, some female athletes who have socially idealized bodies, such as Anna Kournikova, can attain commercial endorsements and celebrity status regardless of actual competitive success in her sport. This type of sexualization of male athletes does not occur as frequently; their images tend to be portrayed in the context of competitive achievements and illustrates the greater social and commercial value placed upon the appearance of women in comparison to men.

Body Objectification in the Sport Environment

Because bodies are the vehicles through which athletes perform and "do" their sport, their bodies are sometimes viewed as objects – objects that are sexualized, viewed and consumed for entertainment and pleasure, and through which physical feats are performed and competitions engaged. Because of the intense scrutiny that

120

exists for athletes within the sport environment, they may internalize this "body as object" perspective and engage in self-objectification. Objectification theory (Frederickson & Roberts, 1997), originally developed to explain the experiences of women in Western societies, suggests that bodies are sexually objectified within sociocultural environments and individuals who internalize the experience may come to see their own bodies as objects and thus experience a variety of negative psychological consequences. These negative psychological consequences include increased body shame and appearance anxiety and decreased internal awareness and flow. In turn, these negative psychological states are thought to increase the risk for mental health conditions such as depression and disordered eating.

Recently, Szymanski, Moffitt, and Carr (2011) proposed a number of core criteria for sexually objectifying environments, including the existence of traditional gender roles, lack of power for women and male domination, emphasis and focus on physical body attributes, and the approval and encouragement of men looking at women. Based upon these criteria, sport environments, in some cases, will be objectifying. Historically, sport has been considered a male preserve and even today most sport organizations are led and controlled by men. Women, when involved, often are adornments (e.g., cheerleaders), placed within the sport environment to be attractive, to entertain, and to be viewed by others. And even when women are the athletes themselves, they often are required to wear tight, revealing uniforms that accentuate their bodies, focus spectators on their appearance (over performance), make them feel self-conscious about their bodies, and sexualize them (Thompson & Sherman, 2010). Moreover, sports such as gymnastics, which emphasize appearance and femininity, may be more objectifying than those without an appearance focus (Parsons & Betz, 2001).

Interestingly, in their original conceptualization of objectification theory, Frederickson and Roberts (1997) suggested that sport participation provides girls and women with an opportunity to focus on the functional performance and capabilities of their bodies, thus having the potential to be an environment that challenges or resists objectification. Although there has not been a great deal of research into the potential protective effects of sport participation, there is some evidence consistent with the idea. Slater and Tiggemann (2012) found that among adolescent girls, sport participation was negatively associated with subsequent self-objectification. That is, the more time the adolescent girls reported participating in sport, the lower their self-objectification was one year later. However, in other cross-sectional studies, findings have not supported a relationship between sport participation and lower levels of self-objectification (e.g., Slater & Tiggemann, 2011), and have suggested that the longer female athletes are involved in sport the more they may be subject to critical comments from coaches about weight, appearance, and eating behaviors (Muscat & Long, 2008). Further, longitudinal data suggests that pressures from coaches and teammates about weight and appearance can lead to increases in body dissatisfaction among female athletes (Anderson, Petrie &, Neumann, 2012). Thus, more research is needed to better understand if and how engaging in sport might serve as a protective mechanism against self-objectification, body image concerns, and ultimately the development of disordered eating behaviors.

Very little research has examined male athletes' experiences of self-objectification, though more has examined body image concerns. One study of male body builders, weight lifters and non-athletes found that body builders had the highest levels of self-objectification (Hallsworth, Wade, & Tiggemann, 2005). Qualitative studies of both male undergraduates (Ridgeway & Tylka, 2005) and male athletes (Galli & Reel, 2009) revealed that men do compare their bodies to others, experience societal pressures to achieve a lean and muscular ideal, and wanted to appear attractive to others. Grieve and Helmick (2008) found that men with high levels of self-objectification reported a stronger drive for muscularity and muscle dysmorphia (e.g., a preoccupation with the belief that one's body is not muscular enough) than men with low levels of self-objectification (Murray, Riger, Touyz, & García, 2010). However, in a test of objectification theory in a sample of male undergraduates, Parent and Moradi (2011) found that although self-objectification was unrelated to drive for muscularity, the extent to which the men internalized the societal masculine body ideal did predict their desire to be more muscular and engage in more muscle building activities. Additional research is needed to further investigate if and how male athletes' experiences of objectification are associated with body image.

The intense focus on body and appearance that results from objectification may be related inversely to cognitive and motor performance (Frederickson & Harrison, 2005; Frederickson, Roberts, Noll, Quinn, & Twenge, 1998; Quinn, Kallen, Twenge, & Fredrickson, 2006), which would have direct ramifications for athletes and other performers. Appearance monitoring, or spending time and energy attending to how one looks, often results from feelings of objectification and can disrupt attention and reduce the cognitive resources that are available for performance. In support, Frederickson and Harrison (2005) found that among girls (10 to 17 years old), self-objectification was associated with poorer performance and technique in softball throwing. Previously, Fredrickson et al. (1998) demonstrated that higher levels of self-objectification were related to lower performance on a standardized math test. Given the importance within athletics of having excellent motor and cognitive processing control, it would be beneficial for researchers to continue to examine the potential linkage between objectification processes and disruptions in physical performance.

Comparing Athletic Ideals and Social Ideals (Not Always A Perfect 'Fit')

Because sports have different physical demands, the size, shape and functionality of athletes' bodies that are needed to perform optimally will vary. For some athletes, the physical requirements for their sport, such as their level of muscularity and/or leanness, align with social and gendered body ideals. For example, male sports (or athletic positions within sports, such as a being a wide receiver on a U.S. football team) that require strength, muscularity, and leanness are consistent with dominant gender body ideologies for boys and men and in line with masculine characteristics of competitiveness, dominance, and independence. Sports thought of as more "gender appropriate" for girls and women, such as figure skating and tennis, although requiring power and strength for performance, tend to reward the athletes who have flexible, graceful, thin bodies. The consistency between "gender appropriate" sports and assumed ideal body types for those sports is not surprising.

For other athletes, there is an inconsistency between the physique that is beneficial for sport performance and what is socially expected and valued. For example, female power lifters need to have strong, powerful and muscular bodies to be able to lift and control large amounts of weight. Female swimmers often have large, muscular arms and shoulders to be able to propel themselves through the water. Female volleyball players and basketball players often are tall and need strong, muscular legs to jump. In all cases, the bodies needed by athletes in these sports to perform at their best may be in contrast to what is expected from society, that is, they tend to be larger, taller, stronger, and more muscular than what is considered to be feminine. For male athletes, the difference is typically in the other direction, that is, being smaller, not as muscular, or being too thin or carrying too much body fat on their bodies is in contrast to the masculine ideal. Male distance runners, for example, are generally slight and lean, and U.S. football players (particularly lineman) may be viewed as obese. Male basketball players may stand out, sometimes uncomfortably, due to their height.

Such inconsistencies between sport and social demands can result in conflicted feelings about one's body, particularly for female athletes (Krane, Choi, Baird, Aimar, & Kauer, 2004; Ross & Shinew, 2008; Russell, 2004). For example, Mosewich, Vangool, Kowalski, and McHugh (2009) interviewed four adult and four adolescent female track and field athletes and asked them to reflect on the meaning of muscularity. The athletes indicated viewing muscularity (especially among competitors) as a sign of strength and something beneficial to performance, yet acknowledged that being too muscular was not desirable socially because it was thought to be 'manly' and detracted from a more feminine appearance. Similarly, Howells and Grogan (2012) interviewed adolescent and adult female swimmers who reported that despite the performance benefits of muscularity, they feared appearing masculine if they were "too" muscular. Although male athletes who do not fit the lean and muscular ideal generally are not viewed as feminine, some may perceive them as "unmanly" because of the strong association between a strong, virile, muscular body and modern day conceptions of masculinity (Drummond, 2002). Thus, it is not surprising to find that male athletes, across multiple sports, view themselves as not being muscular enough and desire a body that is larger and more defined (Raudenbush & Meyer, 2003). For some male and female athletes, real-ideal body conflicts exist that can cause psychological distress and confusion in their sense of self as feminine or masculine.

123

BODY IMAGE AMONG ATHLETES

Understanding Body Image(s)

Body image refers to the perceptions, thoughts, and feelings a person has toward and about his or her body shape, size, and appearance (Cash, 2004). It is multidimensional in nature and includes perceptual, cognitive, affective, as well as behavioral aspects. Perceptual body image is a person's view of his or her size, shape, and appearance, which may or may not reflect reality. Distorted body image perceptions (i.e., seeing oneself in a way that is inconsistent with reality) are commonly associated with negative body cognitions. The cognitive dimension of body image refers to individuals' evaluations about their physical size, shape, and appearance and includes beliefs about certain body parts. For example, an adolescent female athlete may "see" her thighs as big and fat (even though in reality they are not) and think that her thighs are larger than they should be. Often, affective or emotional responses co-occur with body image cognitions. The affective body image dimension relates to the feelings or emotions one has about his or her body and often is measured in terms of level of satisfaction. A male teenage athlete who thinks his upper body is not muscular enough may be dissatisfied with and ashamed of this part of his body because he believes it falls short of the male body ideal.

People often engage in actions or behaviors (i.e., behavioral body image dimension) that are consistent with their perceptions, cognitions, and emotions/attitudes. For example, when body dissatisfied, individuals may engage in appearance checking, wear apparel to reveal or conceal their body size and shape, manipulate their eating and exercise habits to modify their body, engage in pathogenic weight control methods such as self-induced vomiting or taking diuretics, and undergo surgery in order to manage their body and appearance. When it comes to body change strategies, male athletes generally are focused on increasing muscularity and leanness to their satisfaction, whereas female athletes want to be thinner and more toned (but not muscularly large).

Body (Dis)satisfaction among Male and Female Athletes

Because athletes' bodies are in the competitive spotlight, they are often quite aware of their physical size, shape and appearance. Athletes, like non-athletes, report varying degrees of satisfaction with their body shape, size and appearance, though generally are more satisfied with their bodies than non-athletes (e.g., Peden, Stiles, Vandehey, & Diekhoff, 2008; Petrie, 1996). For example, in a 2001 meta-analysis of 78 studies, Hausenblas and Downs found that athletes were more satisfied with their bodies than non-athletes. There are a number of possible explanations for higher body satisfaction among athletes. First, some athletes, because of their physical training, may have bodies that approximate social ideals. If so, they are likely to be more satisfied with their current size and shape. Second, as suggested within the objectification theory (Frederickson & Roberts, 1997) framework, the sport environment may provide a setting or context in which the body's function, rather than appearance, can be central. When that occurs, athletes' physical self-concept may predominate and override appearance-related concerns; a case of function winning out over style. There also are well-documented psychological benefits associated with physical activity and sport participation, including enhanced self-esteem and lower levels of depression (e.g., Greenleaf, Boyer, & Petrie, 2009; Parsons & Betz, 2001), both of which would contribute to more positive feelings towards the body.

Although athletes, compared to non-athletes, may have better body image(s), athletes do report body dissatisfaction and negative body image. Among female athletes, it is common for athletes to report wanting to be smaller or weigh less. For example, Crissey and Honea (2006) analyzed data from the National Longitudinal Study of Adolescent Health and found that 12–18 year old girls who participated in "feminine" sports reported that they felt overweight and were trying to lose weight. Similarly, in a sample of elite female athletes, 54.5% of the synchronized swimmers (Ferrand, Magnan, Rouveix, & Filaire, 2007) and approximately 25% of a mixed sport-sample (Haase, 2011) believed they were overweight. Female collegiate equestrian athletes wanted to weigh an average of 5.0 kgs less than their current weight (Torres-McGehee, Monsma, Gay, Minton, & Mady-Foster, 2011), and female collegiate cheerleaders, regardless of position (e.g., flyer), wanted to be smaller than their current body size/shape (Torres-McGee, Monsma, Dompier, & Washburn, 2012); both findings suggest a high level of current body dissatisfaction.

Body image related issues seem to persist and are perhaps exacerbated when athletes retire. For example, retired female rhythmic gymnasts experienced increased body dissatisfaction after discontinuing their training (Stirling, Cruz, & Kerr, 2012). The former gymnasts reported that they believed thinness was an indicator of success and a competitive advantage, beliefs that some transferred to life after gymnastics. These findings are consistent with previous research with retired athletes (e.g., Kerr & Dacyshyn, 2000; Stephan, Torregrosa, & Sanchez, 2007; Warriner & Lavallee, 2008), though other studies have suggested that body image actually may improve. O'Connor, Lewis, Kirchner, and Cook (1996) found that gymnasts became more satisfied with their bodies in the 15 years after leaving their sport. Because there are reasons why athletes' satisfaction might improve (e.g., removed from the weight/body pressures inherent in the sport environment) as well as explanations to support the opposite (e.g., loss of structured training may lead to weight gain), longitudinal research is needed to determine the temporal sequence of changes that occur in female athletes' body image concerns as they transition from their sport into retirement.

Among male athletes, body dissatisfaction is commonly associated with a perceived lack of muscularity and the idea they are insufficiently lean (Galli & Reel, 2009; Murray et al., 2010). In a qualitative study of current and former competitive male athletes, Galli and Reel (2009) found that most of the men interviewed indicated some level of body dissatisfaction associated with a perceived failure to attain the body ideal for their sport. The importance of the sporting body for men is also evident in results from a study of male college football players (Steinfeldt, Gilchrist,

Halterman, Gomory, & Clint Steinfelts, 2011). Football players with strong athletic identity (i.e., seeing themselves as and valuing their status as an athlete) had higher levels of drive for muscularity in comparison to those with weaker athletic identity. Similarly, among male high school football players, Mackinnon et al. (2003) found that body leanness predicted both perceived athletic competence and body image.

Disturbed body perceptions and dissatisfaction can contribute to an increased drive for muscularity and, in extreme cases, to muscle dysmorphia, which is characterized by an overwhelming belief that one's body is lacking muscularity, engaging in behaviors such as excessive exercise or restrictive eating to increase muscularity and leanness, and disturbed social and personal responsibilities (Murray et al., 2010). Baghurst and Lirgg (2009) found that male collegiate football players, while reporting some symptoms of muscle dysmorphia, did not have the same level of disturbance as male body builders or men engaged in weight training for appearance reasons. Because so few studies have been conducted with male athletes regarding body image concerns, it is unclear as to how theirs may change over time as they retire from sport and change their training regimens. It is possible that, like female athletes, they experience relief from the pressures and messages from coaches and teammates about needing to attain a certain body size and shape. But, also like female athletes, they may suffer from the reduction of physical training, experience weight gain (or a loss of muscularity), and become more dissatisfied with their physical appearance. Longitudinal studies are needed to learn more about the development, maintenance, and change in male athletes' body image.

Sport-Related Factors Associated with Body Image

Although athletes, in comparison to non-athletes, are more body satisfied, they experience body- and weight-related pressures that negatively influence body image (e.g., Anderson, Petrie, & Neumann, 2011, 2012). Athletes are exposed not only to broad social factors that can influence body image, but also to pressures that are unique to the sport environment. For example, sport type may play a role in athletes' body image. There are a variety of suggested categorizations of sport type (e.g., aesthetic, weight-class, ball, endurance) and it is thought that some sport types may expose athletes to greater weight- and body-related pressures than others. For example, aesthetic sports, such as figure skating and synchronized swimming, emphasize and value appearance and attractiveness of athletes' physiques, thus athletes in those sports may face expectations of achieving and maintaining an attractive appearance. Indeed, research indicates that athletes in aesthetic sports have higher self-objectification and body shame than athletes in other types of sports (Parsons & Betz, 2001; Tiggemann & Slater, 2001). Weight-class sports, such as wrestling and crew, require athletes to "make weight" by achieving a specified weight in order to compete in a particular weight division. Athletes who compete in weight-class sports may experience body image disturbances coinciding with their cycle of weigh-ins (e.g., Dale & Landers, 1999). Petrie (1996) compared lean and nonlean athletes to a group of non-athletes on a variety of eating disorder measures, including body dissatisfaction. He found that although the two athlete groups were more satisfied than the non-athletes, they were similar to each other in terms of their body image. Raudenbush and Meyer (2003) found that lacrosse players, in comparison to swimmers, cross-country runners, basketball and soccer players, wanted to gain the most muscle to achieve their ideal physique.

Not all research results support the hypothesis of sport-type differences in weight- and body-related pressures. For example, Hausenblas and Downs' (2001) meta-analysis did not find differences in body satisfaction between athletes in aesthetic, endurance, and ball sports. Among female high school athletes, Karr, Davidson, Bryant, Balague, and Bohnert (2013) found no sport-type group differences among aesthetic/lean (i.e., gymnastics), non-aesthetic/lean (i.e., cross country), and non-aesthetic/non-lean (i.e., softball) sport athletes. It may be that some sports have stereotypical body ideals that are narrowly defined and athletes who are incongruent with these ideals may face a number of weight- and body-related pressures that can contribute to negative body image, regardless of sport type. In sports such as figure skating, there is little variation in the body shape and size of competitive skaters, thus skaters may experience negative body image when they fail to meet the perceived ideal body. Additional research is needed to better understand if there are factors associated with sport type that are consistently associated with body image. Moreover, studies of specific sports may be more fruitful than cross-sport comparisons.

Sport attire and uniforms are another common source of weight- and body-related pressure. In many sports, athletes are required to wear tight and/or body revealing apparel for training and competition. This apparel may be functional in nature, such as allowing for easier movement (Steinfeldt, Zakrajsek, Bodey, Middendorf, & Martin, in press), but in other cases, it may provide no or little performance advantage (Thompson & Sherman, 2010). Regardless of the functional benefit of revealing sport attire, athletes' bodies are often on display via their training and competition uniforms which can contribute to increased self-consciousness, decreased body satisfaction, and disturbed eating attitudes for both male and female athletes (Galli, Petrie, Reel, Chatterton, & Baghurst, in press; Reel, Petrie, SooHoo, & Anderson, 2013). For example, Torres-McGehee et al. (2011) studied female collegiate equestrian athletes and found that the athletes had body image disturbances associated with their equestrian uniform. Similarly, female collegiate volleyball players reported that their tight-fitting, spandex uniforms were a distraction to them during pregame warm-ups and matches (Steinfeldt et al., in press). The volleyball players felt like they were "hanging out" of their uniforms and that all of their imperfections were on display.

Volleyball is an interesting example wherein the uniforms worn by women (spandex shorts or briefs and a form fitting top) are much more revealing than what is worn in men's volleyball. An even more dramatic difference is seen in the sport of beach volleyball. Female beach volleyball players, until 2012, were required to wear bikinis or one piece swimsuits by the international governing body. Male beach volleyball players, on the other hand, wear baggy shorts and tank tops. This

127

difference in uniforms is seen in other sports as well. For example, in track and field events, women often wear more revealing uniforms (e.g., small spandex briefs, sports bras) than men (e.g., tank tops). The trend in women wearing more body revealing uniforms than men is likely associated with social and cultural expectations regarding the value of physical appearance and attractiveness. Women's bodies tend to be appreciated for being (hetero)sexually attractive, whereas men's bodies are more valued for their function and competence. Additionally, historically sport has been considered an environment in which boys and men can demonstrate their masculinity and girls and women have been considered "invaders." Thompson and Sherman (2010) suggested that the more revealing uniforms worn by female athletes were sexual in nature, diminished their seriousness as athletes, and conferred no performance advantages. If the uniforms did help the athletes win, they argued that male athletes would be playing beach volleyball in speedos.

Perceived pressures and weight- and body-related comments from coaches, teammates, judges, and parents can negatively influence athletes' body images (e.g., Anderson et al., 2012; Galli & Reel, 2009). Negative weight- and body-related attitudes and behaviors from coaches can be particularly harmful because athletes typically value and respect coaches' opinions, perspectives, and ideas. Research with female athletes indicates that athletes who perceive that their coaches are critical of their weight or body shape experience negative body image (Coppola, Ward, & Freysinger, in press; Kerr, Berman, & De Souza, 2006; Muscat & Long, 2008). In a qualitative study with eight female collegiate athletes, Coppola et al. (in press) found that athletes perceived that although their coaches encouraged "fit sport bodies" they also made critical comments about their bodies in comparing athletes' bodies to an assumed sport ideal. Further, pressures about appearance and weight from within male and female athletes' sport environments have been associated with increased body dissatisfaction as well as indices of disordered eating (Galli, Reel, Petrie, Greenleaf, & Carter, in press; Reel et al., 2013). Parents can also influence athletes' body image. For example, Fransicso, Narciso, and Alarcão (in press) found that perceived pressure from parents was associated with body image dissatisfaction among elite adolescent female athletes. Additional research is needed to better understand the mechanisms underlying the influences of coaches and parents on athletes' body image.

EATING ATTITUDES AND BEHAVIORS AMONG ATHLETES

Nature and Prevalence of Disordered Eating

Eating disorders are psychiatric conditions that involve unhealthy eating patterns (e.g., binge eating, restrictive dieting), the use of pathogenic weight control behaviors (e.g., vomiting, laxatives, excessive exercise), and disturbances in cognitions and perceptions about weight and self (American Psychiatric Association [APA], 2000). The three primary clinical eating disorders are anorexia nervosa (AN), bulimia nervosa (BN), and eating disorders, not otherwise specified (EDNOS).

The symptoms associated with AN include restriction of food intake so a very low body weight is maintained, body image distortions (including inaccurate perceptions of body weight), intense fear of gaining weight, and body weight influencing self-evaluations (APA, 2000); loss of menstruation has been recommended for removal in the proposed criteria for the *Diagnostic and Statistical Manual – V* (DSM-V). Prevalence of AN is low, though women (0.5% to 0.9%) have higher lifetime rates than men (0.05% to 0.3%; APA, 1994; Hudson, Hiripi, Pope, & Kessler, 2007), adolescents higher rates than young to middle-age adults (Currin, Schmidt, Treasure, & Jick, 2005), and girls greater rates than boys (Ackard, Fulkerson, & Neumark-Sztainer, 2007).

BN is characterized by a recurrent cycle of binge-eating and compensatory behaviors, as well as self-evaluations that are negatively influenced by body shape and weight (APA, 2000); in the DSM-V, it has been proposed that the frequency of binge eating be lowered. During binges, individuals often feel out of control, and then compensate for the large caloric intake through extreme behaviors, such as vomiting, excessive exercising, or use of laxatives. Lifetime prevalence for BN is higher for women (1% to 3%) than the 0.1% to 0.5% noted for men (APA, 1994; Hudson et al., 2007) as well as for adolescents than adults over 20 (Currin et al., 2005); female undergraduates have been identified as a high risk group, with prevalence rates that have ranged from 1.3% to 2.2% (Crowther, Armey, Luce, Dalton, & Leahey, 2008; Keel, Heatherton, Dorer, Joiner, & Zalta, 2006).

EDNOS is the diagnostic designation used when individuals have some, but not all of the symptoms associated with AN or BN (or symptoms are not being experienced at the required level of severity). Binge eating disorder (BED), a current EDNOS diagnosis, is characterized by repeated overeating in which individuals experience distress and feeling out of control, but without the subsequent use of compensatory behaviors. Prevalence rates for general EDNOS have ranged from 2.5% to 3.3% for female undergraduates (Crowther et al., 2008); BED rates generally are higher for women (3.5%) than the 2% rate for men (Hudson et al., 2007).

Although not part of the DSM system, researchers have documented the presence of "subclinical" eating disorders, which are characterized by problematic eating and weight control behaviors, negative beliefs about self, and body image distortions and/or dissatisfaction, but at a level that is less severe than found in the clinical designations. Subclinical prevalence rates are higher than those found for clinical disorders for both men and women (Crowther et al., 2008; Keel et al., 2006) and, for some individuals, may develop into a diagnosable eating disorder (Stice, Ng, & Shaw, 2010). In male and female undergraduates, respectively, subclinical classifications have ranged from 37% to 39% (Cohen & Petrie, 2005; Tylka & Subich, 2002) and binge eating rates from 8.1% to 28.7% (Keel et al., 2006).

Pathogenic Eating among Male and Female Athletes

Male and female athletes have been found to score higher on a range of eating disorder indices than their non-athlete counterparts (Hausenblas & Carron, 1999;

129

Smolak, Murnen, & Ruble, 2000). Prevalence rates for female athletes, at the collegiate and international levels, have ranged from 0% to 6.7% (AN), 0% to 12.1% (BN), and 2% to 13.4% for EDNOS rates (Anderson & Petrie, 2012; Greenleaf, Petrie, Carter, & Reel, 2009; Johnson, Powers, & Dick, 1999; Sundgot-Borgen & Torsveit, 2004). For male athletes at the same competitive levels, prevalence of AN has been reported at zero (0%), whereas rates for BN (0% to 7.5%) and EDNOS (0% to 9.7%) have been higher (Johnson et al., 1999; Petrie, Greenleaf, Reel, & Carter, 2008; Sundgot-Borgen & Torsveit, 2004). Overall, prevalence tends to be higher for elite as opposed to collegiate athletes and for female, in comparison to male, athletes (Anderson & Petrie, 2012; Greenleaf et al., 2009; Johnson et al., 1999; Petrie et al., 2008; Sundgot-Borgen & Torsveit, 2004). At present, there are no credible data for prevalence rates among adolescent athletes, though recent research has suggested that athletes display lower scores across a variety of disordered eating indices than non-athletes (e.g., Martinsen, Bratland-Sanda, Eriksson, & Sundgot-Borgen, 2010).

Like non-athletes, athletes' prevalence rates for subclinical disorders and individual pathogenic weight control behaviors are far higher than clinical designations. In independent mixed-sport samples, a substantial number of male (19.2%; Petrie et al., 2008) and female (25.5%; Greenleaf et al., 2009) collegiate athletes were classified as subclinical (i.e., symptomatic). Similarly, Anderson et al. (2012) reported subclinical prevalence rates that ranged from 20.9% (female collegiate swimmers/divers) to 28.9% (female collegiate gymnasts). Among national/international level athletes, male (1%) and female (4%) athletes were diagnosed with anorexia athletica (AA), which is a subclinical eating disorder designated by low body weight, problematic eating, and excessive concern about body shape and weight (Sundgot-Borgen & Torsveit, 2004). Athletes also admit to binge eating. For example, at a frequency of two or more times per week, 9.3% of male and 7.8% of female collegiate athletes indicate eating uncontrollably to the point of stuffing themselves (Greenleaf et al., 2009; Petrie et al., 2008). What is unknown for athletes, however, is the extent to which disordered eating symptoms ultimately lead to the development of clinical eating disorders.

Athletes also engage in a variety of individual behaviors to control their weight and body size/shape. In mixed-sport samples of male and female collegiate athletes (Greenleaf et al., 2009; Petrie et al., 2008), athletes reported exercising two or more hours per day specifically to burn calories (men – 37%; women – 25.5%) and dieting or fasting two or more times per year (men – 14.2%; women – 15.6%). More extreme forms of weight control were used less frequently: vomiting one or more times per week (men – 5%; women – 2.5%), using diuretics two or more times per month (men – 7%; women – 1.5%), and taking laxatives two or more times per week (men – 7.9%; women – 1%). Given the physical demands of training and competition and the expectations from coaches that exist about fitness, weight, and performance, it makes sense that athletes would rely more on exercise and dieting (two behaviors that can easily be "hidden" within the sport environment or be viewed as an indicator of athletes' dedication to their sport) than laxatives, diuretics, or vomiting. Athletes also may know that these more severe forms of weight control can have serious side effects and interfere more directly with their performances.

Risk Factors Associated with EDs and Disordered Eating

A "risk" factor is defined as a psychosocial, environmental, and/or physical variable that increases the probability of an individual developing an eating disorder (Stice, Ng, & Shaw, 2010), and can only be determined through either longitudinal or experimental studies where the variable is shown to precede (and contribute to) the onset of the disorder (Stice, 2002). Within athlete-eating disorder research, however, the majority of studies have been cross-sectional, thus allowing only for a discussion of the psychosocial correlates of eating disorders.

As discussed earlier in the chapter, the sport environment has been conceptualized as increasing athletes' risk of developing an eating disorder. Expectations from coaches about body size/shape and weight, messages from teammates about food and eating, judges' comments and messages about appearance, and revealing and/or tight fitting uniforms, to name a few, may contribute to the dissatisfaction athletes experience regarding their bodies and their use of disordered eating behaviors. Research with male and female collegiate athletes has demonstrated that pressures from coaches, teammates, and sport about weight, appearance and performance are related to higher levels of body dissatisfaction, dietary restraint, and bulimic symptomatology (e.g., de Bruin, Oudejans, & Bakker, 2007; Galli et al., in press; Reel et al., 2013). In the one longitudinal study to examine the effects of sport environment pressures on female athletes' disordered eating, Anderson et al. (2012) found that pressures about weight, dieting and appearance experienced at the beginning of the athletic season predicted increases in body dissatisfaction at the end of the season; there were no effects from these pressures on the athletes' intent to restrict their caloric intake. These studies validate sport pressures, not only as a correlate, but as a risk factor in the development of at least body dissatisfaction within female athletes.

For female athletes, a number of psychological correlates of disordered eating have been established. For example, dietary intent/restraint (Anderson et al., 2011; Greenleaf, Petrie, Carter, & Reel, 2010), drive for thinness (Hinton & Kubas, 2005; Krane, Stiles-Shipley, Waldron, & Michalenok, 2001), social physique anxiety (Hausenblas & Mack, 1999; Krane et al., 2001), sport anxiety (Holm-Denoma, Scaringi, Gordon, Van Orden, & Joiner, 2009), negative affect (e.g., sadness; Anderson et al., 2011; Greenleaf et al., 2010; Petrie et al., 2009), internalization of societal body ideals (Petrie, 1993; Petrie et al., 2009), overweight perceptions (Haase, 2011), sport position (i.e., being a "flyer" in cheerleading; Torres-McGehee et al., 2012), body image concerns (e.g., body dissatisfaction, body esteem; Anderson et al., 2011; Brannan, Petrie, Greenleaf, Reel, & Carter, 2009; de Bruin, Oudejans, Bakker, & Woertman, 2011; Ferrand, Champely, & Filaire, 2009; Greenleaf et al., 2010; Hinton & Kubas, 2005; Krane et al., 2001; Petrie, 1993; Petrie et al., 2009; Williamson et al., 1995), perfectionism (Brannan et al., 2009), self-esteem (Berry & Howe, 2000; Brannan et al., 2009; Engel et al., 2003; Petrie et al., 2009), exercising to improve appearance (Brannan et al., 2009; Petrie et al., 2009), appearance orientation (i.e., how invested individuals are in improving their appearance; Petrie et al., 2009), perceived athletic competence (Kipp & Weiss, 2013), and ego goal orientation (de Bruin et al., 2009), to name a few, have been associated significantly with a variety of eating disorder indices, including drive for thinness, bulimic symptomatology, and anorexic symptomatology. Similar to findings of research with non-athlete samples, body image concerns, self-esteem and dietary behaviors (and drive for thinness) have demonstrated the strongest and most consistent relationships to the disordered eating outcomes.

Although Petrie and Greenleaf (2012) have suggested that the correlates (or risk factors) of disordered eating for male athletes would be similar to those found for female athletes, few empirical studies have been conducted to examine these potential relationships. For example, Dale and Landers (1999) found that being "in" or "out" of season for collegiate wrestlers was related to their drive for thinness; being in season was associated with higher scores on this dimension. In a mixed-sport sample of male collegiate athletes, higher levels of drive for thinness, body dissatisfaction, feeling ineffective, interpersonal distrust, interoceptive awareness (i.e., difficulty recognizing emotions and feelings of hunger/satiety), and maturity fears were associated with higher scores on the Eating Disorder Inventory (EDI) bulimia subscale (Petrie, 1996). Similarly, bulimic symptomatology was related to feelings of sadness and stress as well as a fear of becoming fat in a sample of male collegiate athletes (Petrie, Greenleaf, Carter, & Reel, 2007); Terry and Waite (1996) reported significant correlations between Eating Attitudes Test (EAT) scores and body shape concerns among male light and heavy-weight rowers. More research is needed with male athletes to determine if the variables proposed by Petrie and Greenleaf (2012) and tested in samples of female athletes actually do correlate with eating disorder indices in the expected directions. Further, for both male and female athletes, longitudinal studies are needed to determine which variables predict the development of eating disorders, act to maintain their presence, and serve a protective function in terms of lowering risk.

CREATING HEALTHY BODY ENVIRONMENTS FOR ATHLETES

Body Appreciation

Body image historically has been framed as negative, that is, the problematic feelings, thoughts, behaviors, and perceptions that individuals have in relation to their body size and shape. Yet, with the advent of the positive psychology movement (e.g., Seligman & Csikszentmihalyi, 2000), it makes sense also to conceptualize body image from an adaptive, healthy perspective. In taking this perspective, Avalos, Tylka, and Wood-Barcalow (2005) identified several qualities of positive body image (or what they called body appreciation), including: (a) being favourably disposed towards one's body regardless of actual physical appearance, (b) accepting one's body despite perceived flaws, weight, or shape, (c) paying attention to bodily needs and behaving in healthy ways towards it, and (d) not accepting unrealistic, societal body ideals. They found, amongst female undergraduates, that body appreciation was related to greater psychological well-being (i.e., self-esteem, optimism, proactive coping), higher body satisfaction/esteem, lower body shame, and lower levels of eating disorder symptomatology. Overall, the women in Avalos et al.'s study felt positively about their bodies, suggesting that not all women are driven by feelings of dissatisfaction.

Within the sport environment, athletes feel positively about their bodies in general (e.g., Hausenblas & Symons Downs, 2001; Peden et al., 2008), but more specifically about how functional they are (Galli & Reel, 2009; Krane et al., 2004; Russell, 2004; Steinfeldt et al., in press). Athletes take pride in being strong and physically fit and being able to perform the skills of their sport against high level competitors. They appreciate what their bodies can "do" (i.e., a high level of athletic, physical, sport concept), though acknowledge that the physical training often shifts their body size and shape away from societal physical appearance ideals that are promulgated through the media. Thus, a focus of research has been on testing prevention programs that help athletes lessen the deleterious effects of societal pressures on their self and body image and reduce their risk of developing an eating disorder.

Studies with non-athletes have demonstrated that prevention programs that (a) target at-risk groups, (b) are interactive and experiential, and (c) are based on effective content (e.g., cognitive dissonance or body acceptance protocols) can result in reduced internalization of societal body ideals, lower dietary intent, decreased body dissatisfaction and eating pathology, and improved negative affect (e.g., Stice, Shaw, & Marti, 2007). Research with athletes has been far more limited, though initial results are promising. For example, among female high school athletes, an 8-week, peer-led training program (Athletes Targeting Healthy Exercise and Nutrition Alternative [ATHENA], Elliott et al., 2004) was associated with healthier behaviors (e.g., decrease in use of diet pills), increased knowledge (e.g., eating disorder consequences), more positive mood, and fewer intentions to engage in unhealthy weight control behaviors (e.g., vomiting). Smith and Petrie (2008) compared cognitive-dissonance and healthy-weight focused interventions in a sample of female collegiate athletes. The athletes attended three 1-hour, professionally-led sessions associated with each intervention. Over the course of the three weeks, the cognitive dissonance group showed decreases in sadness, body dissatisfaction, and internalization of societal appearance ideals.

Becker, McDaniel, Bull, Powell and McIntyre (2012) examined the effectiveness of two evidence-based, three session (60–80 minutes per session) peer-led interventions – cognitive dissonance based and healthy weight-focused that had been modified to address the unique experiences of female athletes. Implemented within an entire NCAA Division III athletic department, they randomly assigned half the athletes from each team to either the cognitive dissonance or healthy weight condition. At a six-week follow-up, they found that both interventions helped to reduce internalization, dietary restraint, bulimic symptomatology, negative affect, and concerns about body shape and weight; several of these positive effects extended

133

to one year post-completion. The results of these prevention program studies suggest that having athletes examine and challenge societal messages about body size/shape and physical appearance, and help athletes develop a healthy approach toward eating can result in improvements in appreciation of body and self, and to decreases in actual disordered eating behaviors. More research is needed to test these and other potential programs (e.g., internet-based interventions) to determine the ideal "dose-response" and what modifications are needed for athletes to make the programs most effective. Further, future studies will need to incorporate control groups to determine if the changes are really due to the interventions or simply to the passage of time.

Rethinking the Social and Gendered Constructions of Athletes' Bodies

Although prevention programming offers hope for increasing athletes' body appreciation, its effects are limited to the athletes who are enrolled in the intervention and by the larger sport culture in which the athletes reside. Thus, it will take changes within the sport culture itself to create broad, meaningful, and lasting improvements in athletes' body appreciation. As discussed earlier in this chapter, gender is socially constructed and determines what is viewed as "masculine" or "feminine," including the body types that are deemed acceptable for each sex. For men, a masculine body is defined through height, muscularity and leanness (Ridgeway & Tylka, 2005); broad shoulders with a V-shaped back, a large chest, and "six-pack" abs are what represent the ideal. Women, on the other hand, have two physical ideals. The first is tall, thin, and willowy, exemplified by runway models. The second ideal is portrayed through the women who model swimsuits and underwear – thin but voluptuous, curvy but with relatively narrow hips and thighs. Thus, through the socialization process, where gender is constructed, boys and girls come to understand that one important way to validate being "masculine" or "feminine" is by having their bodies closely approximate the physical ideal. When there is discrepancy from this ideal, not only do men and women experience body dissatisfaction but they may come to question their masculinity or femininity. Athletes are not exempt from these socially constructed body types.

Through the intense physical training athletes undergo, they shape their bodies, increasing its tone, muscularity, and leanness. Although the physical changes that result from this training are valued from a sport performance perspective (e.g., Krane et al., 2004), for many their muscular and toned bodies are inconsistent with the societal appearance ideal and thus a source of psychological stress that can affect them not only in their social relations but also in their focus and how they feel during their performances (Steinfeldt et al., 2013). Thus, for many athletes there are social, affective, and cognitive costs associated with having a well-developed (and trained) sport body that does not coincide with societal ideals.

So, who determines these body ideals and can they be changed? Can we, as a society, broaden what we appreciate in terms of body size and shape and send messages that there is beauty in the physical bodies of athletes, not just for what they can do, but also how they look? As discussed earlier in the chapter, the sport environment, in particular the messages sent from coaches, teammates, and judges about body, weight and appearance, can influence athletes' views of themselves and their bodies, and determine if they engage in disordered eating behaviors. Thus, a starting place for such "cultural" change is helping those who have the influence to begin to think and behave differently when it comes to discussion around body size/ shape and weight among athletes.

There are several things that can be done within sport to create a body-healthy environment. First, coaches and athletes must come to understand that there is no ideal body weight or body fat percentage that results in superior performance (Bonci et al., 2008), and that within any given sport, there is considerable variability in the body size and shape of high-level performers (Thompson & Sherman, 2010). If coaches and athletes focused less on weight and more on physical fitness, strength, mobility, mental preparation, etc., athletes would begin to become more accepting of how they physically are and likely not engage in pathogenic weight control behaviors. Second, athletic departments can eliminate weigh-ins and weight requirements, except when needed to monitor health during high-intensity training in hot and humid conditions (i.e., monitor hydration). If weigh-ins are done, they should be conducted by medical personnel, in private, and athletes' weights should never be posted. Each athletic department can develop guidelines for when weighing is appropriate, how weigh-ins would be conducted, and how information will be used to benefit the health of the athletes (see Bonci et al., 2008). Third, consistent with the first recommendation, expectations about weight, body size, eating, and appearance should be challenged within each sport because biases exist in terms of how coaches, judges, fans, and others believe athletes from specific sports *should* look. These biases, such as a male cross-country runner should be tall and very lean, influence how athletes are viewed (e.g., will they even be encouraged to pursue a sport in which their body does not coincide with the bias) and what body-change expectations are held for them if they are in the sport (e.g., expectation to lose weight). Instead of making judgments based on physical appearance, athletes could be evaluated on their skills, understanding of competitive strategy, physical fitness levels, psychological preparation, etc. Fourth, examine the revealing uniforms that athletes are expected to wear in training and competition to determine if they provide any performance advantages or if they primarily are being used because they enhance an aesthetic (or sexual) dimension. If no performance advantage exists, then perhaps teams can change to uniforms that do not unnecessarily sexualize the athletes who wear them.

CHAPTER SUMMARY

Female and male athletes face numerous weight- and body-related pressures associated with their athletic performance as well as with gendered social norms and expectations. Although the sport environment may reinforce gendered body ideals and expectations and contribute to weight- and body-pressures, opportunities to promote healthy and positive body images and eating attitudes and behaviors are plentiful. Moreover, sport provides a context in which traditional gender ideologies related to the body can be challenged and changed so that all athletes, regardless of gender, can appreciate their bodies.

REFERENCES

Ackard, D. M., Fulkerson, J. A., & Neumark-Sztainer, D. (2007). Prevalence and utility of DSM-IV eating disorder diagnostic criteria among youth. *International Journal of Eating Disorders, 40,* 409–417.

American Psychiatric Association. (2000). *Diagnostic and statistical manual of mental disorders* (4th ed., text Rev.). Washington, DC: Author.

Anderson, C., & Petrie, T. A. (2012). Prevalence of disordered eating and pathogenic weight control behaviors among NCAA Division I female collegiate gymnasts and swimmers. *Research Quarterly for Exercise and Sport, 83*(1), 120–124.

Anderson, C. M., Petrie, T. A., & Neumann, C. S. (2012). Effects of sport pressures on female collegiate athletes. *Sport, Exercise, and Performance Psychology, 1,* 120–134.

Anderson, C. M., Petrie, T. A., & Neumann, C. S. (2011). Psychosocial correlates of bulimic symptoms among NCAA division-I female collegiate gymnasts and swimmers/divers. *Journal of Sport and Exercise Psychology, 33,* 483.

Avalos, L., Tylka, T. L., & Wood-Barcalow, N. (2005). The body appreciation scale: Development and psychometric evaluation. *Body Image, 2*(3), 285–297.

Baghurst, T., & Lirgg, C. (2009). Characteristics of muscle dysmorphia in male football, weight training, and competitive natural and non-natural bodybuilding samples. *Body Image, 6*(3), 221–227.

Becker, C. B., McDaniel, L., Bull, S., Powell, M., & McIntyre, K. (2012). Can we reduce eating disorder risk factors in female college athletes? A randomized exploratory investigation of two peer-led interventions. *Body Image, 9,* 31–42.

Bonci, C., Bonci, L., Granger, L., Johnson, C., Malina, R., Milne, Ryan, R. R., & Vanderbunt, E. M. (2008). National Athletic Trainers' Association position statement: Preventing, detecting, and managing disordered eating in athletes. *Journal of Athletic Training, 43,* 80–108.

Brannan, M., Petrie, T. A., Greenleaf, C., Reel, J., & Carter, J. (2009). The relationship between body dissatisfaction and bulimic symptoms in female collegiate athletes. *Journal of Clinical Sport Psychology, 3,* 103–126.

Cash, T. F. (2004). Body image: Past, present, and future. *Body Image, 1,* 1–5.

Cohen, D. L., & Petrie, T. A. (2005). An examination of psychosocial correlates of disordered eating among undergraduate women. *Sex Roles, 52,* 29–42.

Coppola, A. M., Ward, R. M., & Freysinger, V. J. (in press). Coaches' communication of sport body image: Experiences of female athletes. *Journal of Applied Sport Psychology.*

Crissey, S. R., & Honea, J. C. (2006). The relationship between athletic participation and perceptions of body size and weight control in adolescent girls: The role of sport type. *Sociology of Sport Journal, 23,* 248–272.

Crowther, J., Armey, M., Luce, K., Dalton, G., & Leahey, T. (2008). The point prevalence of bulimic disorders from 1990 to 2004. *International Journal of Eating Disorders, 41,* 491–497.

Currin, L., Schmidt, U., Treasure, J., & Jick, H. (2005). Time trends in eating disorder incidence. *British Journal of Psychiatry, 186,* 132–135.

Dale, K. S., & Landers, D. M. (1999). Weight control in wrestling: eating disorders or disordered eating? *Medicine and Science in Sports and Exercise, 31,* 1382–1389.

Daniels, E. A., & Wartena, H. (2011). Athlete or sex symbol: What boys think of media representations of female athletes. *Sex Roles, 65,* 566–579.

de Bruin, A. P., Bakker, F. C., & Oudejans, R. R. D. (2009). Achievement goal theory and disordered eating: Relationships of disordered eating with goal orientations and motivational climate in female gymnasts and dancers. *Psychology of Sport and Exercise, 10,* 72–79.

de Bruin, A. P., Oudejans, R. R. D., & Bakker, F. C. (2007). Dieting and body image in aesthetic sports: A comparison of Dutch female gymnasts and non-aesthetic sport participants. *Psychology of Sport and Exercise, 8,* 507–520.

de Bruin, A. P., Oudejans, R. R., Bakker, F. C., & Woertman, L. (2011). Contextual body image and athletes' disordered eating: The contribution of athletic body image to disordered eating in high performance women athletes. *European Eating Disorders Review, 19*(3), 201–215.

Drummond, M. J. (2002). Men, body image, and eating disorders. *International Journal of Men's Health, 1*, 89–103.

Elliot, D. L., Goldberg, L., Moe, E. L., DeFrancesco, C. A., Durham, M. B., & Hix-Small, H. (2004). Preventing substance use and disordered eating: initial outcomes of the ATHENA (Athletes Targeting Healthy Exercise and Nutrition Alternatives) program. *Archives of pediatrics and adolescent medicine, 158*(11), 1043.

Engel, S. G., Johnson, C., Powers, P. S., Crosby, R. D., Wonderlich, S. A., Wittrock, D. A., & Mitchell, J. E. (2003). Predictors of disordered eating in a sample of elite Division I college athletes. *Eating Behaviors, 4*, 333–343.

Ferrand, C., Champely, S., & Filaire, E. (2009). The role of body-esteem in predicting disordered eating symptoms: A comparison of French aesthetic athletes and non-athlete females. *Psychology of Sport and Exercise, 10*, 373–380.

Ferrand, C., Magnan, C., Rouveix, M., & Filaire, E. (2007). Disordered eating, perfectionism and body-esteem of elite synchronized swimmers. *European Journal of Sport Science, 7*, 223–230.

Francisco, R., Narciso, I., & Alarcão, M. (in press). Parental influences on elite aesthetic athletes' body image dissatisfaction and disordered eating. *Journal of Child and Family Studies.*

Fredrickson, B. L., & Roberts, T. A. (1997). Objectification theory: Toward understanding women's lived experiences and mental health risks. *Psychology of Women Quarterly, 21*, 173–206.

Fredrickson, B. L., Roberts, T. A., Noll, S. M., Quinn, D. M., & Twenge, J. M. (1998). That swimsuit becomes you: Sex differences in self-objectification, restrained eating, and math performance. *Journal of Personality and Social Psychology, 75*, 269–284.

Frederickson, B. L., & Harrison, K. (2005). Throwing like a girl: Self-objectification predicts adolescent girls' motor performance. *Journal of Sport and Social Issues, 29*, 79–101.

Galli, N., Petrie, T. A., Reel, J. J., Chatterton, J. M., & Baghurst, T. M. (in press). Assessing the validity of the Weight Pressures in Sport Scale for male athletes. *Psychology of Men and Masculinity.*

Galli, N., & Reel, J. J. (2009). Adonis or Hephaestus? Exploring body image in male athletes. *Psychology of Men and Masculinity, 10*, 95–108.

Galli, N., Reel, J. J., Petrie, T., Greenleaf, C., & Carter, J. (2011). Preliminary development of the Weight Pressures in Sport Scale for male athletes. *Journal of Sport Behavior, 34*, 47–68.

Greenleaf, C., Boyer, E. M., & Petrie, T. A. (2009). Psychological well-being and physical activity: The role of high school physical activity and sport participation. *Sex Roles, 61*, 714–726.

Greenleaf, C., Petrie, T. A., Carter, R., & Reel, J. J. (2009). Female collegiate athletes: Prevalence of eating disorders and disordered eating behaviors. *Journal of American College Health, 57*, 489–495.

Greenleaf, C., Petrie, T. A., Carter, R., & Reel, J. J. (2010). Psychosocial risk factors of bulimic symptomatology among female athletes. *Journal of Clinical Sport Psychology, 4*, 177–190.

Grieve, R., & Helmick, A. (2008). The influence of men's self-objectification on the drive for muscularity: Self-esteem, body satisfaction and muscle dysmorphia. *International Journal of Men's Health, 7*(3), 288–298.

Grogan, S. (2008). *Body image: Understanding body dissatisfaction in men, women, and children* (2nd ed.). New York, NY: Routledge.

Grogan, S., & Richards, H. (2002). Body image: Focus groups with boys and men. *Men and Masculinities, 4*, 219–232.

Haase, A. M. (2011). Weight perception in female athletes: associations with disordered eating correlates and behavior. *Eating Behaviors, 12*, 64–67.

Hallsworth, L., Wade, T., & Tiggemann, M. (2005). Individual differences in male body-image: An examination of self-objectification in recreational body builders. *British Journal of Health Psychology, 10*, 453–465.

Hausenblas, H. A., & Carron, A. V. (1999). Eating disorder indices and athletes: An integration. *Journal of Sport & Exercise Psychology, 21*, 230–258.

Hausenblas, H. A., & Mack, D. E. (1999). Social physique anxiety and eating disorder correlates among female athletic and nonathletic populations. *Journal of Sport Behavior, 22*, 502–513.

137

Hausenblas, H. A., & Symons Downs, D. (2001). Comparison of body image between athletes and nonathletes: A meta-analytic review. *Journal of Applied Sport Psychology, 13*, 323–339.

Hinton, P., & Kubas, K. (2005). Psychosocial correlates of disordered eating in female collegiate athletes: Validation of the ATHLETE questionnaire. *Journal of American College Health, 54*, 149–156.

Holm-Denoma, J. M., Scaringi, V., Gordon, K. H., Van Orden, K. A., & Joiner, T. E. (2009). Eating disorder symptoms among undergraduate varsity athletes, club athletes, independent exercisers, and nonexercisers. *International Journal of Eating Disorders, 42*(1), 47–53.

Howells, K., & Grogan, S. (2012). Body image and the female swimmer: Muscularity but in moderation. *Qualitative Research in Sport, Exercise and Health, 4*, 98–116.

Hudson, J. I., Hiripi, E., Pope, H. G., & Kessler, R. C. (2007). The prevalence and correlates of eating disorders in the National Comorbidity Survey replication. *Biological Psychiatry, 61*, 348–358.

Johnson, C., Powers, P. S., & Dick, R. (1999). Athletes and eating disorders: The National Collegiate Athletic Association study. *International Journal of Eating Disorders, 26*, 179–188.

Judge, T. A., & Cable, D. M. (2011). When it comes to pay, do the thin win? The effect of weight on pay for men and women. *Journal of Applied Psychology, 96*, 95–112.

Kane, M. J., LaVoi, N. M., & Fink, J. S. (2013). Exploring elite female athletes' interpretations of sport media images: A window into the construction of social identity and "selling sex" in women's sports. *Communication and Sport.* 1–31. doi: 0.1177/2167479512473585

Karr, T. M., Davidson, D., Bryant, F. B., Balague, G., & Bohnert, A. M. (2013). Sport type and interpersonal and intrapersonal predictors of body dissatisfaction in high school female sport participants. *Body Image, 10*, 210–219.

Keel, P., Heatherton, T., Dorer, D., Joiner, T., & Zalta, A. (2006). Point prevalence of bulimia nervosa in 1982, 1992, and 2002. *Psychological Medicine, 36*, 119–127.

Kerr, G., Berman, E., & Souza, M. J. D. (2006). Disordered eating in women's gymnastics: Perspectives of athletes, coaches, parents, and judges. *Journal of Applied Sport Psychology, 18*, 28–43.

Kerr, G., & Dacyshyn, A. (2000). The retirement experiences of elite, female gymnasts. *Journal of Applied Sport Psychology, 12*, 115–133.

Kipp, L. E., & Weiss, M. R. (2013). Social influences, psychological need satisfaction, and well-being among female adolescent gymnasts. *Sport, Exercise, and Performance Psychology, 2*, 62–75.

Krane, V., Choi, P. Y. L., Baird, S. M., Aimar, C. M., & Kauer, K. J. (2004). Living the paradox: Female athletes negotiate femininity and muscularity. *Sex Roles, 50*, 315–329.

Krane, V., Stiles-Shipley, J., Waldron, J., & Michalenok, J. (2001). Relationships among body satisfaction, social physique anxiety, and eating behaviors in female athletes and exercisers. *Journal of Sport Behavior, 24*, 247–264.

Kwan, S., & Trautner, M. N. (2009). Beauty work: Individual and institutional rewards, the reproduction of gender and questions of agency. *Sociology Compass, 3*, 49–71

Lorber, J., & Martin, P. Y. (2003). The socially constructed body: Insights from feminist theory. In P. Kvisto (Ed.), *Illuminating Social Life: Classical and Contemporary Theory Revisited* (pp. 279–303; 5th ed). Thousand Oaks: Pine Forge Press.

Mackinnon, D. P., Goldberg, L., Cheong, J., Elliot, D., Clarke, G., & Moe, E. (2003). Male body esteem and physical measurements: Do leaner, or stronger, high school football players have a more positive body image? *Journal of Sport and Exercise Psychology, 25*(3), 307–322.

Martinsen, M., Bratland-Sanda, S., Eriksson, A. K., & Sundgot-Borgen, J. (2010). Dieting to win or to be thin? A study of dieting and disordered eating among adolescent elite athletes and non-athlete controls. *British Journal of Sports Medicine, 44*, 70–76.

Mosewich, A. D., Vangool, A. B., Kowalski, K. C., & Mc Hugh T, F. (2009). Exploring women track and field athletes' meanings of muscularity. *Journal of Applied Sport Psychology, 21*, 99–115.

Murray, S. B., Rieger, E., Touyz, S. W., & De la Garza García, L. (2010). Muscle dysmorphia and the DSM-V conundrum: Where does it belong? A review paper. *International Journal of Eating Disorders, 43*(6), 483–491.

Muscat, A. C., & Long, B. C. (2008). Critical comments about body shape and weight: Disordered eating of female athletes and sport participants. *Journal of Applied Sport Psychology, 20*, 1–24.

O'Connor, P. J., Lewis, R. D., Kirchner, E. M., & Cook, D. B. (1996). Eating disorder symptoms in former female college gymnasts: relations with body composition. *American Journal of Clinical Nutrition, 64*(6), 840–843.

Parent, M. C., & Moradi, B. (2011). His biceps become him: A test of objectification theory's application to drive for muscularity and propensity for steroid use in college men. *Journal of Counseling Psychology, 58*, 246–256.

Parsons, E. M., & Betz, N. E. (2001). The relationship of participation in sports and physical activity to body objectification, instrumentality, and locus of control among young women. *Psychology of Women Quarterly, 25*, 209–222.

Peden, J., Stiles, B., Vandehey, M., & Diekhoff, G. (2008). The effects of external pressures and competitiveness on characteristics of eating disorders and body dissatisfaction. *Journal of Sport & Social Issues, 32*, 415–429.

Petrie, T. A. (1993). Disordered eating in female collegiate gymnasts: Prevalence and personality/attitudinal correlates. *Journal of Sport & Exercise Psychology, 15*, 424–436.

Petrie, T. A. (1996). Differences between male and female college lean sport athletes, nonlean sport athletes, and nonathletes on behavioral and psychological indices of eating disorders. *Journal of Applied Sport Psychology, 8*, 218–230

Petrie, T. A., & Greenleaf, C. (2012). Eating disorders in sport. In S. Murphy (Ed.), *Oxford Handbook of Sport and Performance Psychology* (pp. 635–659). New York: Oxford University Press.

Petrie, T. A., Greenleaf, C., Carter, J. E., & Reel, J. J. (2007). Psychosocial correlates of disordered eating among male college athletes. *Journal of Clinical Sport Psychology, 1*, 340–357.

Petrie, T. A., Greenleaf, C., Reel, J. J., & Carter, J. E. (2009). An examination of psychosocial correlates of eating disorders among female collegiate athletes. *Research Quarterly for Exercise and Sport, 80*(3), 621–632.

Petrie, T. A., Greenleaf, C., Reel, J., & Carter, J. (2008). Prevalence of eating disorders and disordered eating behaviors among male collegiate athletes. *Psychology of Men and Masculinity, 9*, 267–277.

Puhl, R. M., & Heuer, C. A. (2009). Obesity stigma: Important considerations for public health. *American Journal of Public Health, 100*, 1019–1028.

Quinn, D. M., Kallen, R. W., Twenge, J. M., & Fredrickson, B. L. (2006). The disruptive effect of self-objectification on performance. *Psychology of Women Quarterly, 30*, 59–64.

Raudenbush, B., & Meyer, B. (2003). Muscular dissatisfaction and supplement use among intercollegiate athletes. *Journal of Sport and Exercise Psychology, 25*, 161–170.

Reel, J. J., Petrie, T. A., SooHoo, S., & Anderson, C. M. (2013). Weight pressures in sport: Examining the factor structure and incremental validity of the weight pressures in sport – females. *Eating Behaviors, 14*, 137–144.

Ridgeway, R. T., & Tylka, T. L. (2005). College Men's Perceptions of Ideal Body Composition and Shape. *Psychology of Men and Masculinity, 6*(3), 209–220.

Ross, S. R., & Shinew, K. J. (2008). Perspectives of women college athletes on sport and gender. *Sex Roles, 58*(1–2), 40–57.

Russell, K. (2004). On versus off the pitch: The transiency of body satisfaction among female rugby players, cricketers, and netballers. *Sex Roles, 51*, 561–574.

Seligman, M. E., & Csikszentmihalyi, M. (2000). Positive psychology. *American Psychologist, 55*, 5–14.

Slater, A., & Tiggemann, M. (2012). Time since menarche and sport participation as predictors of self-objectification: A longitudinal study of adolescent girls. *Sex Roles, 67*, 571–581.

Slater, A., & Tiggemann, M. (2011). Gender differences in adolescent sport participation, teasing, self-objectification and body image concerns. *Journal of Adolescence, 34*, 455–463.

Smith, A., & Petrie, T. (2008). Reducing the risk of disordered eating among female athletes: A test of alternative interventions. *Journal of Applied Sport Psychology, 20*, 392–407.

Smolak, L., Murnen, S. K., & Ruble, A. E. (2000). Female athletes and eating problems: A meta-analysis. *International Journal of Eating Disorders, 27*, 371–380.

Steinfeldt, J. A., Gilchrist, G. A., Halterman, A. W., Gomory, A., & Clint Steinfeldt, M. (2011). Drive for muscularity and conformity to masculine norms among college football players. *Psychology of Men and Masculinity, 12*(4), 324.

139

Steinfeldt, J. A., Zakrajsek, R. A., Bodey, K. J., Middendorf, K. G., & Martin, S. B. (in press). Role of uniforms in the body image of female collegiate volleyball players. *The Counseling Psychologist*, 10.1177/0011000012457218

Stephan, Y., Torregrosa, M., & Sanchez, X. (2007). The body matters: Psychophysical impact of retiring from elite sport. *Psychology of Sport and Exercise, 8*, 73–83.

Stice, E. (2002). Risk and maintenance factors for eating pathology: A meta-analytic review. *Psychological Bulletin, 128*, 825–848.

Stice, E., Ng, J., & Shaw, H. (2010). Risk factors and prodromal eating pathology. *Journal of Child Psychology and Psychiatry, 51*, 518–525.

Stice, E., Shaw, H., & Marti, C. (2007). A meta-analytic review of eating disorder prevention programs: Encouraging findings. *Annual Review of Clinical Psychology, 3*, 207–231.

Stirling, A. E., Cruz, L. C., & Kerr, G. A. (2012). Influence of retirement on body satisfaction and weight control behaviors: Perceptions of elite rhythmic gymnasts. *Journal of Applied Sport Psychology, 24*, 129–143.

Sundgot-Borgen, J., & Torstveit, M. K. (2004). Prevalence of eating disorders in elite athletes is higher than in the general population. *Clinical Journal of Sports Medicine, 14*, 25–32.

Szymanski, D. M., Moffitt, L. B., & Carr, E. R. (2011). Sexual objectification of women: Advances to theory and research. *The Counseling Psychologist, 39*, 6–38.

Terry, P. C., & Waite, J. (1996). Eating attitudes and body shape perceptions among elite rowers: Effects of age, gender and weight category. *Australian Journal of Science and Medicine in Sport, 28*, 3–6.

Thompson, R., & Sherman, R. (2010). *Eating disorders in sport*. New York: Routledge.

Tiggemann, M., & Slater, A. (2001). A test of objectification theory in former dancers and non-dancers. *Psychology of Women Quarterly, 25*, 57–64.

Torres-McGehee, T. M., Monsma, E. V., Dompier, T. P., & Washburn, S. A. (2012). Eating disorder risk and the role of clothing in collegiate cheerleaders' body images. *Journal of Athletic Training, 47*, 541–548.

Torres-McGehee, T. M., Monsma, E. V., Gay, J. L., Minton, D. M., & Mady-foster, A. N. (2011). Prevalence of eating disorder risk and body image distortion among National Collegiate Athletic Association Division I varsity equestrian athletes. *Journal of Athletic Training, 46*, 431–437.

Tylka, T., & Subich, L. (2002). A preliminary investigation of the eating disorder continuum with men. *Journal of Counseling Psychology, 49*, 273–279.

Warriner, K., & Lavallee, D. (2008). The retirement experience of elite female gymnasts: Self identity and the physical self. *Journal of Applied Sport Psychology, 20*, 301–317.

Williamson, D., Netemeyer, R., Jackman, L., Anderson, D., Funsch, C., & Rabalais, J. (1995). Structural equation modeling of risk factors for the development of eating disorder symptoms in female athletes. *International Journal of Eating Disorders, 17*, 387–393.

AFFILIATIONS

Christy Greenleaf, PhD
Department of Kinesiology
University of Wisconsin – Milwaukee

Trent A. Petrie, PhD
Department of Psychology
University of North Texas

SANDRA KIRBY & GUYLAINE DEMERS

8. SEXUAL HARASSMENT AND ABUSE IN SPORT

INTRODUCTION

There is a powerful tension between two ideas in sport: successful (winning) performance and athlete welfare. Achievement is important in sport and successful performances are the hallmarks of any individual's feelings of well-being and accomplishment. However, when that success comes at the cost of an athlete's well-being, when the imperative to win prevails over the health and wellness of participants, then that sport environment is not a healthy place for athletes. Coaches and authority figures in sport are exploiting others for their own ends when they use power over these athletes for sexual purposes or sexual outcomes (Brackenridge, 2001).

How are the following headlines connected? Long-time assistant basketball coach accused of molesting a team ball boy for a dozen years (Syracuse University); ex-football assistant coach arrested and jailed on new sexual assault charges (Pennsylvania State); Graham James, the "most hated perpetrator" of sexual abuse in hockey (junior hockey), pleads guilty to charges of repeated sexual assaults on two players. In each, coaches were involved. They were the perpetrators, or the knowing bystanders, or the unknowing/unsuspecting "person responsible." And, there is more common ground too. In each case, there were other people who knew or should have known about the breaking or hard-bending of the rules by those who were later charged. In each, the victim(s) got very little justice for taking the courageous steps in speaking out (Kirby & Telles-Langdon, 2012).

From this, it is clear that harassment and abuse are issues in sport. The last two of the accounts, those of Jerry Sandusky (Pennsylvania State Football) and Graham James (Canadian Jr. Hockey) have been high-water or landmark scandals in the US and in Canada, respectively. These cases received wide-spread media coverage and made the public acutely aware of the issues of harassment and abuse in sport.

As authors in earlier chapters have written, sport is a gendered world. From the earliest moments when we try to throw a ball, run a race, jump a bar or swim across a pool, boys are measured against each other and against all girls. Girls are measured against each other. The assumption is that the natural order of things will likely prevail and all but a very few of the boys will be better than all girls. If a boy is not better than a girl, the consequences can be profound, negative and lasting for both. As ludicrous as it sounds, their genders and even their sexualities can be brought into question.

Sport is a social world filled with power relations. At the very top, the International Olympic Committee (IOC) has referential power over the international sport

E. A. Roper (Ed.), Gender Relations in Sport, 141–161.
© *2013 Sense Publishers. All rights reserved.*

federations (IFs) including the International Association of Athletics Federations (IAAF) and the Fédération International des Sociétés d'Aviron (FISA). Where coaches and athletes interact, power also exists. As an award-winning hockey coach, Graham James had authoritative power over the junior hockey players whom he abused: Sheldon Kennedy, Todd Holt and Thereon Fleury. Though coaches have power 'over' athletes, that power unfortunately is not always used to facilitate athlete development (Tomlinson & Strachan, 1996). It can be abused in any number of ways, including through sexual harassment and abuse.

Sport is filled with intercultural relations. The social world of sport consists of nations, cultures and sub-cultures and the interpersonal relationships of those who live within them. Sport makes societies what they are and they in turn make sport what it is. Over the years, sport organizations have been challenged by the women's liberation and anti-racism movements, boycotts of sport at the highest levels, and the exposure of performance-enhancing drug use in sport. Organized sport continues to struggle with the re-establishment of ethical values which, as Brackenridge writes "are supposed to underpin modern sport and to guarantee that the highest possible moral standards...be upheld in sport" (Kirby, Greaves, & Hankivsky, 2000, p. 8).

Following that line of thinking, it can be said that power and gender together in the sport world is not in itself a bad thing. Abuse of power is when social/gender relations go "off the rails" and sport enjoyment, participation and performance suffer. Sport is about health and well-being. It is about the joy of learning sport skills, of racing fast and jumping high. It is about learning how to be a boy and a girl in the world of physical performance. It is about feeling good and being healthy. It is exciting and fun in the moment and its effects last a lifetime. Sport for an athlete should not be, as Brackenridge writes, "a miserable and degrading experience that not only undermines their personal sporting hopes and aspirations but also inflicts long-term damage on their self-esteem and life chances" (2001, p. 4). Everyone seeking to understand gender relations in sport needs to consider how sexual harassment and abuse contaminate healthy relations and damage sport as a social institution.

DEFINITIONS AND THE NATURE AND SCOPE OF THE PROBLEM IN SPORT

The language of sexual exploitation is complex. The language is not only important for naming the issues but also for providing a means for various stakeholders such as researchers, students, parents, athletes, coaches, administrators, lawyers and policy writers and social activists to work together on solving the issues as they arise. All this is made even more complex because what is legal (i.e., the age of sexual consent or prohibited discriminations) varies across international boundaries and across U.S. state lines. Sport is organized in different ways in different countries, making broad-based solutions difficult.

Brackenridge (2001) devotes a complete chapter to the importance of definitions. She suggests that shared understandings and careful language helps to "shape the way a social problem is defined, explained and addressed" (p. 25). The following are a summary of key terms and definitions:

Sexual exploitation – a continuum of sexual discrimination, sexual harassment and sexual abuse where individuals exercise power, some of them sexual, to manipulate, mistreat, and abuse others. Child sexual exploitation occurs when those targeted, the children/youth, are under the age of majority and/or under the age of sexual consent. Included is a range of behaviors from written or verbal abuse to rape, incest, cyber-bullying and economic exploitation of children. Both the production of child pornography and the luring of children online are child sexual abuse (CCCP, 2012).

Sex discrimination/prejudice – attitudes and related behaviors based on negative perceptions of a group's characteristics (e.g., expecting a person to act in a specific way because of her/his gender or sexual orientation). In the sport context, sex discrimination (continuum of sexual harassment and abuse) includes "unwanted, groomed or forced involvement in sexual behavior (including)...the use of gender stereotypes" (Brackenridge, 2001, p. 35) that undermine an athlete's sense of belonging and personal confidence and also hinder her/his athletic performance.

Chilly climate – the social environment where women are consistently treated differently than men in a way that disadvantages women. For example, across the sporting world, women hold fewer positions of power than do men. A chilly sport climate may also be one that is tolerant of but not welcoming to women; one that does not mentor women, nor have policies and procedures for issues such as harassment, employment equity or child care. The concept of chilly climate can also be used to describe the differential and disadvantageous treatment of others in sport, usually minority groups (Brackenridge, 2001). Though more rare, chilly climate can also be used to describe a social environment in sport that consistently advantages women over men.

Sexual harassment – a range of behaviors of a sexual nature by a perpetrator that are unwelcome and/or unwanted by a targeted individual or group. Sexual harassment includes sexual gesturing and comments of a derogatory nature, inappropriate physical touching, sexist jokes and overt sexual behaviors.

Sexual assault – "a term used to refer to all incidents of unwanted sexual activity, including sexual attacks and sexual touching" (Brennan & Taylor-Butts, 2008, p. 1). According to Brennan and Taylor-Butts (2008), the "focus is on the violence rather than the sexual nature" (p. 1) of the behaviors. In the U.S., sexual assault is defined as "any type of sexual contact or behavior that occurs without the explicit consent of the recipient. Falling under the definition of sexual assault are sexual activities (such) as forced sexual intercourse, forcible sodomy, child molestation, incest, fondling and attempted rape" (The

United States Department of Justice, 2013, p. 1). Sexual assault is a form of sexual violence that includes when a person's 'sexual integrity' is violated and/ or when weapons or threats or physical attacks are used against them.

Child sexual assault – sexual violence/sexual assault on underage athletes, those under the age of consent as legally defined in the jurisdiction. In Canada, sections 271 and 272 of the Criminal Code include sexual interference, invitation to sexual touching, sexual exploitation, incest, anal intercourse and beastiality. In Australia, where "sexual abuse is defined as sexual activity between an adult and a child," a child is defined as under 18 years old (Leahy, 2012, p. 118). Leahy also indicates that such sexual activity is "regardless of whether the child understands the sexual nature of the activity (and includes) sexual contact by force or threat of force" (Leahy, 2012, p. 118). Sexual abuse includes acts involving physical contact such as masturbation and sexual touching and acts without touching such as exhibitionism and pornographic photography (p. 118). In the U.S., the National Sexual Violence Research Center (NSVRC, 2012) indicates that there is some preliminary evidence of declining rates of child sexual abuse and other forms of child neglect and mistreatment. Brackenridge (2001) considers the distinction between child and adult athlete to be morally, though not legally, irrelevant when addressing sexual assault within the sport context.

Grooming – "is the process by which a perpetrator isolates and prepares an intended victim. Entrapment may take weeks, months or years and usually moves steadily so that the abuser is able to maintain secrecy and avoid exposure" (Brackenridge, 2001, p. 35). Grooming may also include a quid pro quo, an exchange of benefits for sexual favors.

Sexual coercion – involves persuading someone to engage in sexual activity even after she/he has indicated her/his unwillingness to do so. Sexual coercion is also persuading a child to engage in sexual activity. The persuasion may take many forms, from the very subtle to overt, including social and emotional manipulation, manipulative use of punishments and privileges, and the use of alcohol or drugs.

Lack of sexual consent – consent or the lack of consent make a difference in how sexual activity is understood. Brackenridge (2001) indicates that "sexual contact between an adult/coach and a child/athlete is always wrong; that the abuser is always responsible for his (her) actions" (p. 38). Also, an athlete cannot give 'valid consent' to persons who have authority or a position of trust over them (e.g., coaches). A child below 'the age of consent' cannot consent to sexual activity. "Consent obtained by coercion is invalid" (Archard, 1998, p. 3).

Sexual shakedown of a team – when a person in a position of authority, such as a coach, manager, medical staff member or athletic trainer, engages in sexual interactions with some or all members of a team (Kirby, 2013c). It is not possible in such circumstances for the person in a position of authority over the athletes to gain their consent.

As is evident, many of the definitions are overlapping. These show that individuals may experience more than one form of abuse, more than one time, and by more than one perpetrator. They may experience sexual abuse as children and then again as adults. The abuse may occur over a short time or an extended period of time and the forms of abuse itself may vary over time. Sexual exploitation, the overarching term in this chapter, recognizes the role of authority figures in sport and the way in which they can abuse.

As research and child protection practices are becoming more international and the reach more global, the more complex things are becoming. Age of consent, for example, is not the same in different countries. Moreover, sport is managed in many different social, cultural, religious and economic environments and it is impossible to create a 'one size fits all' set of solutions to sexual exploitation. However, what the research has revealed so far is that the problem of sexual exploitation appears in all societies and is also part of the sport world in those societies. Research has also shown that sexual abuse is a systemic issue in sport, which means that it is entrenched within the world of sport. No one sport is free from the problem. There is also no research that definitively shows one sport to be more risky than another.

PREVALENCE

There are no accurate measures of the amount of sexual exploitation in any nation's population (Brackenridge, 2001). However, Terry and Tallon (2003) indicate that within the U.S., vicitimization studies suggest that the "scope of the problem is extensive" (p. 5). A global study of violence against children was undertaken by Pinheiro (2006). The United Nations Children's Fund (UNICEF, 2007) then commissioned a follow-up focused on sport (Brackenridge, Fasting, Kirby, & Leahy, 2010). While debate continues about the magnitude of the issue of sexual exploitation outside versus inside the world of sport, there is a steadily growing body of evidence about sexual exploitation in sport. This work has proven especially useful in providing an overall sense of the problem in sport.

The research on sexual exploitation in sport is relatively recent and, as suggested above, difficult to compare. According to the research:

- more is known about the sexual exploitation of girls than of boys in sport;
- more females than males experience sexual harassment and abuse in sport (numerous studies);
- there is serious under-reporting of sexual harassment and abuse, particularly by males (Brackenridge, 1997; Kirby et al., 2000; Robinson, 1998);

145

- 29% of 266 elite female and male athletes (Kirby et al., 2000) complained of sexual harassment by men and some women in the sport environment; 51% of 660 elite female athletes experienced sexual harassment (Fasting, Brackenridge, & Sundgot, 2000);
- from a sample of 370 elite and club athletes, 31% of females and 21% of males were sexually abused. Of those, 41% of sexually abused females and 29% of sexually abused males were abused by sport personnel (Leahy, 2012, p. 118);
- just under 1/5th of 210 university athletes in the U.S. reported experiencing sexist or derogatory comments (Volkwein & Sankaran, 2002);
- repeated unwanted sexually suggestive glances (Fasting, 2012), humiliation and ridicule are common forms of sexual harassment experienced by athletes (Fasting et al., 2000; Kirby & Greaves, 1996);
- 21.8 % of 266 elite athletes reported sexual intercourse with authority figures in sport; 8.6% reported forced sexual intercourse; 8.6% reported being sexually assaulted under the age of 16 (child sexual abuse) (Kirby & Greaves, 1996);
- 90% of sexual harassment and abuse is male to female; the other 10% is roughly split between female to male, male to male and female to female (Kirby et al., 2000);
- there is some limited support for a link between penultimate (sub-elite) performance skill and pubescent years (Stage of Imminent Achievement [SIA], Brackenridge & Kirby, 1997) when risk of sexual abuse may be highest;
- harassment by peer university athletes is greater than by coaches (Holman, 1995) or authority figures (Fasting et al., 2000; Fasting, Brackenridge, Miller, & Sabo, 2008);
- there is a high tolerance in sport of sexual harassment (and abuse), hazings, initiations and bullying within teams (Kirby & Wintrup, 2002; Robinson, 1998).

As is evident, there are overlapping information points from the various studies. Most studies were done with elite/high performance athletes on national teams and national development teams or with student-athletes in universities. A small number of studies have been conducted with parents of athletes (Brackenridge, 1997), stakeholder groups, (Parent, 2011) or with a variety of sport organizations (Brackenridge et al., 2007; Parent, 2011; University of Ottawa, 2011). Without comparable approaches, it is difficult to conclude more than that sexual exploitation is a significant problem in sport, the nature of which is not yet fully understood.

Why is sexual exploitation so difficult to measure? First, sport has a reputation as a good place for young people to develop. It is, by and large, a healthy place for athletes and for those who facilitate athletes' participation and achievements. Research on sexual exploitation is not usually welcomed in such environments and at best, is generally considered an unwanted distraction. Second, though the world of sport is quite public, much of the preparation for competition goes on out of the public eye and behind closed doors. Young athletes are often asked to behave as if they are young adults – young ambassadors who have responsibilities for training

146

and competing, for travelling, representing their community or nation, and speaking to the media (Brackenridge, 2001; Kirby et al., 2000). Sexual exploitation of these young ambassadors occurs most often in private and both athletes and perpetrators are reluctant to talk about it at the time and frequently, for many years afterwards. Third, the "Dome of Silence" (Kirby et al., 2000) actively discourages athletes from speaking out. Athletes who do speak out about the violence they have experienced, may not be believed and may suffer consequences such as 'negative progress' in their athletic career and lack of personal support from teammates and other personnel in sport. Fourth, various research codes of ethics make research with victims of sexual abuse, and with children, very difficult. Access to information about what athletes' experience outside of the actual performance of sport is extremely limited (Brackenridge, 2001). Fifth, the researchers and legal scholars have various definitions for sexual exploitation, so comparative work within and across nations is difficult. Research and child protection networks are increasingly working in coordinated ways, however, comparative work across national boundaries and jurisdictional units remains difficult. Despite these difficulties, the private to public shift is underway as athletes are sharing their stories and accounts of athletes' sexual exploitation appear in the press.

SEXUAL EXPLOITATION RISK FACTORS

Research primarily by Brackenridge (1997, 2001) and Cense and Brackenridge (2001) has provided a comprehensive description of risk factors. Are some sports riskier than others? What common characteristics or themes exist as part of the sport culture, athletes' profile and abusers' profile that might assist with understanding where and how sexual exploitation exists?

Sport Culture Risk Factors

A closed sport system is one of the primary risk factors associated with the sport culture. A closed sport system is one where the coach is generally authoritarian in approach and athletes are managed in a tightly controlled, restricted environment with high demands. The athletes typically experience high levels of competition with each other and, because of that, may be largely separated from social support including friends and family outside of sport. Such sports would not be characterized as consultative, either by the coaches or the athletes, and would likely be fairly insensitive to athletes' racial, religious or sexual orientation differences. Fasting et al. (2000) found that there was more abuse by authority figures in women's individual sports that were characterized as more "masculine." For men's sport, few studies exist and no particular sports stand out as riskier. Brackenridge (2001) and Kirby and Greaves (2000) agree that, as yet, there is no real data on risk associated with team or individual sports and that abuse can occur in many places (e.g., at the sport venues during and around the practice times, at the home of the coach, during

147

training, at social events, or on road trips). Research to date shows that one sport is not riskier than another, but that good sport practice to provide safe opportunities for athletes must exist in every sport.

Athletes' Risk Factors

Much of the literature devoted to athletes' risk factors focuses on their vulnerabilities (i.e., past abuse, female athlete triad, minority status) (Brackenridge, 1997; Drinkwater, Loucks, Sherman, Sundgot-Borgen, & Thompson, 2005). Research shows that girls are more at risk than boys in sport, but the underreporting about boys remains a serious problem. There is also some initial research on the vulnerabilities of para-athletes, those athletes who compete with disabilities (Kirby, Demers, & Parent, 2008). Further, athletes who are in the stage of imminent achievement (Brackenridge & Kirby, 1997) and/or rely heavily on the coach or other authority figure while being somewhat distant or isolated from friends and family may be more at risk (Brackenridge, 2001). It does not seem to matter whether the athletes are in a greater stage of undress (e.g., swimming versus rugby) or whether the athletes are in individual or team sports.

Lesbian, gay, bisexual and transgender athletes (LGBT). LGBT athletes are exposed to a particular risk – homophobia. Both Kirby et al. (2000) and Brackenridge and Kirby (1997) agree that homophobia belongs on a sexual harassment and abuse continuum, with its placement dependent on what form the homophobia actually takes. The most reported forms of discrimination appear to be verbal harassment, physical violence, and exclusion. Baks and Malecek (2003) describe the mechanisms of homophobia in sports as a "prisoner's dilemma" – if participants come out of the closet, they experience the hostile sport environment, and if they stay in the closet, sexuality is not addressed and their silence contributes to homophobia and invisibility. Many sport leaders and participants are uncomfortable talking about homophobia in sport (CAAWS, 2007). For many, it is easier to simply deny, ignore or make fun of the issue. In this void of discussion and information–sharing, stereotypes and myths persist. The fear of being outed, of being excluded from the team or accused of being sexually deviant, makes LGBT individuals an easy target for perpretators.

Athletes with disabilities. Athletes with disabilities, like other marginalized groups (e.g., LGBT), are particularly vulnerable to violence and abuse. Sport practice occurs in a variety of settings, and often, the athlete living with a disability may be dependent on the support of a care-giver, an attendant, or a friend. Where a power imbalance exists, particularly when institutional care is involved, there is an increased risk of abuse to people with disabilities. In reviewing the sport disability literature, we were startled by some of the specific vulnerabilities present (Kerr, 1999). For example, physical handling, drug administration, and drug testing for athletes living with disabilities are likely unique and there may be many opportunities for inappropriate

148

touching to occur. Also, though the patterns of sexual abuse may be similar for all athletes, the particular form of abuse of an athlete with a disability may be related to the nature of vulnerability. For instance, while most people have a sexual identity and they may or may not be comfortable in expressing that identity (Kirby & Huebner, 2002), athletes with disabilities may have to fight an uphill battle to have their sexuality accepted. They may have to deal with others who either disbelieve that they can have a sexual identity or outright refuse to accept that there may be a variety of ways to express and experience that sexuality. At this time, there is very little work on the sexual exploitation of athletes with disabilites (Kirby et al., 2008).

Abuser Risk Factors

The majority of the literature devoted to sexual exploitation in sport focuses on the coach as the abuser, however, other individuals in positions of authority are also important to acknowledge (e.g., medical personnel, athletic trainers, or team selectors). As an authority figure, the coach has direct and regular contact with athletes, though often initiates contact with the athlete outside of sport by integrating him/herself into the athlete's family or offering the athlete special privileges outside of the sport context. Disturbingly, athletes do not always see sexual encounters with their coaches as negative (Brackenridge, 2001; Burton Nelson, 1994). Risk factors include where a coach is a boundary challenger – for example, one who tells "off color" jokes, touches athletes unnecessarily, "engages in ambiguous sexual behavior" (Brackenridge, 2001, p. 136) or performs tasks outside the realm of coaching such as massages or counseling an athlete's personal problems. The coach also is in a trusted position and may be able to boundary push without criticism because of a winning record and success with a variety of athletes. Coaches with a sense of impunity and entitlement to know and control everything about their athletes would likely be seen as a risk for the athletes. There is also some research that suggests sexual exploitation by peer athletes may be a risk (Fasting et al., 2000; Holman, 1995), particularly when the sport environment has a tolerance for peer bullying and sexual encounters in sport (Robinson, 1998). Together, the sport culture and athlete and abuser risk factors serve as cautions about the kinds of behaviors that may be problematic in sport.

A dome of silence exists over those in sport, including athletes and coaches. Many are reluctant to expose abuse in sport because of the sheer power "such exposure has to destroy personal, team or even national identities" (Kirby et al., 2000, p. 27). The image of sport is positive; a place where one can play safely, achieve one's potential and share in the challenges and joys of one's teammates. Sport is a place of good values like hard work and honesty of effort and cooperative endeavour. It is also a place of contrasts; of tremendous privacy where one's efforts are made often on long and lonely training paths out of the public eye, and of tremendous publicity where even the most intimate of one's details are known by the public at large. The dedication required of a top-level athlete or a top-level coach contributes to this

149

image. But sexual exploitation contaminates sport. It happens in a very private place, a place protected by the interdependence of the athletes, the intensity of sport, the highly competitive atmosphere, and even the highly symbolic (nationally valued) nature of the activities (Kirby et al., 2000). The sport norm would be suppression of disclosure and exposure. Speaking out about sexual exploitation risks personal criticism, scandal for the sport and the abuser, upset of the tight social relationships of the sport and even personal ostracism from the team. Breaking through this dome of silence is a task not only for the athletes who are sexually exploited, but is a shared task for all who love sport and are committed to safe sport.

PERPETRATORS AND EXPLOITERS

Who Sexually Exploits Children in Sport?

Sexual exploiters in sport are identical to those outside of sport, although sport may provide different opportunities for them to abuse. They may be individuals who deliberately seek children for sexual purposes and do so in a calculated and purposeful manner. These people specifically come to sport because there are opportunities to work as volunteers or in a paid capacity with limited supervision and a great deal of freedom. Or, they may be more opportunistic, as in those who will engage in abusive behavior "if the situation presents itself" (CCCP, n.d., p. 26). They may have a distorted sense of coach-athlete relationship, about appropriate physical contact with athletes, and issues about healthy friendships and intimacy. Sexual exploiters may "believe the athlete is interested in them and that sexual contact is harmless… they do not see their offending as forced or offensive" (CCCP, n.d., p. 26). In either case, the abusers create opportunities for the athletes to be physically close to them. They may look for athletes' vulnerabilities and ways to isolate an athlete from others (e.g., to drive them home, have them live in the abuser's home, or to segregate them for special training). They may also create opportunities for the athlete to be exposed physically in front of them (e.g., in the change room or on the Internet). In any case, the abuser uses his/her position of authority and trust to gain and keep access to athletes. As long as the athlete is silent and no bystanders speak out, and there are no immediate consequences for the abuse, the abusers can continue to justify to themselves why they are good for the athlete (Pascal, 2012).

The Question of Easy Access in Sport

The debate continues about whether paedophiles and other sexual exploiters come into sport because of access to children or whether sport provides opportunities for individuals to become paedophiles, child pornographers or child traffickers. The answer is both.

Those who seek access to children, particularly vulnerable children, can get quite close to athletes as long as there is some coaching skill or voluntary capacity that can provide the route. Although it is more difficult to gain access through the school system, it is not impossible for a skilled abuser. For community and club sport, sport is generally welcoming for those who want to contribute – to drive, to help with events, to fundraise, to do the communications, to chaperone athletes, to clean out facilities after practices and so on. Individuals can volunteer often without going through a criminal screening or even an informal interview.

For the more opportunistic abusers, once the individuals find their place in sport, as coaches or others in positions of authority or with opportunity to be close to vulnerable athletes, they move down the road to becoming a sexual abuser.

Access to athletes continues as long as the following are in place:

– The abuser is a dedicated, award-winning contributor to the sport and to the athletes and the abuser looks just like everyone in sport;
– There are silent bystanders who have not noticed, are not suspicious nor cannot believe that abuse is occurring;
– The sport environment continues forward in an unruffled way – the opportunities for abuse continue to escalate without causing a ripple on the surface;
– The potential for abuse is legitimated by sport practice (e.g., late practice or competition schedules mean athletes have to stay at coach's home; coach offers lots of extra exclusive coaching for an up-and-coming athlete; coach offers to help athlete who is struggling with homework, finances or family issues);
– Those around the abuser do not understand harassment and abuse issues nor do they understand their legal responsibility to report suspicions of abuse (CCCP, n.d.; Kirby, 2013c).

THE CYCLE OF ABUSE AND GROOMING PROCESS

One of the most durable models to explain the abuser profile is Wolf's Cycle of Offending (Fisher, 1994). It had some early support because of the assumption that children who were abused became abusers. As Brackenridge (2001) rightly indicates, this model poorly explains female victims of abuse. The cycle also describes a pattern based primarily on poor self-image. The cycle progresses from poor self-image → expects rejection → withdraws → unassertive → compensatory fantasies → sexual escapism → grooming → outlet → transitory guilt → push away guilt → and back to poor self-image. But, as Brackenridge points out, the determined sex-offender in sport is not operating from poor self-image, but often has a sense of entitlement and uses power to target and abuse athletes.

The grooming process, first flagged by Wolf in 1984 but expanded and applied to sport by Brackenridge (2001), starts from a predator stance. The grooming process is a series of behaviors that some abusers patiently use to engage targeted athletes in sexual behavior. The Predator Cycle progresses from good self-image → good personal skills → expects approval and acceptance → seeks public profile → assertive → assumption of superiority → sexual confidence → increased sense of control → increased self-confidence → and back to good self-image (Brackenridge, 2001). Brackenridge then identified four stages of grooming as targeting, building trust, developing isolation/control and sexual abuse/secrecy. Grooming is perhaps the most insidious of means used by abusers because they target athletes who have existing vulnerabilities such as previous abuse experiences, problems at home, disordered eating, or difficulties in fitting into a team. An abuser then creates an individual relationship with the athlete based first on special treatment and extra attention, friendship, and some seemingly innocuous quid pro quo requests for errands and favors. When the abuser is "sure of the athlete" (sure he/she will be silent, keep a secret), the athlete is then separated from the team members, family and friends through demands to spend time with the abuser. Often, for example, a coach who is grooming an athlete may know more about that athlete than anyone else around them (Starr, 2013). This information is then used to control where, when and how the athlete interacts with the coach. The 'spending extra time' with the athlete converts to 'spending sexual time.' The targeted and now fully compromised athlete is then pressed into secrecy and silence through either being made to feel very special ("I love you and I will divorce my wife for you!") or shaming ("how could you lead me on like this?") or threatening ("if you tell, I will make sure you won't go to Nationals").

The description of the abuse of Sheldon Kennedy by coach Graham James followed the typical grooming and sexual exploitation pattern. In one of the most public cases of sexual exploitation, Graham James groomed 14 year old hockey player Sheldon Kennedy, and other young hockey players (cousins Thereon Fleury and Todd Holt) for sexual abuse. Kennedy described how James helped him with hockey skills, took him on trips, and bought him special clothing. Later, twice weekly special homework/practice sessions turned into opportunities for sexual abuse involving punishments, threats and humiliations (Kirby & Fusco, 1998). These abuses continued, just under the public radar, until Kennedy was 18 years of age. James went to court in 1997, charged by Kennedy and an unnamed player. As is often the case, Kennedy was the first of several to come forward. James went to court again in 2012, this time charged by the two cousins. James began serving his second prison sentence in 2012.

In 2012, in a case that shocked America, Pennsylvania State University became the focal point of child protection in college sport and thrust Dr. Katherine Staley, a research scientist for the Justice Center at the University into the lead for Penn State's Child Sexual Abuse Conference: Traumatic Impact, Prevention and Intervention. In the spirit of open sourcing, much of the conference material was posted on line at *protectchildren.psu.edu* and the archived videos were made widely available. As described at the very beginning of this chapter, Jerry Sandusky was found guilty of 45 counts of child abuse. Sandusky regularly worked with children in The Second Mile Program and contributed to the Pennsylvania State Football program for many years. Problems with his behavior towards at least one child had been identified to members of the University administration more than a decade prior to charges and court. The late head coach, Joe Paterno, along with others in positions of authority, knew about the suspicions. Paterno's inaction may have failed to halt Sandusky's continuation of child sexual abuse. When the case finally did come to court, there were many victims and much damage to all concerned.

An unusual case that links child exploitation in sport with the violence of school shootings occurred in 1996 when Thomas Hamilton shot and killed 16 children and one teacher at the Dunblane Primary School (Bell, 2004). Bell writes that Thomas Hamilton was interested in rifle clubs and in "Boys Brigade" and became more and more involved in Boy Scouts. After some reported issues with his leadership, he was asked to resign and preceded to organize his own boys clubs (16 in total). The clubs were for young boys, Bell writes, who participated in football, gymnastics, swimming and target practice. Brackenridge (2001) noted that while the Scout movement dealt effectively with Hamilton by banning him, once he was with his own unregistered clubs, Hamilton had unsupervised access to children. In other words, Hamilton used sport to attract lots of children. Reports had come to the local police about his sadistic, demanding behavior and some boys complained that he "would do things that made them uncomfortable and would pay them off to keep quiet" (Bell, 2004, p. 3). With no charges laid, Hamilton proceeded to purchase guns and to then murder 17 people. While the children killed were not, in and of themselves, groomed for sexual exploitation, the children participating in the boys clubs were most certainly sexually exploited.

CONSEQUENCES OF SEXUAL EXPLOITATION

For Sport

A principle consequence of sexual exploitation for sport is the loss of what sport means to its participants. Paul Melia of the Canadian Centre for Ethics and Sport writes that while sport has incredible potential, it cannot realize that potential in just any kind of sport. The potential is "realized only in good sport" (2013, p. 1). He argues that principles based on "striving to be the best, striving for excellence, giving everything one has on the field of play to win, also [must] include playing fair, keeping it fun, respecting others, staying safe and giving back" (Melia, 2013, p. 1). A sport environment with sexual exploitation means that sport cannot produce strong, healthy athletes.

Another principle consequence is that organized sport may find itself short of skilled labor. Sport depends upon skilled, though often volunteer workers. Distinctions are needed for when the work is being done by volunteers or by paid workers. The screening process for entry into sport and for job performance must be no less stringent for the volunteer workers. Clear performance criteria and evaluations for all who work in sport would greatly enhance the quality of the sport workplace. On a child protection note, since those who sexually abuse in one environment are known to move along to another environment when things get difficult, and sport is no different, there is cause for concern if volunteers or paid workers in sport move

153

from team to team or region to region with any frequency. Unfortunately, there are cases where a sport organization has quietly asked a person to leave a club because of sexual abuse only to see that same person resurface at a competing club. This practice is known as nimby-ism – the "not in my backyard'" way of handling (mis-handling) sexual abusers. It does not help the sport organization at all because, no matter how quiet the proceedings, word gets out and the sport organization becomes known for taking the easy way out.

A third consequence is that it is tough to coach in an environment that has trouble both ensuring that good coaches get what they need and poor coaches are either trained up or screened out. There is a lot of power in the role of being a coach. Pritchard (2007) writes that coaches have highly important positions in sport – leaders of "small but not inconsiderable empires" (p. 129) – where they have lots of authority and can dictate what they want to happen. While these environments can produce strong athlete performances, they also protect the traditional ways of doing things. Change is not always welcome in sport. Safe sport represents a new approach to how coaches work with athletes and with each other. For example, there are Codes of Conduct in many U.S. national sport organizations including volleyball, gymnastics and swimming. These lay out limits for coaches around such issues as alcohol and drug use, criminal behavior, and sexual boundaries with others, including minors, in the sport. They generally impress upon coaches the need to keep up to date and fully informed on harassment and abuse issues. Sport organizations can help set the standards of good practice using Brake's (2013) two pillars – coaching ethics and athlete welfare. Sport organizations must take a stand against sexual exploitation!

For Athletes

Until all athletes are protected, sport is not completely safe for athletes. While the child protection work in sport does help with risk or threat assessment and can lessen the dangers for athletes, not all sports have equal access to those trained in risk assessment. For those athletes who are exploited, there may simply be no disclosure – no telling of the abuse to anyone. The pressure to remain silent is immense. There is what has been called "the choice of one" (Kirby, et al. 2000), that is – the athletes are faced with a true dilemma of either speaking out and loosing what appears to be a single road to the Olympic Games or remaining silent and put up with the abuse to protect their sport careers. For those who do decide to disclose, just whom do they disclose to? If it is another athlete or a close friend, will the disclosure get into the hands of the trained harassment officer? If so, will there be prompt action to prevent any further harm to the athlete and the start of due process to ensure that the 'accused' is also fully respected by the process? Will sport organizations be open to fully managing the disclosures in a way that first protects the people involved rather than the reputation of the sport? And, once a case is handled according to the policies and procedures and even if the case goes to court, the athlete who is sexually exploited will spend a long time healing. Fortunately there are a number of supports for those who are sexually exploited, and some of them are specific to sport. Athletes are children first and athletes second. As athletes, they have the increasing support of a much wider violence protection network for children – the National Center for Missing and Exploited Children (NCMEC, 2013) in the United States, the Canadian Centre for Child Protection (CCCP, 2012) and the National Society for the Prevention of Cruelty to Children (NSPCC) – Child Protection in Sport Unit (NSPCC, 2002) in the UK.

For the Coach or Other Person in Authority

There is always an inherent vulnerability in the coach–athlete relationship that makes it difficult for those outside that relationship to understand the relationship dynamics. Coaches can "protect themselves" by engaging in good practice. Good coaching practice includes:

– keeping the coaching environment "open" rather than in a closed and secretive space,
– engaging in discussions with athletes, coaches and parents and others in sport about the nature of harassment and abuse and about acceptable standards of behavior,
– ensuring positive and respectful treatment of the athletes is at the center of all good coaching practice, and
– implementing penalties for disrespectful and abusive behavior.

Where professionals are involved, such as medical personnel, sport administrators or professional coaches, there are professional standards of behavior often written into codes of conduct and guidelines for performance. Regular reviews of performance will ensure good performance and also, protect the professional coach as well as the athletes and the sport organization. Just as policies are in place for child protection, they are also there to ensure procedural fairness for all. So, where there is a strong policy environment for child protection, a coach (or other person in positions of authority) who is suspected of sexually abusing an athlete will be able to fully rely on the procedural steps in those policies for the respectful management of the situation.

DEMYSTIFYING THE MYTHS

The most popular myths associated with sexual abuse in sport include the following:

1. *I have never heard a complaint in my sport. We don't have any problems with harassment and abuse.* Sexual exploitation can happen in any sport – individual or team, summer or winter sport, sport for the young and sport for the masters, sport for para-athletes, for LGBT athletes, for all. Every sport needs to provide for the eventuality of a disclosure of sexual exploitation by being fully prepared. Each sport needs to establish widespread informed proactive discussions about

155

respectful sport, engage in ongoing child protection policy development and have good personnel management practices. Having no complaints can mean that there is no safe route for an athlete to disclose abuse, that the pressure to remain silent and 'keep the secret' is very powerful, or that the sport has an 'open secret' environment where everyone knows but nobody talks about abuse.

2. *We know everyone really well in our sport. We are a big happy family. Everybody loves our coaches and all the other support people too. We even love the bus driver! There are no strangers here, so we don't have a problem.* People who exploit children may be attracted to sport because it is where children are, and/ or where they may be able to gain access to children with relative ease. Others are already involved in sport but then sexually exploit children because the opportunity presents itself – an opportunistic abuser. The principle threat is not 'stranger danger' (Brackenridge, 1997), but is a threat from inside the sport organization. Also, though coaches may be seen to be the main issue, abuse can come from other adults in the sport environment. While admirable that everybody gets along and is a happy family, the person who sexually exploits children fits in well to such environments and uses the normalcy of the interactions to hide the abuse activities.

3. *Our coaches are trained and licensed. They even get criminal checks. Many are award-winning. And our athletes have many top-notch performances. Our coaches take special interest in the athletes and often give them lots of special attention. We have nothing to worry about.* Proper qualifications are not related to likelihood of sexual exploitation. However, as part of credentialing, sport organizations can regularly discuss the issues of respectful, value-driven sport, one free of discriminations and abuses. This ensures that the issues are out in the open and may alert people to the signs of abuse. While criminal checks are an excellent part of a child protection program, they are not helpful in identifying those who have not already been charged for sexual exploitation. Since there is a major problem with underreporting of abuse, criminal record checks cannot stand as the only method of prevention. It is ideal when coaches take an interest in the athletes and give them lots of attention, but it should not pass into an unhealthy attention, one where the coach-athlete relationship becomes private and secluded and out of bounds for healthy interactions with others. Unhealthy special attention is to be avoided. Having good practices for prevention of abuse is important. These practices need to be discussed often and understood by all.

4. *When we travel, we always bring a chaperone. The athletes are always supervised. There are always volunteers to help with this. We always have the males stay together and the females stay together. That's the way we ensure no problems will arise.* Sexual abuse can happen anytime and anywhere, including on trips for competition. There may be more opportunity for abusive contact with athletes and therefore, supervision is necessary. Sport organizations should have child protection policies in mind when choosing those who will supervise. Also, abuse happens from male to female, female to female and from male to male. Thus,

segregation by gender is not sufficient to ensure abusive behavior does not occur.

5. *Our athletes are very confident and strong–minded. If a problem existed, they would tell us for sure. We don't have a problem here.* Underreporting is a problem that is not linked directly to the performance or the confidence levels of the athletes. Disclosure is difficult for any athlete and the manner of disclosure may differ depending on the circumstances surrounding an athlete.

6. *A consensual sexual relationship between two adults is none of our business. If the athlete is an adult – with regard to the law – then it is not our job to do anything about his or her relationship with the coach.* Sexual relationships with athletes happen at all levels – youth, high school, college and professional. At the youth and high school levels, such relationships are a criminal offense. At the college or professional levels, it may not be a criminal offense, but it is a breach of coaching ethics and an abuse of power by the coach, even when the relationship is 'consensual' (Brackenridge, 2013; Griffin, 2013).

CONNECTING THE DOTS AND FIGHTING BACK

Prevention: Child Protection and Child Safeguarding

Child protection is everybody's business. Everyone connected to sport must become skilled at connecting the dots. The dots are the red flags about "outside the rules" behavior that in the past (may have) regularly gone unreported (Kirby & Telles-Langdon, 2012). Sport organizations have to provide a clear route by which such reporting can occur. Potential abusers need to feel that they are continually visible and under scrutiny in a sport that wants to protect its participants.

While researchers and activists in sport have paid attention to sexual exploitation for more than three decades, sport organizations are now under considerable pressure to rapidly change their social and cultural environments. Connecting the dots, as described in the previous paragraph, is an important part of how sport organizations can take some responsibility. For example, the Cal Ripken, Sr. Foundation (CRSF) formalizes the importance of taking responsibility by underlining individual compliance. The CRSF is a foundation to help disadvantaged young people learn critical life lessons and build character through baseball and softball-themed programs. They have produced a child protection policy template that includes space for a signature indicating that each individual has read and agrees to abide by the policy (CRSF, 2013). Parent (2011), in her comprehensive study of the sexual harassment and abuse in sport in the Province of Quebec, discovered that respondents perceived a lack of clear leadership from their sport organizations. Parent also recognized their perceptions of a prevailing sense of indifference toward the issues, a belief that insufficient time, resources and competence were available for prevention planning, and an overall lack of comprehensive measures in place to prevent sexual harassment and abuse. What this amounts to, she wrote, is "a lack of rules regarding behavior management in sport organizations" (Parent, 2011,

157

p. 144) and recommended that sport organizations establish external barriers (e.g., for recruitment) and internal barriers (e.g., behaviors management).

Once We Know: Managing the Cases

Speaking out about child sexual exploitation is difficult. Walking away from or doing nothing about suspected child sexual exploitation makes one complicit in that abuse (Brackenridge, 2001). In many countries, such as Canada, it is also illegal to let suspected child abuse go unreported. Thus, when athletes disclose their experiences with sexual abuse, or an onlooker reports about something disturbing he/she has witnessed, the "reporting" has begun. A safe sport environment is one of immediate support whereby the harassment officer is immediately contacted, really listens to the disclosure/report, and conducts an accurate recording of the disclosure. The sport-specific sexual harassment policies and legal rights and responsibilities then should 'click into place' with steps immediately taken to reduce the opportunity for any further harm and to commence the fact finding investigation.

Since the sport culture is one of keeping the "Dome of Silence" over the negative experiences and events, an organization's first response to suspected abuse may well be to 'wish it away' or to minimize the account. However uncomfortable this may be for sport organizations, reporting is only the first of a number of actions that together will ensure the case is handled appropriately, efficiently and respectfully. Sport has the ability to offer a safe environment for all. The capacity to protect the "young people in sport and through sport" (Tiivas, 2013, p. 5) is built through conscious effort and skill. Creating a safe place, where participants can thrive, is the goal for child protection.

CHAPTER SUMMARY

Paul Melia (2013) wrote that when sexual exploitation in sport is reported but nothing is done, it is tragic for the athletes and for sport. Sport has lost its way and is out of touch with its foundational values Melia continues, and when people in sport cannot determine what the right thing to do is, then we have a crisis in sport.

Modern sport is not particularly equitable. Vulnerabilities can appear when inequities exist and power is not equally shared. Sexual exploitation in sport is an abuse of power by those with authority over others, where the "outside the rules" behaviors take the form of sexual discrimination and sexual comments, sexual touching, sexual assault, bullying and cyber-bullying, hazing and initiations, and child sexual exploitation and child trafficking. Sexual exploitation of girls and boys in sport makes everyone shine the light on sport. It is in this light that we see the violent underbelly of sport, the damage and the roots of it – we see what is wrong with sport and what needs to happen to make sport better.

One approach to breaking the pattern of negative behaviors is through the use of children's rights and, more broadly, human rights, to eliminate discrimination and other forms of violence in sport (David, 2005). Sport researchers and child protection experts are increasingly working in coordinated ways, though comparative work across national boundaries and jurisdictional units remains difficult. The children's rights and human rights approach is complimented when countries work across social, cultural and political mandates to find shared ways of making sport safe for all.

Sexual harassment is the problem that 'hits sport in its guts.' Sexual harassment is in sports' backyard. Harassment-free sport is good for society and good for its participants. The challenge is to act proactively to make sport harassment-free for all its participants. (Kirby, 1995, p. 61)

REFERENCES

Archard, D. (1998). *Sexual consent*. Oxford: Westview.

Baks, B., & Malecek, S. (2003). *Invisible: Synopsis on homophobia and discrimination on sexual orientation in sport*. Retrieved from European Gay and Lesbian Spot Federation website: http://www.eglsf.info/EGLSF_Public_Documents/EGLSF_synopsis_on_homophobia_2003pr.pdf

Bell, R. (2004). The Dunblane massacre. *Crime Library: Criminal Minds and Methods*. Retrieved from http://www.trutv.com/library/crime/notorious_murders/mass/dunblane_massacre/index.html

Brackenridge, C. H. (2013). *Myths about sexual abuse in sports*. Retrieved from Moms Team website: http://www.momsteam.com/health-safety/myths-about-abuse-in-sports

Brackenridge, C. H. (2001). *Spoilsports: Understanding and preventing sexual exploitation in sport*. London: Routledge.

Brackenridge, C. H. (1997, Nov). *Inaugural Address to Cheltenham and Gloucester College of Higher Education,* Cheltenham, England.

Brackenridge, C. H., Fasting, K., Kirby, S. L., & Leahy, T. (2010). *Protecting children from violence in Sport: A review with a focus on industrialized nations*. Retrieved from the UNICEF Innocenti Research Centre website: http://unicef.hu/c/document_library/get_file?p_l_id=13438&noSuchEntryRedirect=viewFullContentURLString&fileEntryId=24654

Brackenridge, C. H., & Kirby, S. L. (1997). Playing safe? Assessing the risk of sexual abuse to elite child athletes. *International Review of Sociology of Sport, 32*(4), 407–418.

Brake, D. L. (2013). *Going outside Title IX to keep coach–athlete relationships in bounds*. Retrieved from Safe4athletes website: http://safe4athletes.org/component/k2/item/2-going-outside-title-ix-to-keep-coach-athlete-relationships-in-bounds

Brennan, S., & Taylor-Butts, A. (2008). Sexual assault in Canada 2004 and 2007. *Canadian Centre for Justice Statistics Profile Series, 19*, 1–20.

Burton Nelson, M. (1994). *The stronger women get, the more men love football*. New York: Harcourt Brace.

Cal Ripken Sr. Foundation. (2013, March 19). *The National Center for Missing and Exploited Children (NCMEC) issues new standards for protecting child athletes from sex abuse*. Presentation presented at the Safe to Compete: Protecting Child Athletes from Sexual Abuse Summit, Alexandria, VA.

Canadian Association for the Advancement of Women and Sport (CAAWS). (2007). *Seeing the invisible, speaking about the unspoken*. Retrieved from the Canadian Association for the Advancement of Women and Sport website: http://www.sportlaw.ca/wp-content/uploads/2011/03/a-Equity-Discrimination-Seeing-the-Invisible-Speaking-About-the-Unspoken-A-Position-Paper-on-Homophobia-in-Sport-for-CAAWS-2006.pdf

Canadian Centre for Child Protection (CCCP). (2012). *A 10 year review of Canada's tipline for reporting the online sexual exploitation of children*. Retrieved from Cybertip!ca website: https://www.cybertip.ca/pdfs/CTIP_10YearReport_en.pdf

Canadian Centre for Child Protection (CCCP). (n.d.). *Commit to kids: A program to help child-serving organizations prevent sexual abuse*. Winnipeg: CCCP.

CBC News (2011, Oct 25). Neepawa hockey team disciplined for hazing. Retrieved from http://www.cbc.ca/news/canada/manitoba/story/2011/10/25/mb-neepawa-natives-hockey-hazing.html

Cense, M., & Brackenridge, C. H. (2001). Temporal and developmental risk factors for sexual harassment and abuse in sport. *European Physical Education Review, 7*(1), 61–79.

Crouse, K. (2013). Abuse victim seeks ouster of U. S. swimming officials. *New York Times.* Retrieved from http://www.nytimes.com/2013/05/24/sports/kelley-davies-currin-seeks-ouster-of-usa-swimming-officials-after-coachs-abuse.html?_r=0n

David, P. (2005). *Human rights in youth Sport: A critical review of children's rights in competitive sports.* New York: Routledge.

Drinkwater, B. L., Loucks, A., Sherman, R. T., Sundgot-Borgen, J., & Thompson, R. A. (2005). *International Olympic Committee (IOC) consensus statement on the female athlete triad.* Retrieved from the Olympic Movement website: http://www.olympic.org/content/news/media-resources/manual-news/1999–2009/2005/11/09/ioc-consensus-statement-on-the-female-athlete-triad/

Fasting, K. (2012). Sexual harassment and abuse in Norwegian Sport. In C. H. Brackenridge, T. Kay, & D. Rhind (Eds.), *Sport, children's rights and violence prevention: A sourcebook on global issues and local programmes* (pp. 112–117). London: Brunel University Press.

Fasting, K., Brackenridge, C. H., & Sundgot-Borgen, J. (2000). *Sexual harassment in and outside of sport.* Oslo, Norway: Norwegian Olympic Committee.

Fasting, K., Brackenridge, C. H., Miller, K. E., & Sabo, D. (2008). Participation in college sports and protection from sexual victimization. *International Journal of Sport and Exercise Psychology, 16*(4), 427–441.

Fisher, D. (1994). Adult sex offenders: Who are they? Why and how do they do it? In T. Morrison, M. Erooga, & R. C. Beckett (Eds.) *Sexual offending against children: Assessment and treatment of male abusers* (pp. 1–24). London: Routledge.

Griffin, P. (2013, March 26). Coaches, athletes and sex: Not a good game plan [Web log post]. Retrieved from http://ittakesateam.blogspot.ca

Holman, M. (1995). *Female and male athletes' accounts and meanings of sexual harassment in Canadian interuniversity athletics* (Unpublished doctoral dissertation). University of Windsor, Ontario, Canada.

Kerr, A. (1999). *Protecting disabled children and adults in sport and recreation: The guide.* Leeds, UK: The National Coaching Foundation.

Kirby, S. L. (1995). Not in my backyard: Sexual harassment in sport. Canadian Woman Studies/ Les Cahiers de la Femme, 15(4), 58–62.

Kirby, S. L. (2013a). In women's sport, who are the women? In G. Demers, L. Greaves, S. Kirby & M. Lay (Eds.), *Playing it forward: 50 years of women and sport in Canada* (pp. 46–61). Toronto, Canada: Canadian Feminist History Society.

Kirby, S. L. (2013b). Abuse in sport: What makes athletes so vulnerable? Paper presented at the Safe Sport Leadership Conference. Colorado Springs, CO, USA.

Kirby, S. L. (2013c, March 19–20). Safe sport: Vulnerable athletes, sexual abuse and the need for child protection. Paper presented to the Safe to Compete: Protecting Child Athletes from Sexual Abuse. National Centre for Missing and Exploited Children, Alexandria, VA.

Kirby, S. L., Demers G., & Parent, S. (2008). Vulnerability/prevention: Considering the needs of disabled and LGBT athletes in the context of sexual harassment and abuse. *International Journal of Sport and Exercise Psychology, 6*(4), 406–427.

Kirby, S. L., & Fusco, C. (2000). Are your kids safe?: Media representations of sexual abuse in sport. In S. Scraton & B. Watson, (Eds.) *Sport, leisure and gendered spaces* (pp. 45–73). Eastbourne, UK: LSA Publication No.67.

Kirby, S. L., & Greaves, L. (1996, July 11–14). *Foul play: Sexual abuse and harassment in sport.* Paper presented at the Pre-Olympic Congress, Dallas, Texas.

Kirby, S. L., Greaves, L., & Hankivsky, O. (2000). *The dome of silence: Sexual harassment and abuse in sport.* Halifax, Canada: Fernwood.

Kirby, S. L., & Huebne, J. (2002) Talking about sex: Biology and the social interpretations of sex in sport. *Canadian Woman Studies, 1*(3), 36–43.

Kirby, S. L., & Telles-Langdon, D. (2012). Connecting the dots: What the Graham James story has to teach us. *Coaching Canada, 19*(1), 50–51.

Kirby, S. L., & Wintrup, G. (2002). Running the gauntlet: An examination of initiation/hazing and sexual abuse in sport. In C. H. Brackenridge & K. Fasting (Eds.), *Sexual harassment and abuse in sport: International research and policy perspectives* (pp. 65–90). London, England: Whiting and Birch.

Leahy, T. (2012). Sexual abuse in competitive sport in Australia. In C. L. Brackenridge, T. Kay & D. Rhind (Eds.), *Sport, children's rights and violence prevention: A sourcebook on global issues and local programmes* (pp. 118–122). London: Brunel University Press.

Melia, P. (2013). *Losing our way*. Retrieved from the Canadian Centre for Ethics in Sport website: http://www.cces.ca/en/blog-17-losing-our-way-

National Centre for Missing and Exploited Children (NCMEC). (2013, March 19–20). Program for Safe to Compete: Protecting Child Athletes from Sexual Abuse. Alexandria, VA.

National Sexual Violence Resource Centre (NSVRC). (2012). *Understanding child sexual abuse definitions and rates*. Retrieved from http://nsvrc.org/sites/default/files/NSVRC_Publications_TalkingPoints_Understanding-Child-Sexual-Abuse-definitions-rates.pdf

National Society for the Prevention of Cruelty to Children (NSPCC). (2002). Protecting Children: A guide for Sportspeople. Leeds, UK: Coachwise Solutions.

Parent, S. (2011). Disclosure of sexual abuse in sport organizations: A case study. *Journal of Child Sexual Abuse, 20*(3), 322–337.

Pascal, C. (2012, July 9). Negligent bystanders to sexual abuse. *Toronto Star*. Retrieved from http://www.thestar.com/opinion/editorialopinion/2012/07/09/negligent_bystanders_to_sexual_abuse.html

Pinheiro, P. S. (2006). *World report on violence against children*. Geneva, Switzerland: United Nations Secretary-General's Study on Violence Against Children.

Pritchard, A. (2007). Coaches. In C. H. Brackenridge, A. Pritchard, K. Russell & G. Nutt (Eds.), *Child welfare in football: An exploration of children's welfare in the modern game* (pp. 124–134). London: Routledge.

Robinson, L. (1998). *Crossing the Line: Sexual harassment and abuse in Canada's national sport*. Toronto, Canada: McClelland and Stewart.

Starr, K. (2013, May 24, 2013). When did the system fail Kelly Davies Currin and the rest of us? *Huffington Post Sports*. Retrived from http://www.huffingtonpost.com/katherine-starr/when-did-the-system-fail_b_3328817.html.

Terry, K. J., & Tallon, J. (2003). *Child sexual abuse: A review of the literature*. Retrieved from Sjpcommunications.org/files/pastoralcare/reviewofliterature.pdf

The United States Department of Justice. (2013). *Sexual assault*. Retrieved from http://www.ovw.usdoj.gov/sexassault.htm#sa

Tiivas, A. (2013). *Child protection in sport unit USA swimming*. Paper presented at the Safe Sport Conference. Retrived from http://www.usaswimming.org/_Rainbow/Documents/f9d50826-74e2-4b1d-b29e-4f461381217e/Tiivas_Presentation.pdf

Tomlinson, P., & Strachan, D. (1996). *Power and ethics in coaching*. Ottawa, Canada: Coaching association for Canada.

United Nations Children's Fund (UNICEF). (2007). *Exercising Rights: Preventing and eliminating violence against children in sport*. (Eds. Brackenridge, C. H., Fasting, K., Kirby, S. L., & T. Leahy). Florence, Italy: UNICEF Innnocenti Research Centre.

United Nations Children's Fund (UNICEF). (2007). *Exercising rights: Preventing and eliminating violence against children in sport*. Florence, Italy: UNICEF Innocenti Research Centre.

University of Ottawa. (2011). *A study of national and provincial sport organizations' athlete protection and harassment policies and procedures*. Retrieved from http://www.sante.uottawa.ca/pdf/AstudyofNationalandProvincialSportOrganizations.pdf

Volkwein-Caplan, K., & Sankaran, G. (2002). *Sexual harassment in sport: Impact, issues and challenges*. Oxford, UK: Mayer and Meyer Sport.

AFFILIATIONS

Sandra Kirby, PhD
Associate Vice President (Academic) and Dean of Graduate Studies
University of Winnipeg

Guylaine Demers, PhD
Department of Physical Education
Laval University

GERTRUD PFISTER

9. DEVELOPMENTS AND CURRENT ISSUES IN GENDER AND SPORT FROM A EUROPEAN PERSPECTIVE

INTRODUCTION

Games and dances, various forms of gymnastics, physical activities and performances (i.e., sport in a broad sense) have always existed and continue to exist in all societies. However, the numerous and various body and movement concepts have culture-specific patterns as they "embody" a society's norms and values and reflect the dispositions and expectations of particular social groups. Sports and games are embedded in and subject to social structures in general and the gender order in particular. They adapt to prevailing habits and tastes according to gender, age and social status.

When writing about sport, one has to address the challenge of meanings and translations as the term is defined differently depending on country and culture. Here I use *sport* in a broad sense, ranging from elite sport to sport for all (including recreational physical activities). This chapter has a main focus on sport developments and systems and practices in Europe, which differ decisively from the concept and organization of sport in the United States.

GENDER CONCEPTS AND MOVEMENT CULTURES: HISTORICAL DEVELOPMENTS

Since most societies have been, and still are, dominated by men, it is hardly surprising that men have taken the leading role in the development of various physical exercises and sports. Nonetheless, women have often been able to develop their own movement cultures, and there have always been women who have succeeded in achieving their demand to participate in men's sports. This is true for traditional cultures, as well as for societies in Greek and Roman Antiquity, in the Middle Ages and in the Renaissance.

Gendered Physical Activities in Traditional Societies

The body and movement cultures of pre-industrial societies depended on people's environment and circumstances of life, and were often related to work and warfare as well as to religion, rituals and magic. They were characterized by a paucity of

E. A. Roper (Ed.), Gender Relations in Sport, 163–180.

rules, a lack of regulation and bureaucracy, and an absence of abstract performances and records. Since men dominated and continue to dominate in most societies, they have usually played the leading role in the various physical cultures. Nevertheless, women in pre-industrial societies were involved in many physical activities, among them endurance sports such as running and combat sports like Naginata, a Japanese specific form of fencing. However, their participation varied in accordance with the division of labor between the sexes as well as with norms, values, and relations of power (Pfister, 2004).

In ancient Greece, sport, war and religion were closely interconnected, which explains the exclusion of the "weak sex" from both the gymnasium (where mind and body were educated) and the Panhellenic Games. Women were not even allowed to watch the Olympics, the most important religious festival in honor of Zeus. However, girls did participate in a running contest in honor of Hera, and women in Sparta underwent physical training in order to become healthy mothers of strong sons.

In the Middle Ages and in the early modern period, sports and games were played in many European countries as preparation for war and/or in conjunction with festivals, though the regional economic, social and cultural differences in Europe and the class divisions in medieval societies prevented the emergence of a single prevalent system of physical activity. Despite the predominance of male power, some women achieved privileged status at court or in a nunnery. Some of these women rode horseback and enjoyed the sport of falconry and others played simple ballgames. Aristocratic women also played an ancillary role at the medieval tournaments that were an important aspect of the life of a medieval knight. Tournaments served not only to harden the warrior's body and prepare it for battle; they were also vivid symbolic demonstrations of the social order. It was important that women be present at these tournaments to admire and encourage the combatants and to acknowledge men's right to rule.

In towns, the most popular sports – archery, wrestling, and fencing – were also related to the exigencies of warfare. That meant, generally, the exclusion of women from these sporting activities that were a prominent part of urban life; but women were occasionally allowed to compete among themselves in an archery contest, especially in Flanders and in Holland. Throughout Europe, archery competitions were important social events that would have been painfully incomplete had admiring female spectators been excluded.

Among the peasantry, women were so essential in the struggle for mere survival that it seemed only natural for them to share in many of the sports of their fathers, husbands, and sons. Women appear in medieval documents not only as dancers, but also as participants in the widely popular (and wildly chaotic) game of folk soccer. In England, France, Germany, Switzerland, and Italy, girls and women ran races for smocks and similar prizes. However, there was a common feature at sporting events – girls and women were positioned as members of the audience; their primary role was to admire the physical prowess of male participants in contests of strength, endurance and skills (Christensen, Guttmann, & Pfister, 2001; Guttmann, 1991).

164

It must be admitted, however, that our picture of movement cultures in pre-industrial societies is far from complete. If women appear far less frequently than men, one reason for their absence is that men have written the histories and interpreted the documents (which, in turn, were produced mostly by men). To gather evidence of women's sports and physical activities, it is often necessary to glean the historical field after conventional historians have finished their harvest.

The Emergence of Gymnastics/Turnen and Sports in the 18th and 19th Centuries

In the late 18th and early 19th centuries, Western political, economic, and social institutions were decisively altered by new forms of technology and production, by the philosophical currents of the "Age of Reason" and by the French Revolution and the wars which followed. Work began to move from fields and households to factories and offices, changing the nature of the family which had traditionally combined economic and domestic functions. Faith in scientific rationality, especially in the form of medicine and biology, began to replace religion as the basics of society's conception of the gender order. All of these changes, however, tended to increase rather than decrease the perceived differences between men and women. Although a few voices called for greater equality between the sexes, most Europeans believed that men and women were by nature complementary opposites. The myth of men's strength and women's weakness was generally accepted. The doctrine of "separate spheres" sent men into the political and economic realms while women, especially those of the middle class, were expected to devote themselves to the home and the church. As reactions to these new challenges and demands, various concepts of physical activities and sports emerged (Pfister, 2003).

The most important initiative came from the German pedagogue, Johann Christoph Friedrich GutsMuths (1759–1839), a charismatic teacher and the inventor/collector of numerous physical exercises and games. His book, *Gymnastics for Youth* (1793), was translated into many languages and became the 'bible' of physical educators. However, girls do not appear in his "bible" and did not attend his school.

GutsMuths had a decisive influence on Friedrich Ludwig Jahn (1758–1852) and his "German Gymnastics," referred to as Turnen. Jahn and his adherents aimed to liberate Prussia from the French occupation (as an outcome of the Napoleonic wars) and to overcome the feudal order that had cut Germany into a patchwork of antagonistic states. Turnen included exercises on apparatus (among them parallel bars, the balance beam, and climbing poles), athletics (e.g., running, wrestling, rope skipping, swimming and hiking), and numerous games. The Turners did not strive for records but for training of the whole body as a preparation for war. Turnen was defined as a "men-only affair." Turnen spread to many European countries, and was "nationalized" (e.g., in the form of "Sokol," a gymnastics organization in Slavic countries). In contrast to sport organizations, the various Turner organizations (e.g., in Germany, Belgium or France) had a political and national impetus. In Germany, the Turners participated in the 1848 revolution fighting for human rights, some even for democracy. After the failure of the revolution, many Turner emigrated to the U.S., taking their concept of physical education to their new home country.

Another form of gymnastics was "invented" by the Swedish physical educator, Per Henrik Ling (1776–1839). He created an alleged scientific system of simple exercises intended to promote balance, harmony, and health that was to be used by soilders in particular. Although Ling envisioned his program as solely for men and boys, Swedish gymnastics eventually became the seedbed of women's physical education (e.g., in England and Finland). Swedish entrepreneurs then brought this Gymnastics system to the U.S., where it was taught in the Boston Normal School of Gymnastics and introduced to girls' schools in the city.

In France, the evolution of gymnastics took a militaristic turn under the guidance of Francisco Amoros (1770–1848), a Spanish officer who immigrated to France and established a training school at which exercises were conducted by military command. The Ecole de Joinville (1852), where physical educators were trained, was under the army's control, and many of France's physical educators were former army officers. The predictable result of this military emphasis was the almost complete neglect of girls' and women's gymnastics.

In the 19th century, the British transformed their traditional physical pastimes into what we now recognize as modern sport. Sport enforces quantification and a comparison of performances as well as a striving for records. British educators used sport, particularly soccer and rugby, in the boys' boarding schools as a means of "taming" the students. The boys were expected to learn to adhere to rules. Sports were an essential part of "muscular Christianity" (i.e., the basis of moral manhood).

Girls and women were not entirely excluded from the nascent sports culture of the 18th and 19th centuries. Some of them participated in rural cricket matches. Lower-class women in London often engaged in boxing matches, to the delight of the mostly male spectators. On the whole, however, modern sports were considered to be a "masculine preserve."

Over the course of the 19th century, however, there was increasing concern about the effects of industrialization and urbanization on girls' and women's health. Gymnastics became increasingly considered a means of enhancing beauty and health, and preparing young women for marriage. Phokion Heinrich Clias (1782–1854), a propagandist active in Switzerland, France, and England, coined the term *calisthenics*, meaning gentle exercises which claimed to enhance appearance without violating morality and propriety. In the second half of the century, girls' and women's gymnastics and physical education spread in many European countries. In view of the political tensions and the armed conflict that threatened, girls' schools began to include gymnastics in their curriculum, in particular because of the desire for healthy mothers to give birth to strong sons who were needed as soldiers. The exercises were still restricted to simple movements which followed the motto: head up, legs down and closed. In addition, women were accepted (although not as full members) in gymnastics clubs (e.g., in France and Germany). In these countries, even some independent gymnastics clubs for women began to emerge (Christensen et al., 2001; Guttmann, 1991).

THE TURN OF THE 20TH CENTURY: NEW ROLES FOR WOMEN AND THE TRIUMPH OF MODERN SPORTS

With industrialization and the accompanying modernization, the situation for women changed rapidly from the end of the 19th century onwards. Women's movements gained influence and their demands for women's rights had a considerable impact. Universities opened their doors to female students, and educated women began to enter the professions. Sport became fashionable, particularly for men, but for women too. However, women's sport participation was influenced by such factors as culture, religion, and social class. In Spain, for example, where the Roman Catholic Church exercised great authority, it was only aristocratic or upper-middle-class women who indulged in such pastimes as golf, tennis, and skiing. In the liberal democracies of Northern and Western Europe, women playing "feminine" sports found a measure of acceptance.

Track and field provides an excellent example of the barriers faced (and eventually overcome) by female athletes in Europe. In Germany, the first track and field contests for women were met with strong opposition. When the Berlin sports club, "Comet," staged a women's sport event in 1904, the club hoped to lure a large number of sensation-hungry spectators through the turnstiles. The 400-meter race did, indeed, generate revenue and publicity, but it also raised a number of questions about the appropriateness of the race. When the race was repeated, with the added attraction of some French participants, there was less public interest than expected. The official journal of the German Track and Field Federation took the "ladies race" as an occasion to condemn women's competitions. The runners' style was satirized as a "duck waddle" and their efforts were written off as a misunderstanding of female emancipation. Despite the initial failures to inaugurate women's track and field in Germany, interest in such events and in women's sport in general was growing.

In France and other countries, large numbers of women caught "cycling fever" and a number of them actually competed in bicycle races (which were discontinued at the turn of the 20th century). Soccer was also played by women in England and France. However, throughout Europe there was still widespread opposition to women participating in strenuous sports. Critics, such as Baron Pierre de Coubertin, the most famous French sports official, relied on an arsenal of medical, moral, and aesthetic arguments.

Despite the opposition, women's sports movements started to emerge in many European countries before or during World War I. French women staged a number of athletic events as early as 1914–1918. In England, the beginnings of women's participation in modern sports can be traced to the women's colleges and to London's polytechnic schools, where sports clubs for female students were founded. Some of these students even participated in the Women's Olympiads which were organized by the International Sporting Club of Monaco in Monte Carlo in 1921, 1922, and 1923.

In addition to the financial costs associated with sport involvement, many people from the working class were excluded due to the nationalist leanings of clubs and

167

federations. As a reaction, workers founded their own Turnen and sports movement in the 1890s. In the international and national workers' sports federations, female members generally had the same rights as male members, at least on paper. However, positions of power and influence were held exclusively by men.

The growing importance of women's sports and increasing athletic performance demanded decisive changes in sports clothes. In the 19th century, as a rule, physical exercise and sport took place in everyday clothing or in long skirts, but the popularity of the bicycle forced a change in costume for safety's sake. In the early decades of the 20th century, the opposition to women wearing trousers was gradually overcome. The controversy surrounding sports dress was not merely a debate about clothing, but an issue of women's roles and men's power (Christensen et al., 2001; Guttmann, 1991).

20th Century Society, the Gender Order and Women's Gymnastics and Sports

World War I and its aftermath brought profound political, economic, and social change, including changes in gender relations. In most European nations, women moved a step forward on the path toward legal equality. Nonetheless, even in countries in which women achieved the right to vote and hold office, they were still often regarded as "the second sex." Professional women suffered discrimination and housewives had to acknowledge their husbands as the head of the family.

In the 1920s, a new, more athletic ideal of femininity was proclaimed. Short hair, a tanned body, and narrow hips became fashionable. The "liberation" of the body was purchased, however, at a cost. Women internalized aesthetic ideals that required considerable effort to accomplish. And yet, while the "new woman" was celebrated in glamour magazines, novels, and films, broad sections of the population clung to traditional conceptions of femininity. For women whose lives were a daily struggle for economic survival and for women who were essentially wives and mothers, the ideals propagated by the mass media were wholly unrealistic or did not make sense.

In the postwar years, sports achieved a new zenith of popularity in Europe and beyond. The globe was spanned by a network of international sports federations including the International Olympic Committee (IOC – 1894), the International Soccer Association (1904) and the International Amateur Athletic Federation (IAAF – 1912). Despite critical opposition, in many countries sports became recognized as "the religion of the 20th century." Women were by no means immune to the fascination with sports, and large numbers of them engaged in increasingly strenuous contests.

Although few people doubted that girls and women should be physically active for the sake of their health, their participation in highly competitive sports led to fierce controversies. At the core was the debate over the compatibility of competition and motherhood. The weightiest arguments against strenuous sports came from medical experts, in particular gynecologists, who inveighed against competition and against participation in "manly" sports such as soccer. Again and again members of the medical profession complained about the female athlete's diminished fertility, her disinclination to bear children and her "masculinization."

The Olympic Games were a highly visible arena for the controversies surrounding the appropriateness and desirability of women's sports. Although Coubertin had revived the Games in 1896 as a purely male enterprise and continued to oppose women's participation to the day of his death in 1937, females competed in golf, tennis, pistol shooting, horseback riding, and other disciplines in the 1900 Olympic Games in Paris. According to French sources, 58 women took part in 11 sports, but the Games in 1900 were an exception (Pfister 2000; Wilson, 1996).

Prior to World War I, women were limited to sports which the men of the IOC deemed appropriately feminine. In the 1920s, the struggle was over track and field; the IAAF and the IOC wanted to keep the "core" of the games – the stadium – free from the contamination of female athletes. This decision encountered resistance from the Fédération Sportive Féminine Internationale (FSFI), which Alice Milliat, a French translator, and a group of male supporters of women's sports had founded in 1921. Between 1922 and 1934 the FSFI organized four Women's World Games. In response to the challenge from the FSFI, the IOC reluctantly inaugurated women's track and field at the 1928 Olympic Games in Amsterdam (Quintillan, 2000).

In Olympic sports, the opportunities for women varied from country to country. In Germany, women were encouraged to participate in sports contests, including those in track and field. As early as 1919, the German Sports Authority called upon its member clubs to create sections for female athletes; even so, women's soccer continued to be taboo. In France, however, where a variety of female sports federations had been founded, women not only competed in track and field, they also formed soccer teams and played in national and international tournaments. In other parts of the continent, including Scandinavia, women's gymnastics flourished, while other women's sports were less widely accepted. During Spain's brief republican period (1931–1939), the shackles that had inhibited the growth of women's sports were loosened, only to be tightened again when General Franco imposed a Fascist dictatorship upon his people.

The national differences in sport opportunity can be observed in Olympic participation of Germany, Norway and Spain. It was not until 1948 that a Norwegian woman took part in any track and field event, while almost half of the women on Germany's 1928 Olympic team competed in track and field events. One of Germany's competitors was Lina Radke who won the first-ever women's 800-meter race and the first gold medal in athletics for Germany. It was not until after World War II that Spain sent a single female athlete to the Olympics.

Toward the end of the 1920s, the mass media began to celebrate the achievements of female athletes, at least when they competed in fashionable sports. Among the early idols were the flamboyant French tennis player, Suzanne Lenglen; the German airplane pilot, Elli Beinhorn, who made headlines not only with her round-the-world flights but also because of her marriage to a famed automobile racer; and Sonja Henie, the beautiful Norwegian "Ice Princess," who skated her way from the

Olympic Games to a career in Hollywood. The headlines that announced Gertrud Ederle's successful swim across the English Channel were comparable to those that celebrated Charles Lindbergh's solo flight across the Atlantic.

While the achievements of female athletes continued to be met with a mix of fascination and doubt, gymnastics/calisthenics were gradually transformed into an almost entirely female domain with millions of adherents. Throughout Europe, a variety of systems and schools were propagated, some emphasizing health and hygiene, others more intent on the aesthetics of human movement. Strongly critical of modern sports and their obsession with quantified achievement, the proponents of gymnastics were concerned principally with the quality of the movement experience, the form and shape of the body, and the harmonious development of the whole person. Some of the numerous gymnastics schools were influenced by modern dance; others aimed at teaching women the "right" movements and postures. Although the gymnastics movements in Europe propagated a rather traditional image of womanhood, it spoke to many who believed that it offered an essentially feminine movement culture. In addition, gymnastics appeared to be a physical activity without competition, but this claim did not hold true for long as gymnastics was eventually introduced into the Olympic program in 1984 (Christensen et al., 2001; Guttmann, 1991).

Women's Sports under Fascism

With the Fascist ideologies espoused by the dictatorial regimes of Mussolini's Italy, Hitler's Germany, and Franco's Spain, a new gender order based on biologist thinking emerged. With varying degrees of success, these regimes sought to reduce women's aspirations and to once again focus on their roles as wives and mothers.

Although all Fascist regimes redefined and restructured the gender order and their sport politics, the changes were most radical in Germany. In addition to health, Nazi physical education was intended to inculcate an ideology of racial superiority, military preparedness, and strong leadership. The Nazis coined the term "political physical education" which meant that sport was to be used to prepare men for their roles as soldiers and women for theirs as mothers. In Nazi discourse and in the medical literature it was influenced by, discussions of women's sport centered on one question: What enhances and what diminishes a woman's reproductive function? Although Nazi ideology had originally been opposed to sports competitions for women, Hitler realized the propaganda advantages of successful athletes. His regime supported female athletes in a number of ways, as shown at the 1936 Olympic Games in Berlin, where Germany fielded the most successful team of female athletes (Christensen et al., 2001; Guttmann, 1991).

Developments after World War II

After the devastation and deprivation brought about by World War II, the peoples of Europe turned eagerly to sports, which, even in occupied Germany, represented a more attractive world than the ubiquitous ruins of the postwar era. With the gradual return of ordinary life came a call for women to resume the domestic roles they had been forced to abandon by the exigencies of war. The Fifties were a decade that re-emphasized the traditional ideals of home and hearth.

In the 1960s, student revolutions, the women's movement, sexual liberation, the pill, as well as new fashions such as jeans and t-shirts, contributed to women's emancipation. Sport ideologies, organizations and practices in this time were strongly influenced by the ideological struggles of the Cold War. The performance of the Soviet Union's female athletes at the 1952 Olympics (in Helsinki) astonished the world. For the next several decades, athletes from the Communist regimes of Eastern Europe continued to dominate women's events at the Olympic Games.

Olympic success was the result of a number of interrelated factors: the centralized search for athletic talent, which began with the systematic recruitment of children; scientific research designed to maximize performance; the concentration of economic resources on sports; the high prestige and social security granted to successful athletes; material rewards to athletes (e.g., travel abroad); and medical manipulation through drugs. As a result of Communist sport bureaucrats' pursuit of gold medals and world championship victories, female athletes trained to the point where they no longer seemed, in Western eyes, to be women. But this did not bother the sport officials. Questions about the deep voices of swimmers were answered with the response: "We came here to swim, not sing."

The concentration on elite athletes in Eastern Bloc countries took place at the expense of recreational sports. Facilities available to ordinary citizens were poor and time for sports participation was scarce. Women were triply burdened; their vocational, domestic, and political obligations left them little time or energy for sports participation (Christensen et al., 2001; Guttmann, 1991).

In East and West, there was renewed resistance against women taking up sports. Women were discouraged, for example, from playing soccer or participating in weightlifting or boxing. It was not until 1972 that soccer federations accepted female players. The IOC waited another twenty years before introducing women's soccer into its program, and it was 2012 before women were finally admitted to all sports at the Summer Olympic Games.

SPORTS TODAY: DOES GENDER STILL MATTER?

Sport Participation

Despite the dramatic changes in societies, gender norms and sports in recent decades, the gender gap has not totally closed. Girls and women are by no means as likely as men and boys to be physically active in their leisure. While both genders are engaged in different sports, there are considerable gender differences with regard to visibility, finances, leadership and power.

It has to be taken into consideration that the sport system in Europe differs dramatically from the sport systems in other parts of the world, particularly from the U.S. where equal access of male and female students is enforced in the school system. In the Northern and Western European countries, sport federations and clubs are the main sport providers and are responsible for recreational physical activities (at all competitive levels) for males and females and all age groups. These clubs and federations are civil society associations based upon the principles of democracy, volunteering, and autonomy, and as a result, the State has no influence on the gender representation of their membership or leaders. Sport organizations are supported by public subsidies because sport promises to provide public benefits such as health and social integration.

Despite seemingly equal opportunities for males and females, girls and women are a minority of sport participants. According to the results of a representative survey conducted in the countries of the European Union (EU), women are on average less physically active than men and a minority among sport club members (European Commission, 2010). However, there are tremendous differences with regard to the country and type of sport; the intersecting categories of social class, education, ethnicity and gender each contribute to inequalities with regard to sport participation.

A good indicator of sport involvement in the EU is the frequency of physical activity. Results from the EU survey indicate that 43% of the male population in EU countries reports playing sport at least once a week, whereas only 37% of women report activity at this level. Forty nine percent of the male and 57% of the female respondents indicated that they never, or less than once a month, participate in sport activities (European Commission, 2010). Among 15–24 year olds, 19% of the young men and only 8% of the young women were found to engage in sport five times a week or more; and 71% of the young men and 50% of the young women engage in sport at least once a week. In most countries, men are overrepresented among the individuals who are physically active more than three times a week. Only in Denmark, Finland and Sweden do slightly more women than men report a high physical activity rate. Sixteen percent of the male and 8% of the female respondents of the EU survey were members of a sport club. These percentages are much higher in some countries. In Germany, for example, around 30% of the population is a sport club member and the percentage of women among the members is 39% (European Commission, 2010; Pfister, 2010a).

Bottenburg, Rijnen, and Sterkenburg (2005) indicated that the popularity of different types of sports in Europe varies considerably depending, among other things, on tradition and environment. For example, team handball is especially popular in Denmark and Germany, ice skating in the Netherlands, rugby, basketball and judo in France, and darts in England. Some of these traditional sports (e.g., handball and skating) are popular with both genders, while others (e.g., rugby and darts) are considered men's sports.

In the last few decades, women have gained access to all sports and are now participating in activities once thought to be exclusively male (e.g., marathon running, soccer, rugby, water polo, boxing, weightlifting and ski jumping). Nevertheless, sports that require great skills and risk taking such as motor sports, parkour, skateboarding or kite-surfing are still domains of young men. Gymnastics, aerobics, and dance, as well as equestrian sports, continue to attract far more women than men.

Currently, the spectrum of sports available to women is far broader than in the past, although large gender differences exist depending on the region and the country. In Europe, soccer is the most important sport with regard to the number of players, but also with regard to media interest and money involved. The 53 soccer federations in Europe have 12.6 million adult members; among them are 8% women (more than 1 million). More than 10 million children play soccer, of which 9% are girls. However, there are large differences between the various countries. Girls and women make up 22% of all players in Norway; in Germany the proportion is 15%, and in Greece 1%. With one million female members, the German Soccer Federation is the largest organization catering to women's soccer worldwide. In recent years, not only have the numbers of female players increased, but so too have the numbers of women and men who are fans of women's soccer. Seventeen million Germans watched the Japan-Germany Game at the World Championship in 2011. This event gained considerable media attention worldwide and attracted millions of viewers.

Despite the growing popularity of women's soccer, the players, just as the female athletes in most other sports, are "semi-professionals," meaning that many of them get financial support, but not enough to make a living. Many players and athletes are students; others are gainfully employed, often half time in order to have enough time for training and competing in their sports. In contrast, in some of the men's sports (e.g., car racing – formula one) and particularly soccer, successful athletes can earn a fortune.

This mapping of the sport participation in European countries shows clearly that the world of sport is (still) gendered with male and female domains, and that women seem more willing than men to enter the other gender's spheres. Boys and men have reacted to the "feminization" of traditionally male sports by searching for new challenges and creating new and extreme sports which provide a space for *doing* masculinity. Sport participants are always doing gender, the question is whether a "de-gendering" of sport is possible, not least because male and female participants will present different images and will give their activities different meanings (Pfister, 2010c).

The populations in European countries include migrants coming from different countries, often countries with a majority of Muslim inhabitants. Sport habits and tastes are dependent on the ethnic backgrounds as migrants bring their sport-related attitudes and practices to Europe. As the situation in Germany shows, migrant girls and women are largely underrepresented among the physically active population. In contrast, migrant boys (e.g., boys with a Turkish background) are as highly involved in sport (in particular soccer) as their German peers (Pfister, 2010b). However, in several European countries, specific sport programs for migrant women have been developed, and various initiatives have been launched to encourage female migrants to become members of sport groups or clubs.

WOMEN, SPORT AND POWER

The gender hierarchy in key executive positions of sport organizations has been on the agenda of women's sport advocates for decades, but with little success. Recent studies indicate that the executive boards of sport federations at the international as well as national levels are still male domimated (Comité International Olympique., Loughborough University, 2010; Pfister, 2006b).

In a project supported by the European Union, international and national sports federations were investigated with the following results: the most prestigious sport organization, the IOC, has approximately 17% women among its members. Ninety five percent of the more than 70 international organizations were headed by a male president and the percentage of women among the members of the executive boards was on average less than 10%. In addition, examination of the gender breakdown among board members of 62 national federations of six selected sports in 11 European countries revealed that only three of the federations had a female president and 19% of the federations were governed by "men only" boards. In most federations, women are a small minority in positions of power. Norway is the only country where all of the six sports federations had more than 25% women as members of their executive committees (Pfister, 2011).

Coaching: Is It Still a Men's Profession?

In Europe, the situation of coaches is very diverse depending particularly on the age and gender of the athletes, the level of competition and the sport. Numerous instructors working at a "sport-for-all" level are volunteers or paid per hour. Many women are engaged in these types of "coaching." In contrast to the large numbers of women as instructors at the sport-for-all level, an overwhelming majority of coaches in elite sport are men. Comprehensive statistics about the gender of coaches in European countries do not exist, but there is information available (e.g., about the coaches in the Olympic delegations) which provides insight into the gender proportion in this profession.

At the 2012 Olympic Games, all of the men's teams (of all countries) and 43 of the 48 women's teams competing at the Games were coached exclusively by men. The 407 German athletes, 44% of them women, were coached by 46 men and five women, with the five female coaches responsible for women-only sports. Among the participants in the latest representative survey in Germany, 13% of the coaches in elite sport were women, who, with few exceptions, were in charge of female athletes (Digel, 2010). LaVoi and Dutove (2012) have provided an overview of studies on the obstacles faced by, as well as the support provided for, female coaches. However, their work refers mostly to a North American context, where coaches are employed by colleges and universities. In European countries, coaches work mostly for sport federations, clubs or athletes. With few exceptions, their salaries and working conditions are poor, and this may also be one of the reasons why women do not chose this occupation. Research in the European sport context indicates numerous instances of discrimination which women face in the coaching profession, including gender stereotyping and discriminatory recruitment strategies including the practice of "homosocial reproduction" (selecting candidates that most closely reflect those in power) (Pfister, 2013).

Causes and Explanations

If we want to change the current gender arrangements and provide women with opportunities to "play with the boys," we have to know about the reasons for the underrepresentation of women in the various fields of sport. However, there is not just one reason, and no simple explanation. At first sight, women's roles in sport seem to be the result of their individual choices, but a closer look reveals that gender hierarchies are embedded in intersecting traditions, cultures, structures and institutions, and interwoven in social arrangements and individual lives. Unpacking gender in the various areas of sport and in the manifold cultures of Europe will result in a bricolage, a puzzle which needs much more work in order to get it completed (Pfister, 2010c).

When referring to men and women and their opportunities, behavior and decisions, we have to be aware that there are tendencies and averages that vary according to society and culture, but that there are large individual differences between women with regard to their interests, prospects, resources and so on. The same is true of men. Both are dominated by and contributing to the gender order of a society. Gender can be defined as:

> a process of social construction, a system of social stratification and an institution that structures every aspect of our lives because of its embeddedness in the family, the workplace and the state, as well as in sexuality, language and culture, [and – most importantly – in sport]. (Lorber 1994, p. 5)

Gender is integrated in identities, staged and negotiated in interactions. The current gender order provides "scripts" for everybody to "do gender" because gender is not something we have or are, but something that we permanently do. From this perspective, the engagement of men and women in sport is not self-evident, normal and natural but subject to changes as women and men proceed through life-long socialization processes. Several intertwined theoretical approaches may help to understand gender inequality in sports and societies whereby the distribution of work is the decisive issue (Pfister, 2010c).

175

Modern societies organize work in a specific way. From the 19th century onwards, with the emergence of industrialization and factories, places of employment became increasingly separated from homes and families, which resulted in a gendered segregation of work. Men went out to work in offices or factories while women stayed at home and took care of the children. Housework was (and still is) unpaid – nor is it considered to be "real" work. These gender arrangements are integrated in discourses and practices legitimized by biologism. Biologist thinking refers to the belief that bodily characteristics, the female body or black skin, are indicators of cognitive and social abilities and that the biology or "nature" of women and men legitimizes their positions in families, organizations and institutions – and explains the unequal distribution of power in society as a whole (Pfister, 2013).

The seemingly normal and natural gender arrangements can be unmasked by history. Since the 19th century, we have observed a continuous "intrusion" of male domains by women, from space flight to boxing. However, men do not seem to be willing to "conquer" female domains such as housework or synchronized swimming. Even today, women are engaged in child care more than men, and family responsibilities make it much more difficult to combine life, work and leisure. These responsibilities also have an impact on women's opportunities of becoming involved in sport – as participants, athletes, coaches or leaders.

Sport Participation and Sport Choice

An individual's choice of sporting activities depends on complex, interacting processes and conditions. People will take part in sporting activities when the activity is suited to their aptitudes, tastes, expectations and aspirations and when it promises rewards. Sporting habits and competencies are acquired during life-long socialization processes which are influenced by the intersections of gender, social class and ethnicity. Here the environments (i.e. schools, clubs, peer groups and informal sporting spaces), as well as the policies of sports institutions, are of major importance because they may provide options – but may also impede access to sport for all and elite sport alike.

Girls and boys develop specific sporting "tastes" and abilities which fit into the current gender cultures of the various countries. In recent decades, horseriding stables have become female spaces while skateboard parks have become male domains. Soccer, too, is in many countries a male space where women and girls – as "latecomers" and outsiders – are often not welcome. As long as soccer is labeled "male," boys and men (at least those who are good at the game) gain self-affirmation, while female players have to defend their choice of taking up a men's sport or face the consequences of being labeled a lesbian. The growing interest of women in the game, however, serves to challenge the seemingly "natural gender" of soccer. However, in many countries, women who play soccer are met with institutional discrimination (i.e., lack of financial resources), as well as insufficient infrastructure, administration and organization.

Gender Inequality among Leaders and Coaches

There is no doubt that not only individual choices, but also the discrimination rooted in the institutions and cultures of the various sports impede access to and the advancement of women as leaders and coaches (Pfister, 2006a). In addition, the aforementioned gender segregation of work has a decisive influence on women's (and men's) positions in the labor market and decisions about their role as a leader or coach. Pfister (2006a, 2006b) argued that the gender hierarchy in executive positions is also, at least partly, caused by various marginalization processes. Women who aspire to key executive positions are often labeled unreliable leaders/coaches and excluded because the men in charge assume that women should prioritize their families and/or cannot invest the time, flexibility and energy required of such important positions. Other factors which may also play a role are stereotypes, defense mechanisms (attempts to preserve soccer as a male space), discrimination processes and the reluctance of men to give up their posts.

There is also literature (Hovden & Pfister, 2006) which indicates that some women are not interested in getting involved in sport organizations. This, however, raises several questions: Are the incentives (power) not as attractive for women as they are for men? Is the workload too heavy? Are there problems to combine care for a family and working as a leader or a coach? Are women discouraged by prejudices, stereotypes, discrimination and an "organizational culture" orientated to the needs of men? The culture of an organization determines not only the way people interact with each other but also, in general, the distribution of work and the expectations which members and leaders have of each other. Organizational culture is created, enacted and also "gendered" via discourses, symbols, rituals and practices in everyday situations and relates to aims, corporate identities and modes of operation. Modern organizations emphasize equal opportunity, but they reproduce gender hierarchies via the notion of the "ideal leader," whose characteristics and behavioral patterns are derived from men's capabilities and life circumstances. The gendered nature of organizations is thus masked by the assumption of a "disembodied and universal leader, who is actually a man, exposing hegemonic masculinity" (Acker, 1990, p. 139). Women are marginalized since their aspirations and personal circumstances are not taken into consideration.

As research indicates, the "ideal leader" of a sport organization is a person with a long and continuing commitment to sport, with extensive networks, the knowledge and attitude of an insider and a "demonstrative" investment of energy and time (Acker 1990; Pfister 2006b, 2010a). Time and flexibility are considered to be useful benchmarks for measuring the quality of a person's work, as well as his or her commitment. Many women do not have long careers and large networks in sport organizations; they may also have difficulty attending long meetings at odd hours, and their abilities may not be suited to the tasks which are "sex typed." In short, many women are perceived to not have the characteristics of an "ideal leader."

The way new personnel are recruited is part of the "culture of the organization." Executive positions in sport are often filled by means of co-option (i.e. appointing a person by general agreement or adopting the principle of "homosocial reproduction"). In addition, organizations prefer candidates that reflect the members of the group, and improve its image and power. In a male-dominated world, women are different; they may even be regarded as "troublemakers," especially if they promote women's rights. However, it must also be considered that in some sports, only a small group of women are qualified and available for higher positions and that, as already mentioned, women may not be interested in taking on leadership positions.

Some of the barriers indicated above also refer to coaches. Women who intend to work as top-level coaches may meet similar problems to those of women aiming for leadership positions. In addition, in most countries and in most sports very few women have the licenses which are required for coaching an athlete or a team in elite sport. Women also face considerable barriers during the qualification processes in most sports because the training as a coach is adapted to the (sporting) biographies, the competencies and (sporting) performances of men, as well as to male norms and values. Courses are mostly co-educational and the teachers are men. Many women feel marginalized in this male-dominated environment. However, women-only courses, which were very successful in Germany, have the image of being not as good or not "tough" enough.

Another reason for the lack of female top coaches may be the small number of women aspiring to coach at a high level. As research indicates, an overwhelming majority of female coaches do not want to coach male athletes, and this decision limits their job opportunities. In addition, the anticipation of the working conditions – in particular working in the evenings and on weekends, as well as the travelling – may not encourage women to aim for a coaching career (Pfister, 2013).

GENDER AND SPORT: NEW ISSUES

There are many more gender issues which influence women's and men's opportunities to participate in sport. Currently, the dress codes of female athletes are a contested issue. On the one hand, some sport federations try to force female athletes (e.g., beach volleyball) to wear "sexy" clothes in order to attract (male) audiences. On the other hand, sport federations (e.g., Iran) demand an "Islamic attire" of their female athletes. In addition, Muslim women who have "embodied" their faith may choose to wear a hijab when participating in sports. While certainly an issue in need of continued discussion, there is a growing trend to allow women to choose their sport dress according to their religious beliefs (Pfister, 2010b).

Problems which do not only concern girls and women, but also boys and men, are homophobia and sexual harassment. As sport has a focus on the body and allows or even demands body contact, it seems to be an area where sexual abuse – often by coaches – occurs quite frequently. In Europe (but also worldwide) there are numerous studies not only on the forms of harassment and abuse, but also on means of prevention (Brackenridge, 2001). Degrees of homophobia depend on countries and cultures. Whereas LGBT (lesbian, gay, bisexual, transgender) athletes are more accepted in many Northern and Central European countries, homophobia is still an issue in some cultures and in some sports.

Intensive debates have emerged regarding gender verification and eligibility criteria. New questions being addressed include: Should women with hyperandrogenism participate in women's events although they may have a higher androgen level than the majority of female athletes? Is it fair to exclude transgender athletes from participation in competitive sport? It is hopeful that discussions surrounding these questions will continue and focus on solutions that are fair and inclusive.

An additional point of discussion surrounds the experiences and opportunities of pregnant athletes and of female athletes with children. Current questions revolve around training and pregnancy and how pregnant women are supported by the sport system. Due to the high demands on time and energy, some perceive the roles of athlete and mother to be incompatible. However, examples show that mothers can quite soon resume their training and continue to be successful in their sports. It is important, however, that sport organizations set this, as well as a host of other topics, on their agenda.

CHAPTER SUMMARY

Throughout the 20th century, sport has become a worldwide movement. Today, elite sport symbolizes ability and superiority, it is believed to represent groups and nations, and it has become big business. However, in Europe there is also a strong "sport for all" movement which attracts large parts of the general population. Although traditional sports and games as well as modern sport were inventions and domains of men, women have gained slow but continuous access to all levels and forms of sport. However, in many areas – from sport participation to leadership – gender gaps still exists. The reasons for the continued gender inequality in sport are similar to the reasons for gender hierarchies in other areas of society. However, in the last few decades, the integration of women in sport has increased. It is to hope that these developments signal increasing gender equality in all areas and at all levels of sport.

REFERENCES

Acker, J. (1990). Hierarchies, jobs, bodies: A theory of gendered organizations. *Gender and Society, 4*(2), 139–158.

Bottenburg, M., Rijnen, B., & Sterkenburg, J. (2005). *Sports participation in the European Union: Trends and differences.* Nieuwegein: Arko Sports Media.

Brackenridge, C. H. (2001). Spoilsports: Understanding and preventing sexual exploitation in sport. London: Routledge.

Christensen, K., Guttmann, A., & Pfister, G. (Eds.). (2001). *International encyclopedia of women and sports*, Vol. 1–3. New York, NY: Macmillan Reference.

Comité International Olympique, 2010 International Olympique. *Gender equality and leadership in Olympic bodies: leadership and the Olympic Movement 2010. Women, Loughborough University: Comité International Olympique, 2010.* University: Comité International Olympique.

Digel, H. (2010). *Berufsfeld trainer im Spitzensport.* Schorndorf: Hofmann.

European Commisson. (2010). Sport and physical activity. Retrieved from http://ec.europa.eu/sport/library/documents/d/ebs_334_en.pdf

Guttmann, A. (1991) *Women's sports: A history.* New York: Columbia University Press.

Hovden, J., & Pfister, G. (2006). Gender, power and sports. *Nora: Nordic Journal of Women's Studies, 14*(1), 4–11.

LaVoi, N. M., & Dutove, J. K. (2012). Barriers and supports for female coaches: An ecological model. *Sports Coaching Review, 1*(1), 17–37.

Lorber, J. (1994). *Paradoxes of gender.* New Haven: Yale University Press.

Pfister, G. (2000). Women and the Olympic Games. In B. Drinkwater (ed.), *Women in Sport* (pp. 3–19). Oxford: Blackwell Science.

Pfister, G. (2003). Cultural confrontations: German turnen, Swedish gymnastics and English sport: European diversity in physical activities from a historical perspective. *Sport in Society, 6*(1), 61–91.

Pfister, G. (2004). The role of women in traditional games and sports. Retrieved from http://library.la84.org OlympicInformationCenter/OlympicReview/2000/OREXXVI31/OREXXVI31zg.pdf

Pfister, G. (2006a). Women and leadership positions: Theoretical reflections. In G. Doll-Tepper, G. Pfister & S. Radtke (Eds.), *Progress towards leadership: Biographies and career paths of male and female leaders in German sports organisations* (pp. 9–53). Köln: Sportverlag Strauss.

Pfister, G. (2006b). Women as leaders in sports: International tendencies. In G. Doll-Tepper, G. Pfister & S. Radtke (Eds.), *Progress towards leadership: biographies and career paths of male and female leaders in German sports organisations* (pp. 55–70). Köln: Sportverlag Strauss.

Pfister, G. (2010a). Are the women or the organisations to blame? Gender hierarchies in Danish sports organisations. *International Journal of Sport Policy, 2*(1), 1–23.

Pfister, G. (2010b). Outsiders: Muslim women and Olympic Games: Barriers and ppportunities. *The International Journal of the History of Sport, 27,* 2925–2957.

Pfister, G. (2010c). Women in sport: Gender relations and future perspectives. *Sport in Society, 13*(2), 234–248.

Pfister, G. (2011). Gender equality and (elite) sport. Report by the Council of Europe. Retrieved from Retrieved from http://www.coe.int/t/dg4/epas/resources/texts/INF25%20Gender%20equality%20and%20elite%20sport.pdf

Pfister, G. (2013). Outsiders: Female coaches intruding a male domain. In Pfister, G., & M. Sisjord (Eds.). *Gender and sport: Changes and challenges* (pp. 71–103). Münster: Waxmann.

Quintillan, G. (2000). Alice Milliat and the women's games. *Olympic Review, 26* (2–3), 27–28.

Wilson, W. (1996) The IOC and the status of women in the Olympic Movement: 1972–1996. *Research Quarterly for Exercise and Sport, 67,* 183–192.

AFFILIATION

Gertrud Pfister, PhD
Department of Nutrition, Exercise and Sport
University of Copenhagen

CONTRIBUTING AUTHORS

Karen Appleby, Ph.D. is an Associate Professor in the Department of Sport Science and Physical Education at Idaho State University (ISU). She earned her doctorate in sport psychology from the University of Tennessee in 2004 and has been teaching at ISU ever since. She teaches classes in sport psychology, research and writing, marketing and management in sport, and sport sociology. While her research interests are diverse, the majority of her research is focused on gender issues in sport. For example, Dr. Appleby has published papers on the experience of female athletes in socially defined "masculine" sports (i.e., female rock climbers) and the experiences of elite female athletes and motherhood. Dr. Appleby is also committed to providing hands-on opportunities for girls in her community to participate in sport and physical activity. She is currently the co-event coordinator for the ISU celebration of National Girls and Women in Sports Day (NGWSD). This event provides opportunities for approximately 300 girls (grades K-6th) to take part in both traditional and non-traditional sports and physical activities. In her spare time she loves to race her bike, run on the trails with her dogs (Rufus and Knox), and cross country ski with her husband (Sam) in the Idaho mountains.

Akilah R. Carter-Francique, Ph.D. is an Assistant Professor in the Department of Health and Kinesiology at Texas A&M University. Her research scholarship, teaching, and service focus on intersections of race/ethnicity, gender, and sport/physical activity. As a former collegiate athlete and sport administrator, current issues of diversity and social justice, participation and representation, and access and opportunity continue to influence and shape her work. Dr. Carter-Francique is also the co-founder and director of *Sista to Sista*™ which is a co-curricular leadership development program designed to foster a sense of connectedness amongst Black female collegiate athletes. Through monthly group discussions and service activities, Black female collegiate athletes are provided an opportunity to learn about themselves as a racial and gendered minority within the context of sport, share their voices and experiences as women of color, and use their sport participation as a platform to give back to the community.

Guylaine Demers, Ph.D. has been a Professor in the Department of Physical Education at Laval University since 2001. She is the Director of the undergraduate coach education program, namely the Baccalaureate in Sport Intervention. Dr. Demers takes particular interest in issues of women in sport, coach education and homophobia in sport. She currently sits on CAAWS board of directors and on the editorial board of the *Canadian Journal for Women in Coaching*. She was a key contributor to the development and implementation of the new competency-based National Coaching Certification Program in Canada. Dr. Guylaine Demers is actively involved in promoting gender equity and coach education in sport within her home province of Québec. She currently serves as Chair of Égale-Action, Quebec's Association for the Advancement of Women in Sport and Physical Activity. Her work and achievements have been recognized both provincially and nationally. Dr. Demers made the 2010 *Globe and Mail* newspaper's annual list of Canada's Top 50 in sport. She was named recipient of the 2009 YWCA's Women in Sport Award for her accomplishments in Québec for the advancement of women in leadership positions and in 2007 and 2010, she was named one of CAAWS' Most Influential Women in Sport and Physical Activity in Canada.

Leslee A. Fisher, Ph.D. is an Associate Professor of sport psychology at the University of Tennessee. A former track-and-field and volleyball athlete, Dr. Fisher completed two master's degrees (counselor education and adult fitness) and a doctorate in sport psychology. To date, Dr. Fisher has published 59 academic and applied manuscripts and has numerous national and international presentations. Dr. Fisher's research focuses on the integration of cultural studies and sport studies, particularly the newly emerging field of cultural sport psychology. She has published her research in *The Journal of Sport and Exercise Psychology*, *The Sport Psychologist*, *International Journal of Sport and Exercise Psychology*, *International Journal of Sport Psychology*, *Women in Sport and Physical Activity Journal*, and *Athletic Insight*. In addition, Dr. Fisher has served as the Secretary/Treasurer of the Association for Applied Sport Psychology (AASP). She is also an AASP Fellow, an AASP-certified sport psychology consultant, a National Board Certified Counselor and a limited licensed professional counselor.

Courtney L. Flowers, Ph.D. is a Professor in Sport Management at the University of West Georgia. She earned her Doctorate of Philosophy in Physical Education, Sports, and Exercise Science from the University of New Mexico. She also holds a M.S. degree in Sport Administration from Grambling State University and a B.S. in Biology from Mississippi Valley State University. Her research is guided by analyzing legal aspects of sport and the sociocultural perspectives on sport surrounding minority women and Historically Black Colleges and Universities. Dr. Flowers brings an array of sport experience to her teaching and scholarship including golf administration, athletic conference administration, and NCAA Division I athletic academic advising. In addition to her teaching and research, she is a member of the American Alliance for Health, Physical Education, Recreation, and Dance, the North American Society for the Sociology of Sport, and the North American Society for Sport Management.

Elaine Foster, MPE-AA has been heavily involved in sport throughout her life – from team sports to individual activities and outdoor adventures. She obtained her bachelor's degree in physical education with an emphasis in exercise science, and her Master of Physical Education-Athletic Administration degree from Idaho State University. Her academic interests include women in sport and physical activity, health promotion among women, and assessment in physical education. Elaine has worked as a personal trainer, coach, and physical activity instructor. She currently works at Idaho State University in Pocatello, Idaho as an adjunct instructor for the Sport Science and Physical Education department where she has taught courses in physical education foundations, anatomy and physiology, activity techniques, and professional development.

Christy Greenleaf, Ph.D. is an Associate Professor in the Kinesiology Department at the University of Wisconsin – Milwaukee. She completed her undergraduate work in psychology at Bowling Green State University, her master's degree at Miami University (Ohio), and her doctoral work at the University of North Carolina at Greensboro. Dr. Greenleaf's research focuses on body image, eating attitudes and behaviors, and weight stigma within exercise and sport contexts. She is a Fellow of The Obesity Society and American Alliance for Health, Physical Education, Recreation and Dance and is an American College of Sports Medicine Physical Activity in Public Health Specialist. Dr. Greenleaf is an active figure skater and is a competitive member of an adult synchronized skating team.

Alicia Johnson, M.S. is a Sport Studies doctoral student at the University of Tennessee, Knoxville (UTK) concentrating in Socio-Cultural Studies. At UTK, she works with the Center for Sport, Peace, and Society, which is currently the cooperative partner for the U.S. State Department's Empowering Women and Girls through Sports initiative. She earned her M.S. in Counseling Psychology with a concentration in Athletic Counseling from Springfield College in 2012. While at Springfield College, Alicia served as an Academic Coach for athletes at an underserved high school through AmeriCorps. In 2010, she obtained her B.S. in Exercise Science, with minors in Biology and Sports Medicine, from Minnesota State University, Mankato. While there, Alicia was on the competitive cheerleading team and was captain of the football and basketball sideline cheerleading teams. In 2009, Alicia was a summer research intern for the University of Minnesota's Tucker Center for Research on Girls and Women in Sport.

Kerrie J. Kauer, Ph.D. is an Associate Professor with the Department of Kinesiology at California State University, Long Beach. Her research focuses on gender, sexuality, and the body as it relates to sport and human movement.

Sandra Kirby, Ph.D. has been working on issues of sexual harassment and abuse in sport, child protection in sport, and gender equity for most of her adult life. Dr. Kirby identifies as an athlete and a sport scientist. She represented Canada at the 1976 Summer Olympic Games in Montreal, Canada and has continued as a competitor in the sports of rowing and cross country skiing. As an academic, she found her voice first as a feminist dedicated to issues of equality and violence against women during the women's movements and later in the women and sport movement, on exactly the same themes. She has experienced first-hand many of the changes the contributors to this book write about. Dr. Kirby has authored a number of books including the *Dome of Silence: Sexual Harassment and Abuse in Sport* (2000), the first book ever published on the topic. She is also part of the International Task Force on Harassment and Abuse in Sport, chaired by Professor Celia Brackenridge of the UK. Dr. Kirby is privileged to be part of a group of activist/scholars working to make sport a safe and fair experience for all participants.

Susannah Knust, Ph.D. earned her doctorate in Sport Psychology and Motor Behavior from the University of Tennessee, Knoxville in 2013. She worked with University of Tennessee athletes as a Sport Psychology Consultant during her studies. Her Master's degree in Sport Studies was earned from Western Michigan University in 2009. She completed her Bachelor's degree in Spanish Education at Calvin College in 2002 and was a Spanish teacher for seven years. She has coached softball at Cornerstone University and Grand Rapids Christian High School. She is originally from Grand Rapids, Michigan. She currently works with Soldiers as a Master Resilience Trainer-Performance Expert in the Comprehensive Soldier and Family Fitness program.

Vikki Krane, Ph.D. is a Professor with the School of Human Movement, Sport, and Leisure Studies at Bowling Green State University. She also is an affiliated faculty member with the Women's Studies and American Culture Studies programs. Her research focuses on gender, sexuality, and sport. Dr. Krane has been the editor of *The Sport Psychologist* and the *Women in Sport and Physical Activity Journal* and currently is on the editorial boards of the *Psychology of Sport and Exercise, The Sport Psychologist,* and *Qualitative Research in Sport and Exercise.* She is a fellow of the National Academy of Kinesiology and the Association of Applied Sport Psychology.

Nicole M. LaVoi, Ph.D. is a Senior Lecturer in the area of social and behavioral sciences in the School of Kinesiology at the University of Minnesota, the Associate Director of the Tucker Center for Research on Girls and Women in Sport and the co-founder of the Minnesota Youth Sport Research Consortium. Dr. LaVoi's research has focused on the effect of adult behaviors (parents and coaches) on children and youth, the physical activity of underserved girls, the barriers experienced by female coaches, and media representations of girls and women in sport. Dr. LaVoi has published book chapters, research reports, and a number of peer reviewed articles, was a contributing author of *The 2007 Tucker Center Research Report: Developing Physically Active Girls,* and has helped produce and develop "Concussion and Female Athletes: The Untold Story" in conjunction with Twin Cities Public Television.

Trent A. Petrie, Ph.D. is a Professor in the Department of Psychology and the Director of the Center for Sport Psychology at the University of North Texas. His research interests include eating disorders and body image in athletes, psychosocial antecedents of athletic injury, professional issues in sport psychology, and the influence of motivational climates. He is a licensed psychologist in Texas and a certified consultant through the Association for Applied Sport Psychology (AASP). He is a Fellow of both AASP and the American Psychological Association (APA), and is the current Past-President of Division 47 (Exercise and Sport Psychology) of APA.

Gertrud Pfister, Ph.D. earned her doctorate in history, followed by another doctorate in sociology. From 1980 to 2000, she was employed as a professor at the University of Berlin and was appointed to a professor position at the University of Copenhagen in 2001. Dr. Pfister conducted several large national and international research projects; she has published more than 200 articles and 20 books. Dr. Pfister plays a leading role in various sport-related scientific communities. From 1983 to 2001 she was president of the International Society for the History of Sport and from 2004 to 2008 she was the head of the International Sport Sociology Association. Currently, she is a member of the executive board for Women Sport International. All of her life, Dr. Gertrud Pfister has been active in sport, in particular in skiing, tennis and long distance running.

Theresa Walton, Ph.D. is an Associate Professor in the School of Foundations, Leadership and Administration at Kent State University. Her research focuses on investigations of power relationships and the ways those relationships are both resisted and maintained within mediated sport narratives. In particular, she has examined media discourse of gender equality in sport, women's amateur wrestling, and elite distance running. More recently, she has investigated how high school girls navigate and understand their embodied identities. Her work has been published in the *Sociology of Sport Journal*, the *Women in Sport and Physical Activity Journal*, the *Journal of Popular Culture* and *Sport, Education and Society*.

ABOUT THE EDITOR

Emily A. Roper, Ph.D. is an Associate Professor in the Department of Health and Kinesiology at Sam Houston State University. Dr. Roper earned her doctorate in cultural studies with an emphasis in sport psychology from the University of Tennessee, Knoxville and her M.S. in sport psychology from the University of Toronto. Her research focuses on gender, sexual identity, and sport. In particular, she has examined the representation of physically active females in children's and young adult literature, environmental barriers women and girls face engaging in outdoor physical activity, and women's career experiences in sport psychology. Dr. Roper's work has been published in *Research Quarterly for Exercise and*

Sport, Women in Sport and Physical Activity Journal, Sex Roles, the *Journal of Applied Sport Psychology, The Sport Psychologist, Research in Dance Education,* and *Athletic Insight.* She has also contributed to several books including *Cultural Sport Psychology: From Research to Practice, Contemporary Sport Psychology,* and *The Oxford Handbook of Sport and Performance Psychology.* Dr. Roper served as the Publications and Information Division Head for the Association for Applied Sport Psychology (AASP) from 2010 to 2013 and as an associate editor for *Athletic Insight.* She was the recipient of the 2001 AASP Dissertation of the Year Award and 2013 SHSU College of Education Researcher of the Year Award.